Michigan State Library

TA 668.Q38 1974 C.1 The plastics

the
plastics
architect

the plastics architect

arthur quarmby

pall mall press

The Pall Mall Press
5 Cromwell Place, London SW 7

First published in Great Britain
© 1974 by The Pall Mall Press, London
ISBN 0 269 02825 0

Filmset by Typesetting Services Ltd, Glasgow, Scotland
Printed in Great Britain by Butler and Tanner Limited, Frome

contents

CHAPTER 1	introduction	7
CHAPTER 2	materials history	11
CHAPTER 3	materials	18
CHAPTER 4	fabrication technology	31
CHAPTER 5	historical applications	44
CHAPTER 6	spatial enclosures	63
CHAPTER 7	component construction	115
CHAPTER 8	sculptural applications	143
CHAPTER 9	prospective work	161
CHAPTER 10	in conclusion	183
	bibliography	193
	list of illustrations	195
	name index	201
	subject index	206

For Jeannie

CHAPTER 1 introduction

This book is an attempt to provide a basic tool for architects and designers in the use of plastics in building. To bring together an outline of the materials and fabrication techniques, and a review of the most important projects and structures which have been designed over the past twenty years.

To me plastics are a constant source of delight as a whole range of fascinating man-made materials with every colour from transparency right through the spectrum both translucent and opaque, with unlimited choice of texture from jewel-like smoothness through velvety flock to a harshness equalling exposed aggregate concrete, and with tensile strengths from rubbery glue right through to a glassy brittleness.

Plastics materials are unique in that they permit the designer to create structures which are transparent, translucent or self-coloured. They can offer a strength-to-weight ratio up to a hundred times higher than that of any other material. They can be produced with uni-directional or multi-directional strength, and can have locally-increased stiffness or flexibility built in. All basic types are water and vapour-proof, unlike the majority of traditional building materials. You name it, and within normal physical laws, you can have it.

These are man-made materials which can be tailored almost at will for any particular job—and this in itself is a problem. Firstly because the architect is accustomed to designing within the properties of available materials, and when these constraints are removed the problem is far more difficult. Rather like the difference between traditional jazz with its rigid framework around which one can improvise, and certain types of more modern jazz where the framework is removed and the musician is faced with the task of creating from nothing. Or put more simply in normal building terms, the difference between designing a building on a difficult site where the very difficulties tend to create the solution, and that of designing on a flat, featureless site where everything has to come from within.

The second problem is that as virtually anything is possible with plastics materials they still tend to be used, especially in theoretical projects, as cure-alls. The fact that a proposal is feasible does not necessarily mean that it is practical or economical, and these factors may be underestimated if the designer is not equipped with an adequate knowledge of materials, processes and costings.

For example it would be quite possible to calculate the wildly varying wind stresses around the surface of a pneumatic structure, or the differing tensile stresses on the skin of a suspension structure, and then construct the fabric of the skin accordingly with locally tailored strengths. This is not particularly difficult, but to the best of my knowledge it has never yet been done because it is too expensive. With the size of structures we use at the moment it is still far more economical to choose a fabric which is capable of handling the highest stress which will be imposed upon it in any location.

Again, it is normally possible to obtain small runs of rigid shell structures fairly economically on simple moulds. But the finish will not be very good, the quality control may be reduced, and the unit cost will be very much higher than would be the case if a more sophisticated production process were employed. However to tool up for the more advanced process will in many cases be so expensive that a production run to equal the total demand for the structure for a whole country may be required in order to amortize these costs effectively and achieve the maximum possible economy.

Plastics materials can be cure-alls, but only in very special circumstances. In the normal run of building applications only a very small part of their real potential can be deployed, and this applies to the fabrication processes even more than to the materials.

At last we have materials capable of offering the possibility of the real mass-production of economical, sophisticated structures, and the fabrication technology of injection moulding, press moulding, extrusion, vacuum forming and rotational casting to enable us to do it. Unfortunately most of these techniques will remain beyond our reach until we succeed in organizing the gigantic market for building into viable units—or until the computer-control of this production reaches the stage where the moulding tools which are at present incredibly expensive can be produced cheaply and automatically, thus freeing the machine from the constraint of standardized bulk production.

Despite these difficulties and shortcomings in the present situation we can still use plastics materials and processes to turn building on its head, to rethink architecture and to question the whole basis of function and construction.

To ask why we build cavity walls when we have composite plastics materials on the market which could in many respects do a far better job at literally one tenth of the cost? To ask why we put patch upon patches with our roofs, when it would be possible to produce a unit to fulfill all the functions of decorative finish, strength, insulation and weatherproofedness in one go? To ask why cars have power-operated windows and buildings do not, and why we pay such high prices for the caves we call home? To ask why we live as we do, and how we would like to live if only we could free our minds from the clutter of our upbringing, experience and habit? To ask what buildings are for anyway, when we have the ability to control the climate under vast yet very economical enclosures?

We are not really very clever, are we? Not when the houses we live in are more cramped than those of our grandparents because the increase in building costs outstrips the growth of personal wealth, and not when the simplest village in the hills is an object lesson to us in environmental design.

How often do we stand back from our surroundings and look at them dispassionately? Try it and see, and ask whether the environment would have really been much worse without architects, and without planning and building controls. Try even looking at shanty towns in central America or Africa and ask whether, making due allowance for the difference in financial investment, they are really worse than the council estates of England or the monstrous high-rise housing projects of France or Russia, as places to live?

We design out of habit, we do not think, we do not question. Many of us graduate with a set of ideas which have been planted in us at college and which we then use, virtually unchanged, throughout our careers.

For this one can perhaps blame architectural education which, even more than other forms of education, is aimed at the situation as it exists now, rather than at what it could be or what it will be in twenty years time, when the students are at mid-career.

The real purpose of architectural education is as concealed by the academic course, no matter how liberal, every bit as much as the doctrine of Christianity is obscured by the teachings of the Church. Or perhaps the real purpose is not even fully appreciated at all in the first place. A student attends an architectural college in order to obtain the blessing of society which will then permit him to practice as an architect and earn a modest living. That is the regular pattern.

If the student is lucky, and only a few are, something else will happen to him during the six or seven years of the course. The lucky few experience a situation which brings out and develops their innate ability. This happens in rare cases and quite erratically, because such development is not the prime purpose of the architectural course.

It happens in the oddest and most unexpected way. We can all remember students with a flair for draughtsmanship who were successful at the beginning of a course but who gradually slipped further and further back, having relied too heavily on their insubstantial gifts. Then others—to all intents and purposes a little ordinary perhaps, no real ability, trailers at the tail end of the year—suddenly exploding with imagination and ability.

Anyone who teaches architecture has seen this occur, and many of us wonder why and how and whether, if we were clever enough, we could bring this about in all students?

The only clue I have as to what really happens is a suspicion that it is very closely bound up with self-confidence. I remember a student in my year of no particular ability who on one occasion made a big stand against a major project which was set by the college. He did a sarcastic half-day sketch and then disappeared for six weeks. A new extra-low mark was especially introduced for his effort, but immediately afterwards he started producing eccentric designs which were totally incomprehensible to staff and students alike. He got high marks for this work and from then onwards never looked back.

If the production of high-fliers were the principal aim of architectural education, then with careful study we might find ourselves able to bring out this sort of ability in the majority of students, rather than in the minority.

We should be trained to think, to question, to rebel, and above all to understand something of the excitement which every subject holds. Then perhaps we should not be so ready to design out of habit, to accept society as it stands, and meekly to give way to the official whose ruling is always unhesitatingly and unshakably what the book says.

Then, too, perhaps we should be more able to exploit to the full the opportunities which lie before us in the use of plastics materials and technology in order to change the built environment of the world for the better in terms of the quality and delight of living.

CHAPTER 2 materials history

In 1664 Robert Hooke the English 'experimental philosopher' and prolific inventor, Curator of the Royal Society and assistant to Robert Boyle, wrote these words:

> 'I have often thought that probably there might be a way found out to make an artificial glutinous composition much resembling that excrement out of which the silk worm wire-draws his clew.'

Other dreamers probably had similar ideas, but the real birth of the plastics industry was delayed until the second Great Exhibition in 1862 at which Alexander Parkes exhibited his new material which he called Parkesine.

Parkes was a man of a similar type to Hooke. Trained as an art metal worker, he rapidly became manager of the casting department of a Birmingham firm where his fertile and restless imagination generated an endless flow of ideas and inventions. Indeed he speedily amassed the amazing total of eighty patents, which led him to abandon his post and live on the sale of licences.

Many of these inventions were naturally concerned with metallurgy; he invented a number of alloys and devised a well-known process for the de-silvering of lead which is still in common use. However in 1846 (when he was thirty-three) he had diversified from metals into rubber, at a time when the rubber industry was a bare twenty-five years old and when vulcanization, the technique which gives rubber its bounce and increases its resistance to heat, was quite new.

The vulcanization then developed (by Goodyear and by Hancock) was a high-temperature technique, and Parkes developed the idea of introducing a system for coating fabric with rubber in the cold. And followed it up in the same year by a patent for reclaiming the material from waste.

His familiarity with rubber technology, with sulphur chloride, which he was subsequently to use as a plasticiser for cellulose nitrate, and with the milling, calendering and extrusion of rubber and gutta-percha was undoubtedly of great importance in his next step, the development of Parkesine.

Cellulose nitrate (or guncotton) had been discovered some years before, but its explosive properties had been of prime interest. Parkes altered the manufacturing process slightly, and produced as a result a material capable of being moulded into decorative items. The jury of the Great Exhibition awarded him a bronze medal for the material, described as 'the product of a mixture of chloroform and castor oil which produces a substance hard as horn, but as flexible as leather, capable of being cast or stamped, painted, dyed or carved...'.

Parkesine was received with such enthusiasm, that by 1866 Parkes was able to launch a company for its exploitation with a capital of £100,000 ($240,000). However he appears to have been less successful as a businessman than as an inventor, for the company was in liquidation within two years due, some would claim, to the inventor's insistence that the price of Parkesine be pegged to one shilling per lb and to his determination to prove the speed of the process. Cheap, substandard materials were used and the finished articles were produced before the material had been fully formulated, with the result that a flood of faulty products was returned to the factory.

Parkes returned to metallurgy and specialized largely in this work until his death in 1890, and the story of Parkesine moves to the United States where the problem of the shortage of ivory was causing such concern to the manufacturers of billiard balls that one company had offered a prize of $10,000 to anyone who could develop a suitable substitute material.

John Wesley Hyatt, a printer working in Albany, New York, decided to accept the challenge and spent several years attempting to solve the problem. Like Parkes and his successors in England, Hyatt had no formal education in chemistry. This proved to be no barrier to him, and he is quoted as saying that 'some successful experiments I might never have made if I had been familiar with the danger theories of some learned men'. He started by bonding layers of fabric or paper pulp coated with shellac without success, but finally ended up in 1869 with a billiard ball made of cellulose nitrate, as Parkes had done two years before.

Hyatt's balls were originally coated with a colouring film of virtually uncontaminated guncotton... 'consequently a lighted cigar applied would at once result in a serious flame and occasionally the violent contact of the balls would produce a mild explosion like a percussion guncap. We had a letter from a billiard saloon proprietor in Colorado mentioning this fact and saying that he did not care so much about it but that instantly every man in the room pulled a gun'.

Work continued to overcome this and other problems, which were finally resolved in 1870 by the association of camphor as a solvent generating a product which was completely viable commercially, and which was given the name of Celluloid.

The early development of plastic was characterized by original research in Europe and commercial exploitation in the United States, where the commercial success of Celluloid led to a search for other new materials which might prove just as profitable.

However before moving on to subsequent developments, it would be as well to remind budding inventors that this is only one case of many where lasting fame has been awarded not to the inventor, but to the commercial exploiter—to the man who cashed in on the idea. Perhaps that is unkind (and in Parkes' case the cash did not last long), and perhaps it would be more just to say that the laurels go to he who realizes the potential of an idea and puts it into practice.

Many materials which today are household words in plastics were discovered long before the Great Exhibition of 1862—styrene in 1831, melamine in 1834, vinyl chloride in 1835 and polyester in 1847. However in not one of these cases did the inventor appreciate the potential of his materials, and none of them was really exploited until well into the twentieth century.

The next major advance in the development of plastics materials was not until 1907 when Leo Baekeland, a Belgian chemist working in the United States, took out the first of his 119 patents on phenol-formaldehyde, the material which came to be known as Bakelite.

Once again we record the success of a man who took an existing, well-known invention, modified it, and exploited it in ways which those who had gone before had never dreamed of.

Variations on the phenol-formaldehyde theme had been known of since 1872; indeed a chunk of the material was kicking around in my home town of Huddersfield as long ago as 1890. However Baekeland found a way of controlling the fast reaction between phenol and formaldehyde which enabled the material to be moulded, and developed applications ranging from gears to gramophone records, from switches to solenoids.

Baekeland's financial success encouraged chemists to work on further synthetic materials, and especially materials which could overcome the inadequacies of Bakelite—the fact that unless laminated with paper or cloth it was brittle, and that its colour potential ranged all the way from brown to black.

Before awarding the customary honours to the next exploiter, it is only fair to record that in the years between the liquidation of the Parkesine Company and the turn of the century, many of the real inventions in plastics had been made. They are unsung, but they are there. Injection moulding patented by the Hyatt brothers in 1872; polyvinylchloride by Baumann in the same year; the screw extruder by Gray in 1879; polymerised methylacrylate by Kohlbaum in 1880; ureaformaldehyde by Hölzer in 1884; cellulose acetate by Cross and Bevan in 1894, and polycarbonate by Einhorn in 1898.

This latter is a prime example of the curious progress of materials developments in plastics, for it was not put on the market until 1959. In that year I brought back a polycarbonate jug from Germany—only to have it dismissed by British industry with the words 'Oh yes, polycarbonate. We've known about it for years'. Now, after twelve years of slogging development, polycarbonate is slowly becoming a real success in the building industry.

However the story is told of a similar material which had been made up into transparent bricks, and at a demonstration it was claimed that the material would stand up to gunfire. A pistol was produced and fired at the construction, which resulted in some very neat little holes. A voice from the back then called out 'What happens if you kick it?' 'What happens if you kick it indeed—why nothing, except you are likely to get sore toes', was the reply. The questioner got up, walked forward and gave the wall a great kick—and it promptly shattered.

I am assured that this story has no basis in fact, but that it is one of many which circulate in the plastics industry, having been devised by the representatives of certain organizations to frighten potential customers away from their rivals.

Returning now to conventional history, ureaformaldehyde, which had been known since 1884, was patented by Hans John in the United States in 1918 as an adhesive and as a suitable material for the impregnation of textiles. A variation of this development enabled him to produce a transparent, hard material, and led to the search for a synthetic substitute for glass, a search which has not yet been entirely successful.

The pace now hots up somewhat. A failing British company switched in desperation from cyanide production to the exploration of new chemicals, and wound up with the first commercially successful moulding powder— 'a simultaneous condensation of urea, thiourea and formaldehyde'—which could be used to impregnate cellulose pulp and wood flour. The ground-up results of this mixture were marketed in 1928, but suffered from a tendency to deliquesce and to smell when heated.

The next major development was that of melamine—first discovered in 1834, but now used as the basis of a range of new resins (some of which form the surface coating of decorative laminates, the backing being a laminate of paper and Mr. Baekeland's Bakelite), by companies in Germany and Switzerland.

We move on now to 1929, when William Chalmers was working on a substitute for glass at McGill University, Montreal. He found that a hard, clear material was produced by the polymers of methacrylic ethylester and methacrylic nitrile, and his discovery was rapidly taken up by major companies in the United States and Britain, to be developed as polymethylmethacrylate and marketed at a modest cost in 1934. Just in time to be used as a synthetic glazing material for the aeroplanes of the Second World War.

The First World War emphasized the essential nature of a large scale chemical industry in any belligerent country, while the Second World War brought the plastics industry to full stature.

Up until this time, plastics chemists had been groping in the dark. The basic monomers had been known for almost a century but neither they nor the mechanism of polymerization were understood. It was still the time of the so-called 'pick and mix'—choose a few chemicals, stir them up and

1820	Hancock invented prototype of modern mill, for processing rubber
1831	Earliest description of styrene
1834	Liebig first isolated melamine
1835	Pelouze nitrated cellulose
1835	Regnault prepared vinyl chloride
1839	Goodyear discovered vulcanization of rubber
1845	Bewley designed extruder for gutta-percha tubes
1845	Schönbein nitrated cellulose in the presence of sulphuric acid
1847	Berzelius made first polyester
1859	Butlerov described formaldehyde polymers
1862	Display of Parkesine at Great Exhibition in London
1865	Schützenberger acetylated cellulose
65	Parkes's main patent for his Parkesine process
1866	Parkesine Co. established
1866	Berthelot synthesized styrene
1868	Parkesine Co. liquidated
1869	Spill registered Xylonite Co.
1870	Hyatt's basic celluloid patent
1870	Establishment of Hyatt's Albany Dental Plate Co. (later to become Celluloid Manufacturing Co.)
1872	Hyatt Brothers patented first plastics injection moulding machine
1872	Bayer reported reaction between phenols and aldehydes
1872	Baumann reported polymerization of vinyl chloride
1872	'Celluloid' registered as a trademark by Hyatt
1873	Caspery & Tollens prepared various acrylate esters
1874	Spill wound up Xylonite Co.
1875	Daniel Spill Co. established
1877	British Xylonite Co. established
1878	Hyatt introduced first multicavity injection mould
1879	Gray granted patent for first screw extruder
1880	Kahlbaum polymerized methylacrylate
1884	Hölzer isolated urea-formaldehyde condensation products
1884	Hyatt won patent action against Spill
1884	Chardonnet silk (first artificial silk) produced
1892	Viscose silk developed by Cross and Bevan
1894	Cross and Bevan produced industrial process for manufacture of cellulose acetate
1898	Einhorn described polycarbonates
1899	Continuous cellulose nitrate film first made by casting on a polished drum
1899	Kipping began his researches into organo-silicon compounds
1899	Smith published patent on phenol-formaldehyde composition
1899	Kritsche and Spitteler patented casein plastic and established Galalith
1901	Röhm awarded doctorate for his thesis on acrylate polymers
1901	Smith discovered alkyd resins by reaction of glycerol and phthalic anhydride
1905	Miles prepared secondary cellulose acetate
1909	Baekeland granted his 'Heat and Pressure' patent for phenolic resins
1912	First emulsion polymerization patent—applied to isoprene
1912	Klatte synthesized vinyl chloride and vinyl acetate from acetylene
1912	Ostromislenski patented polymerization of vinyl chloride
1915	First production of synthetic rubber (methyl rubber) at Leverkusen
1918	John patented urea-formaldehyde condensation resins
1919	Eichengrun produced cellulose acetate moulding powder
1921	Eichengrun designed modern injection moulding machine
1922	(c.) Staudinger began work on macromolecules
1924	Discovery and preparation of polyvinyl alcohol
1925	Earliest (unsuccessful) U.S. attempt at commercial production of styrene
1926	Eckert and Ziegler marketed modern plastics injection moulding machine
1927	Commercial production of polyacrylates
1928	Commercial production of urea-formaldehyde moulding powder (Beetle) began
1928	Carothers started his researches on polymers and polymerization
1928	Copolymerization of vinyl chloride and vinyl acetate
1929	Industrial research on styrene and polystyrene initiated in Germany
1929	Birth of British Plastics Federation
1930	Semon plasticized p.v.c.
1930	Injection moulding of polystyrene in Germany
1931	Formation of Institute of Plastics Industry
1931	Neoprene discovered by Carothers
1931	Initiation of I.C.I. research leading to high pressure polythylene
1931	Bauer and Hill separately began investigating esters of methacrylic acid
1931	Hyde began research on organo-silicon polymers
1932	Screw pre-plasticization in injection moulding patented
1933	Crawford devised commercial synthesis for methyl methacrylate
1933	Carleton Ellis patent on unsaturated polyester resins
1933	Butadiene-styrene rubber introduced
1934	First commercial production of Perspex
1935	Henkel made melamine-formaldehyde resins
1935	Staudinger proposed three phase addition polymerization process
1935	Troester produced first extruder designed for thermoplastics
1937	Polyurethanes first produced
1938	Full-scale production of nylon
1938	Observation of polytetrafluoroethylene
1938	Polymerization of caprolactam (Nylon 6)
1939	Commercial production of polyethylene
1939	First patent (in Germany) on epoxides
1940	Production of p.v.c. in U.K.
1941	Rubber Reserve Co. (U.S. Govt) initiated synthetic rubber industry of U.S.A.
1941	Whinfield and Dickson invented polyethylene glycol terephthalate (Terylene)
1942	Dow Corning made silicones industrially
1943	Pilot plant production of p.t.f.e.
1943	Castan's patent on epoxides
1946	Polyurethane elastomers introduced
1947	Initiation of Du Pont research programme on polyformaldehyde
1950	First large scale production of Teflon (p.t.f.e.)
1952	Macdonald established conditions for production of commercial polyformaldehyde
1953	Staudinger received Nobel prize for his work on macromolecules
1953	Ziegler made polyethylene using organo-metallic catalyst
1954	Natta made high molecular weight, stereoregular polypropylene
1954	Synthesis of cis-polyisoprene (synthetic natural rubber)
1956	Schnell published results on polycarbonates
1956	Plant scale production of high density polyethylene
1959	Polyformaldehyde came onto the market
1959	Polycarbonates came onto the market

1 A chronology of plastics, with one hundred dates.

see what happens. Just like the empiric method of structural experiment—kick it about and see if it stands up.

This state of affairs is perfectly illustrated by the development of polystyrene. The monomer—styrene—was discovered in 1830 and the polymer in 1845, but it was not until shortly before the Second World War (and, significantly, shortly after the publication of Staudinger's theories that plastics materials were composed of giant molecular chains) that commercial production of the material was commenced.

Polyethylene, discovered in Britain in 1933 and in commercial production by 1939, is a sort of odd man out in this situation. In what we think of as a typical British way, the discovery was made by chance, and in its final stages was the result of a small leak in the apparatus which admitted just enough oxygen to complete the material. Without polyethylene the development of radar during the war might well have been impossible.

In Germany, the need to be independent of materials from outside Europe acted as a tremendous spur to the plastics industry, and led to a very great expansion in the production of polystyrene, a wide range of vinyl plastics, and methacrylates. British production of p.v.c. was not commenced until the fall of Malaya and the consequent loss of supplies of natural rubber—which in addition generated the development of the synthetic rubber industry, to match that already advanced in Germany. And not only in Britain and Germany; in the United States production of all synthetic rubbers in 1942 amounted to 3,600 tons, but by 1945 the US production of one British-developed range alone was 725,000 tons.

After the war a quiet period was followed by a change of direction in the search for new plastics materials. Up until this time a material was discovered and then means of exploitation were investigated. Now however in a number of cases the desired properties were defined, and a suitable product was developed accordingly. Polyurethane, discovered by Bayer in the search for a material comparable to nylon, was a typical example of this trend.

Despite the fact that exceptions still arose—on the face of things polypropylene was one such case, being the subject of a design competition for suitable applications—the tendency has grown since the fifties (and is still increasing) for new or modified materials to be produced tailored to a specific need. And in this lies the future of the plastics industry.

2 Common plastics materials, their abbreviations and families.

Term	Abbreviation	Thermoplastic	Thermosetting	Term	Abbreviation	Thermoplastic	Thermosetting	Term	Abbreviation	Thermoplastic	Thermosetting
Acrylonitrile-butadiene-styrene plastics	ABS	•		Phenol-formaldehyde	PF		•	Polystyrene	PS	•	
Carboxymethyl Cellulose	CMC	•		Poly(acrylic acid)	PAA	•		Polytetrafluoroethylene	PTFE	•	
Casein	CS	•		Polyacrylonitrile	PAN	•		Poly(vinyl acetate)	PVAc	•	
Cellulose acetate	CA	•		Polyamide (nylon)	PA	•		Poly(vinyl alcohol)	PVAL	•	
Cellulose acetate-butyrate	CAB	•		Polybutadiene-acrylonitrile	PBAN	•		Poly(vinyl butyral)	PVB	•	
Cellulose acetate propionate	CAP	•		Polybutadiene-styrene	PBS	•		Poly(vinyl chloride)	PVC	•	
Cellulose nitrate	CN	•		Polycarbonate	PC	•		Poly(vinyl chloride-acetate)	PVCAc	•	
Cellulose propionate	CP	•		Poly(diallyl phthalate)	PDAP		•	Poly(vinyl fluoride)	PVF	•	
Cresol-formaldehyde	CF		•	Polyethylene	PE	•		Poly(vinyl formal)	PVFM	•	
Diallyl phthalate	PDAP		•	Polyethylene terephthalate	PETP	•		Silicone plastics	SI		•
Epoxy, epoxide	EP		•	Poly(methylchloroacrylate)	PMCA	•		Styrene-acrylonitrile	SAN	•	
Ethyl cellulose	EC	•		Poly(methyl methacrylate)	PMMA	•		Styrene-butadiene plastics	SBP	•	
Melamine-formaldehyde	MF		•	Polymonochlorotrifluoroethylene	PCTFE	•		Styrene-rubber plastics	SRP		•
Perfluoro(ethylene-propylene) copolymer	FEP	•		Polyoxymethylene, polyacetal	POM	•		Urea-formaldehyde	UF		•
				Polypropylene	PP	•		Urethane plastics	UP		•

POSTSCRIPT

It is odd, to say the least, that the plastics world should pay homage to men such as Parkes, Hyatt and Baekeland as founders of the industry when they were not primarily inventors of new materials but rather exploiters who recognized the potential in the work of others.

It is unfortunate for the original discoverers that these three should be given all the credit when they were also the ones who made all the profit.

Odd that the plastics industry should appreciate the past importance of applications development, while relegating it to a minor role today. For nowadays the bulk of the effort, both physical and financial, is applied to materials development and applications research is, by comparison, neglected. Perhaps this situation will be righted by over-production, or perhaps it will be realized that the planning of future capacity can and should stem from applications innovation and expansion.

materials   CHAPTER 3

Plastics materials are man-made substances which do not exist in nature. They are, generally speaking, organic materials—that is they are based upon carbon (although there are a growing number of exceptions to this rule). They are high polymers—giant molecules made up of small simple repetitive units assembled into large groups. As their name implies, they are plastic at some stage of their production, and at that stage can be moulded in shape by a variety of techniques.

The carbon atom is the basis of the vast majority of plastics materials. It may be described as a hard ball with four equally spaced valences or connectors to which other atoms may be attached.

For example, the hydrogen atom has a single valence, so four hydrogen atoms can be connected to a single atom of carbon. This produces methane.

Alternatively two atoms of oxygen, with two valences each, may be connected to one atom of carbon, producing carbon dioxide.

A further possibility is for one carbon atom to link to a second carbon atom. If this is done with two valences, the others being attached to hydrogen atoms, the result is ethylene. If three valences connect the carbon atoms instead of two, we have acetylene.

Substances in which these multiple links of valences exist are described as being unsaturated, which means that under certain circumstances the valences may be detached and linked to other materials—or to other molecules of the same type which may be around.

For example, the ethylene monomers described above may be linked together to form a chain, thus forming the material known as polyethylene. (The name polyethylene is often abbreviated to polythene.)

A long chain of monomers (the simplest group of atoms from which the chain is built) is known as a polymer, and if very long indeed it is known as a high polymer.

The odd valences at the end of the chain may be closed off by individual atoms or groups of atoms, or the end of the chain may be connected to its beginning.

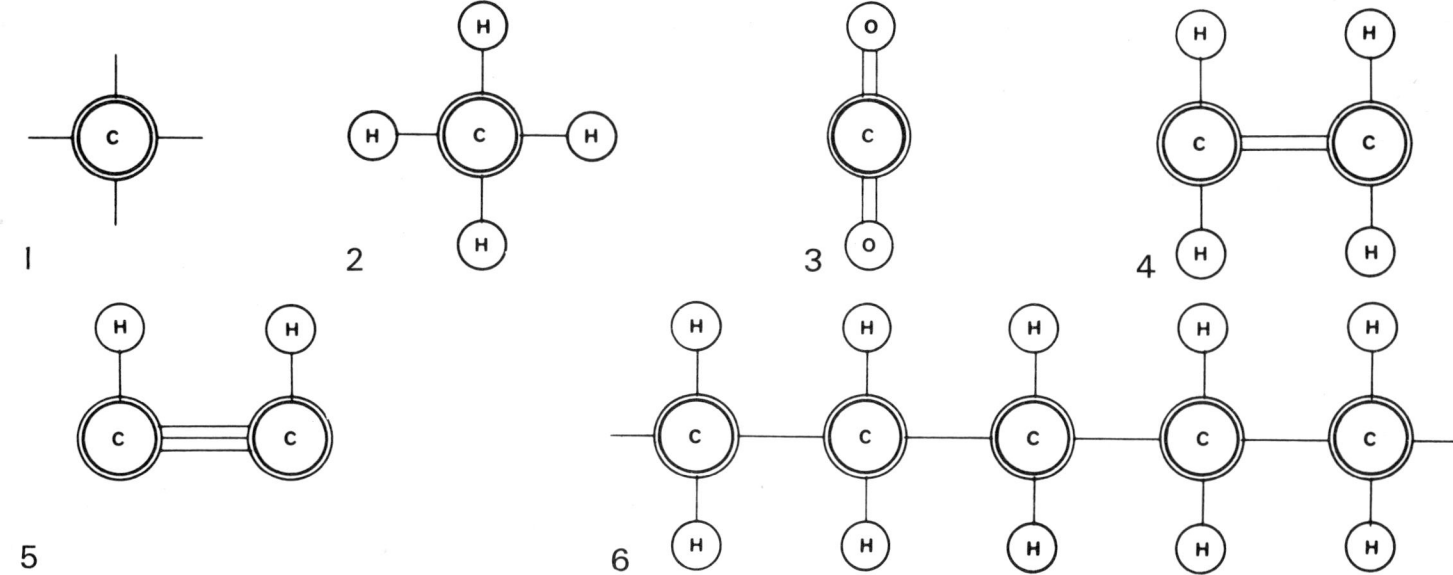

A material such as polyethylene consists of a very large number of such chains, chains which are extremely strong in themselves but do not have firm links with adjacent chains.

This means that the chains can and do slide past each other, and when this happens the material changes its shape. For example, if a piece of polyethylene is loaded, the chains can move in relation to each other, and when the load is removed they may not return entirely to their original position. This is the phenomenon known as creep.

If heat is applied the material softens and eventually flows, and can then be moulded into a new shape. This results from a loosening-up of the chains which can then slide about quite easily; rather like warming up a canful of tinned spaghetti.

This material therefore belongs, by definition, to the group known as the thermoplastics, materials which can be softened by the application of heat, and which when cooled will harden—in some examples to the point of brittleness. Materials which can also be repeatedly softened and then hardened by the application of heat and by subsequent cooling.

Thermoplastic materials—for example polystyrene, polyvinylchloride (p.v.c), polyamide (nylon) polypropylene, polymethylmethacrylate (acrylic) and many others—can normally be recovered and re-used relatively easily (with some exceptions) on account of their ability to be repeatedly softened and hardened. This does not apply to the next group, the thermosetting plastics.

Starting again from molecular structures, it will be appreciated that in certain circumstances the molecules (or monomers) can be linked to other molecules not only in a chain, but also in the form of a network. (Note that for ease of presentation chemical structures which are three-dimensional are represented in two-dimensional fashion.)

This network is created by a very strong chemical link between the chains which prevents sliding and generates a material which is rigid at

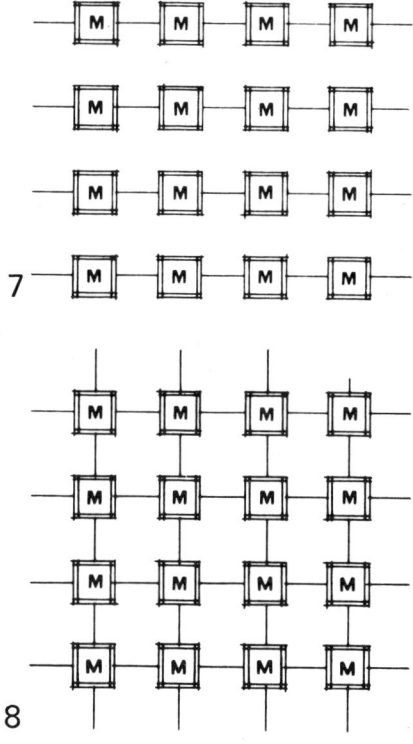

3 1. Carbon atom 2. Methane 3. Carbon dioxide 4. Ethylene 5. Acetylene 6. Polyethylene 7. Thermoplastic structure 8. Thermosetting structure.

all temperatures (except those at which the material is destroyed), and one which in consequence is far less subject to creep.

Moreover as the molecules are very closely packed there is no room for even a solvent to enter between the chains and cause dispersal. The materials are therefore generally insoluble.

Such cross-linked materials belong to the thermosetting group of plastics. They are initially thermoplastic in character but a chemical reaction (often but not always generated by heat) forms the cross-linkages, creating a hard material which cannot afterwards be resoftened.

COMMON THERMOPLASTICS

1. *Low density polyethylene* is a tough material which is unaffected by water and is resistant to a wide range of corrosive chemicals. The maximum safe working temperature is 70°C. It is naturally colourless and translucent, but pigments can be incorporated to give a virtually unlimited range of colours. Polyethylene is commonly moulded by extrusion or injection moulding, but may also be supplied in powder form for rotational casting and conversion into light-weight foam.

2. *High density polyethylene* is a crystalline form of polyethylene which is three to four times as strong and rigid, has a softening point nearly 40°C higher, and is more transparent. It can be processed in the same way as low density polyethylene.

3. *High molecular weight polyethylene* is composed of very long chains with molecular weights of up to 4 million. Its toughness, abrasion resistance, and impact resistance make it suitable for high-stress engineering applications. It is light in weight, and has excellent chemical resistance.

4. *Polypropylene* belongs, like polyethylene, to the family known as the polyolefins. This is the lightest known plastic, with a specific gravity of 0.90. It has a waxy feel and a high gloss with a harder surface than high density polyethylene. It softens at around 30°C higher than high density polyethylene, but stiffens appreciably at lower temperatures. Polypropylene may be processed in the same way as polyethylene, and is employed very widely in injection moulding.

5. *Polyvinyl chloride* or p.v.c. is perhaps the most versatile and also one of the cheapest of plastics materials. It is available in a range of flexibility from rubbery to rigid, depending upon the amount of plasticiser added. (Plasticiser is a substance which may be added to many thermoplastic materials and which acts as a lubricant between the molecular chains.)
Rigid p.v.c. is used for pipework, rainwater goods and cladding panels. In plasticized form, it is used for wall and floor coverings, etc. It is transparent and has a full colour range.
It is now possible to achieve localized plasticity, and window sections are produced in a rigid grade of material with flexible closure strips, all in one operation.
In all its grades p.v.c. is unable to support combustion, but tends to decompose when heated. It softens at about 75°C.
P.v.c. compounds are specially formulated for an extremely wide range of applications, and are employed in extrusion, blow moulding

(into bottles particularly) vacuum forming, injection moulding, calendering, and in paste form for coating fabric (air-supported structures, tension structures) and for rotational casting. Also used in expanded form (i.e. foam), both rigid and flexible.

Post-chlorinated p.v.c. has improved high-temperature resistance, and may be used for hot water pipes.

P.v.c. film may be metallized for lightweight mirrors.

6. *Polystyrene* is a hard, brittle material which is easily recognized by the way in which it rings when tapped. It is crystal clear and has an excellent colour range. Various modified grades have been developed which are variously described as toughened, medium impact and high impact.

Polystyrene has a relatively low softening point and is very extensively used in injection moulding, also extrusion, blow moulding and vacuum forming. When stretched it forms a tough film used in packaging, and may also be expanded into beadboard or extruded into a cellular foam.

7. *Acrylics* The best-known member of this family is polymethylmethacrylate. Glass-clear and with a complete colour range, the material is used extensively for rooflighting, illuminated signs and light fittings. It is extremely tough and light, its light transmission exceeds that of glass, and it is highly weather-resistant. It softens at temperatures of over 80°C, and its fire resistance is not very good.

Common moulding techniques include injection moulding and extrusion, and especially vacuum forming and blow moulding from sheet form.

8. *Polyamide*, or nylon. Best known in fibre form, nylon is tough, with good resistance to wear and a low coefficient of friction. It can be used at higher temperatures than most thermoplastics and can be moulded into dimensionally stable components (locked-in stresses can be caused by the stretching or compression of material during the moulding process. These stresses remain after the material has set hard and can generate subsequent deformation.) Very many different formulations of nylon are available, the material having been extensively tailored for different applications. Commonly used in extrusion and injection moulding.

9. *Cellulose acetate* is similar to Celluloid but has reduced flammability. It is used most commonly in sheet form, but also as rods and tubes and for packaging films, spectacle frames, light fittings and door furniture. Triacetate is used for films and also for fibres.

10. *Polyvinyl acetate* (P.V.A.) One of the oldest of the vinyl plastics, limited in use on account of its low softening point. It is employed extensively in the formulation of emulsion paints.

11. *Acetal copolymer.* Chemically inert, and strong at sustained high temperatures. It is used in carburettors and other automobile parts, also for taps and ball valves, and is capable of replacing metal in a number of high stress and high temperature applications. Formed by extrusion, injection moulding and blow moulding, the material is translucent to opaque.

12. *Polytetrafluorethylene* (P.T.F.E.) A moulding material with a very wide temperature range, resistant to chemical action and with a coefficient of friction (against itself) equal to that of wet ice. A high molecular weight polymer which is moulded at temperatures above 350°C. Best known as a coating for domestic pans.

13. *Acrylonitrile butadiene styrene* (ABS). A very high impact relative of polystyrene which is used for bonnets, boot lids and bodies in the automobile industry, and which can be expected to find extensive applications in building in addition to the plumbing fittings already available. Electroplated ABS (commonly chrome plated) is used for car radiators, grilles and door handles. The colour range is limited and weather resistance is only moderate (but may be improved by a surface coating of P.V.F.).

14. *Polyvinyl fluoride* (P.V.F.) A rather expensive material with a high softening point which is very resistant to weather, chemicals, light and abrasion. Chiefly used as a transparent coating to g.r.p. panels or shells and to plywood, for external use.

15. *Polycarbonate*. Clear (with a slight amber tint) and with a very high impact strength, tensile strength and ductility. It may be worked cold, like a metal. Dimensionally stable, it is virtually self-extinguishing and has a high softening point. Relatively high cost; may be injection moulded, blow moulded or cast into film. Used as a vandal-proof substitute for glass.

16. *Polyimide*. A specialized family of materials which may be used in the temperature range from 150°C to 400°C. Samples have been unaffected after twelve months in air heated to 275°C. Insoluble in all known solvents and infusible, so cannot be moulded by any conventional techniques. However processes have recently been developed for fabricating enormous mouldings. The price of the material currently puts it beyond the reach of the building industry, but it is extensively used in space technology.

17. *Polyethylene terephthalate*. Extruded directly as fibre, film or strip; glass-clear and with a very high melting point. As a film it may have locked-in two-way stresses which can be released by heating (useful for applications such as drum skins and shrink-wrapped food etc.). However, the film is generally further processed, generating phenomenal strength and stability. Used for meteorological balloons and, when metallized, for stratosphere research balloons and lightweight mirrors. Opaque film with a light surface texture is used for drawing office materials.

COMMON THERMOSETTING PLASTICS

1. *Phenol formaldehyde,* or phenolic. Cheapest of the thermosetting materials, phenolic is used with paper to form the base of decorative laminates such as Formica and Warerite, as a water-resistant adhesive for wood and with wood flour, asbestos or cotton flock, for the production of electrical insulating, and for a variety of building applications such as black W.C. seats.

	Clarity/ transparency potentiality	Compressive strength (where relevant) p.s.i. × 1,000	Tensile strength (where relevant) p.s.i. × 1,000	Modulus of elasticity (in tension) (where relevant) p.s.i. × 100,000	Thermal movement in./in. per °C. ×10⁻⁵	Softening point °C.	Water absorption ⅛ in. thickness % in 24 hours	Burning rate (inflammability)
Thermoplastics								
Polythene (low density)	cloudy translucent	cold flows	1-2·3	0·17-0·35	16-18	85-87	0·015	very slow
Polythene (high density)	cloudy translucent (film-transparent)	2-4	3·1-5·5	0·8-1·5	11-13	120-130	0·01	very slow
Polypropylene	transparent to translucent	8·5-10	4·2-5·5	1·3-2	6-8·5	150	0·01	slow
Nylon	cloudy transparent	7-14	7-12	1·5-4	8-15	melt 220-264	0·4-3·3	self extinguishing
Acrylic	glass clear	12-20	7-11	4·5	5-9	80-98	0·3-0·4	slow (drips flame)
Rigid p.v.c.	glass clear	8	8·5	3·5	5	82	0·05	self extinguishing
Flexible p.v.c.	glass clear	—	—	—	—	—	0·5-1	self extinguishing
Polystyrene (normal)	glass clear	11·5-16	5-12	4-6	6-8	82-103	0·03-0·4	slow
Polystyrene (high impact)	glass clear	4-9	2·5-7	2·5-4·5	3·4-18	78-100	0·1-0·3	slow
ABS	translucent	2·5-11	2·5-9	1·0-4·1	6-13	85	0·1-0·3	slow
Polycarbonate	glass clear	11	8·5-9·5	3·2	6·6	165	0·3	self extinguishing
Acetal	translucent	18	10	4·1	8·1	175	0·12	slow
Cellulosics	glass clear	according to type	according to type	according to type	10-15	70	according to type	slow
Thermosets								
Phenolic (without filler)	transparent	10-30	7-8	7·5-10	2·5-6	—	0·1-0·2	very low
Phenolic (with filler)	opaque	22-40	6·5-8·5	8-12	3-4·5	—	0·3-1·0	very low
Urea	transparent	25-35	6-13	15	2·2-3·6	—	0·4-0·8	self extinguishing
Melamine	transparent	40-45	—	—	4	—	0·1-0·6	self extinguishing
Polyester (glass fibre reinforced)	translucent	18-25	9-20	5-8	2-3	—	0·01-1	slow
Epoxy	amber transparent	15-30	5-12	2-6	4·5-6·5	—	0·05-0·1	moderate to self extinguishing
Polyurethane	glass clear	according to grade	—	—	—	—	—	slow
Comparison Materials								
Mild steel	opaque	110-130	70·6	300	0·126	—	—	—
Aluminium	opaque	50-60	12	103	0·240	—	—	—

4 The main properties of plastics.

Material	Density		Compressive stress at yield point		Tensile strength		Coefficient of linear expansion		Thermal conductivity	
									k value (at 50°F) Btu.in/ft²h °F	λ value (at 10°C); k.cal/m h °
	lb/ft³	g/l	lb/in²	kg/cm²	lb/in²	kg/cm²	per °F	per °C		
Expanded polystyrene	1	16	10	0.7	18	1.26	$3\text{-}4 \times 10^{-5}$	$5.4\text{-}7.2 \times 10^{-5}$	0.24	0.03
Expanded polystyrene	1.5	24	18	1.26	28	1.96	4×10^{-5}	7.2×10^{-5}	0.23	0.029
Expanded polyvinyl chloride	2.5	40	40	2.8	70	4.9	3×10^{-5}	5.4×10^{-5}	0.24	0.03
Expanded polyvinyl chloride	4.5	72	130	9.1	230	16.1	3×10^{-5}	5.4×10^{-5}	0.24	0.03
Foamed urea formaldehyde (U.F.)	0.5	8	Very low	Very low	Very low	Very low	5×10^{-5}	9×10^{-5}	0.24	0.03
Foamed phenol-formaldehyde (P.F.)	2	32	8	0.56	14	0.98	0.6×10^{-5}	1.08×10^{-5}	0.28	0.035
Foamed phenol-formaldehyde (P.F.)	3.5	56	34	2.38	19	1.33	0.6×10^{-5}	1.08×10^{-5}	0.27	0.034
Foamed polyurethane (carbon dioxide blown)	2.5	40	40	2.8	30-50	2.2-3.5	$1.5\text{-}3.5 \times 10^{-5}$	$2.7\text{-}6.3 \times 10^{-5}$	0.27	0.034
Foamed polyurethane (fluorinated hydrocarbon blown)	1.5	24	25	1.75	40-80	2.8-5.6	$1\text{-}4 \times 10^{-5}$	$1.8\text{-}7.2 \times 10^{-5}$	0.17	0.021
Expanded ebonite	4	64	40	2.8	40	2.8	3×10^{-5}	5.4×10^{-5}	0.20	0.025

The colour range is limited to brown and black (the lighter grades being adversely affected by ultraviolet light). High temperature resistance—rocket nose cones of modified P.F. successfully withstand atmospheric re-entrance temperatures. Phenol formaldehyde is commonly fabricated by compression or transfer moulding, and also by machining.

2. *Urea formaldehyde*, or urea. A tough material with an unlimited colour range, used for cups, tumblers and electrical fittings. Urea forms the base of a range of stoving enamels for coating kitchen ware and refrigerators etc., and is used as an adhesive in the production of plywood and chipboard. Compression and some injection moulding.

3. *Melamine formaldehyde*, or Melamine is closely related to Urea. It has

Thermal resistivity		Maximum temperature recommended for continuous operation		7 days water absorption	Water vapour diffusance		Behaviour in fire
/k	1/λ	°F	°C	vol. %	at 65°F lbft² h atm/in†	at 18°C g/cm² h mmHg/cm	
.2	33.3	175	79	3.0	0.011	1.79×10^{-5}	Softens and collapses. Flame retardent grade available.
.4	34.5	175	79	2.5	0.007	1.14×10^{-5}	
.2	33.3	150	66	3.0	0.0038	0.62×10^{-5}	Collapses and generally burns with difficulty.
.2	33.3	150	66	3.8	0.002	0.326×10^{-5}	
.2	33.3	212	100	Fairly high	0.136	22.4×10^{-5}	Resistant to ignition.
6	28.6	266	130	High	0.140	22.8×10^{-5}	Highly resistant to ignition.
7	29.4	266	130	60	0.115	18.7×10^{-5}	
7	29.4	225	107	4.3	0.096	15.6×10^{-5}	Generally inflammable but relatively flame retardant forms are available.
9	47.6	210	99	5.5	0.021	3.42×10^{-5}	
0	40.0	122	50	1.5	0.0002	0.0326×10^{-5}	Flame retardant.

5 Typical properties of cellular plastics used in building.

broadly similar properties but requires a higher moulding temperature, is harder, stronger and more resistant to staining. Tasteless, non-flammable and non-toxic, melamine is best known as the surfacing material for decorative laminates such as Formica and Warerite, but is also widely used for domestic crockery.

4. *Epoxide resins* (Epoxy) are very versatile materials which, unlike the three previous examples, do not require high pressure moulding. Epoxides have good adhesion and excellent mechanical and electrical insulation properties. They are widely used in the formulation of paints and other surface coatings, and in the production of self-levelling very thin screeds for flooring, both in decorative and high wear applications. However their major application is still in the manu-

facturing of adhesives, solders and jointing compounds. Metal-filled epoxides can operate at temperatures of up to 200°C, and can be electroplated.

5. *Polyester resins* are similar to the epoxides in that they can be moulded at low pressure, have good electrical and mechanical properties and chemical resistance, and have a complete colour range. However they are also considerably cheaper, and rather simpler and more versatile to handle. Polyester/glass laminates (g.r.p.) are used for vehicles, pipes, ducts, furniture and building shells and components.

THE SILICONE PLASTICS

These are exceptional in that their molecular chain is based upon the silicon and not the carbon atom. They cannot therefore be classed entirely as organic materials, and they offer the first suggestion of a breakthrough in the tailoring of inorganic atoms to form new man-made materials.

Silicone materials may be thermoplastic or thermosetting depending upon the type of side linkages applied, and products range from oils to thermoplastic solids, from rubbers to thermosetting resins.

The silicon–oxygen combination, the base of the silicone range, is remarkably stable and silicones can in consequence withstand severe temperature, ultraviolet, and infra-red conditions.

The chief plastics use is in the formation of low-pressure laminates in conjunction with glass fibres which can withstand temperatures of well over 250°C indefinitely. The most common building application makes use of the hydrophobic properties of the materials in the production of water-repellent treatments for buildings.

Silicone plastics are at the moment too expensive for general use, but their continued development may suggest the possibility of an eventual solution to the problem of fire in plastics structures.

RADIATION CROSSLINKING

The tailoring of plastics materials has resulted in the production of specialized formulations which blend the characteristics and properties of thermoplastic and thermosetting materials.

In addition it has been possible for a number of years to crosslink certain thermoplastic materials by subjecting them to nuclear radiation. This may have the effect of knocking off certain atoms, leaving open valence points which link to similarly produced open valences on adjacent chains, converting the thermoplastic to a thermoset. This results, in the case of polyethylene for example, in increased stiffness and temperature resistance.

However, the technique cannot be applied to all thermoplastic materials. In some cases components of the main chain get knocked off, resulting in conspicuous loss of strength.

REINFORCED THERMOPLASTICS

Reinforced thermosetting resins are well known to designers, but reinforced thermoplastics have so far been little used in building. The addition of reinforcement to any plastics material results in increased stiffness, impact resistance and tensile strength, and also helps to control the thermal movement of the material. These are the very factors which restrict the use of thermoplastics in building, and the only reason for the limited penetration of reinforced thermoplastics into the building market has been the lack of development by manufacturers.

However glass reinforced nylon has been used experimentally in the injection moulding of car bodies, and glass fibre reinforced polycarbonate for injection moulded window frames. Asbestos fibre reinforced p.v.c. is in limited use in cladding applications in building.

REINFORCED THERMOSETTING RESINS

Theoretically any plastics resin may be reinforced with virtually any fibre material, resulting in a material with increased stiffness, tensile strength and stability.

In practice, however, many of the possible combinations are impracticable on account of cost, or blending or moulding difficulties.

Nevertheless, as the table shows, the range of useful reinforced plastics materials is far wider than is generally supposed.

FOAMS

Very many plastics materials can be expanded into low-density foams which are amongst the best heat insulators available, and some of which have a high strength-to-weight ratio and may be impermeable to moisture vapour.

The principal foams used in building are polyurethane and polystyrene, and these are employed for thermal and acoustical insulation and as the structural cores of sandwich panels.

Foams can be produced from selected polymers, with properties ranging from very flexible to extremely rigid, and may have open or closed cell structures. (With an open cell structure the interstices are interconnected and the material can breathe, and can consequently soak up and transmit moisture. In a closed cell structure the interstices are separated from each other and the material may be impermeable.)

The thermal insulation of foamed plastics is governed, generally speaking, by the density. However if the density becomes too low, the cell size may increase to such a point that convection currents form in each cell, lowering the insulation properties.

The gas with which the interstices of the foam are filled becomes a further element governing the thermal insulation of closed cell foams. Some of the heavier gases such as fluorocarbon give higher thermal insulation properties than the more commonly used gases such as carbon dioxide. It should perhaps be appreciated just how high the thermal insulation of plastics foams is—for example a $\frac{1}{2}''$ panel of skinned polyurethane can equal the insulation of a normal $11''$ cavity wall.

As a further example, a number of modifications of the British Railways relay room system have been used in the Antarctic. The shells are $1\frac{1}{2}''$ thick (two skins of $\frac{1}{8}''$ g.r.p., $1\frac{1}{4}''$ expanded phenolic foam) and the thermal insulation is so effective that the windows often have to be opened in external temperatures of $40°$ below freezing. This despite the fact that expanded phenolic, used for its fire resistant properties, is one of the poorer plastics foam insulators.

One important point should be made in concluding this section on materials. Plastics are not cheap; they are made by some of the most complex and expensive plant in the whole of chemical engineering, but a little can go a very long way. And in a world of galloping inflation they are unique as building materials in that their price is steadily falling.

Their future as basic building materials becomes more assured almost daily as the range of properties and manufacturing processes is extended, and as the plastics industry becomes more skilful in building further new materials from basic atomic building blocks.

PLASTICS WASTE

According to the Batelle Institute, plastics materials in general garbage run to only 2·5% of the total and will not reach 5% until 1980. However these are percentages by weight rather than volume, and as plastics are noted for an extremely high volume-to-weight ratio, they tend to minimize the seriousness of the situation.

As one plastics chemist said 'people keep on asking us to make the stuff more and more resistant to everything—weather, chemicals, vandals, the lot—and then they moan that it doesn't fall apart when they dump it'. In his opinion the major problem lies not with plastics but with people.

His attitude is certainly valid in the case of certain Sicilian city authorities who, according to the *New York Times,* have developed a splendid technique for disposing of all the city garbage. They tie it up in plastic bags and throw it into the sea. The prevailing currents then carry the bags across the Straits of Messina to Calabria. Now the Calabrians are threatening to collect the offending bags, hire helicopters to airlift them back to Sicily, and drop them on Messina. As the R.I.B.A. *Journal* commented, the seagulls may fly high in Mobile, but this is ridiculous.

However the 'people' aspect of waste is only one side of the problem, the plastics themselves being the other.

Relatively little can be done with thermosetting materials—their molecular structures are so close that it is not possible for a solvent to get in to break them up, and they do not burn at all well. The only practical proposition is to pulverize them to a powder and put it in holes in the ground (and is it true that we are excavating more holes than we are filling?). There is just one small consolation to this—the powder will be inert, and dangerous chemicals will not leach out into the soil.

The picture is a little brighter with the thermoplastics. Generally speaking they are not so resistant to the elements as the thermosets—those polyethylene bags on the beach will yellow and crack and eventually break up with the action of the sun and the sea—and considerable work is being carried out in the development of photosensitive thermoplastics, which gradually degrade under sunlight.

Unfortunately this degradation tends to allow some of the potentially dangerous chemicals to leach out—fluorine for example, or lead, which is used as a stabilizer.

Similar chemicals may be released into the atmosphere by burning thermoplastics—chlorine is released by burning p.v.c. and this is so

Reinforcement	Plastics Material	Moulding Method	Uses and Characteristics
Paper	Phenolic	Compression moulded into sheet form	Used for flat sheets as back-up for decorative or as industrial laminated sheet. Moulded by batch process in multi-daylight high pressure presses
Paper	Polyester	Compression moulded into sheet form	Used for flat sheets as decorative laminate. Can be continuously produced on heated drums, at little more than atmospheric pressures. Printed surfacing paper is used to obtain decorative effects
Paper	Epoxide	—	—
Cotton (cloth or loose fibres)	Phenolic	Compression moulded into a finished shape	Formed and used exactly as conventional phenolic mouldings, but the cotton fibres (or fabric) help to stabilise the material and reduce brittleness, thermal movement
Sisal	Polyester	Compression moulded into a finished shape	Moulded with matched polyester tools under low pressure or normal matched metal tools in a compression moulding press. Some tendency towards water sensitivity. Lower cost, higher bulk factor than glass fibres. Much lower tensile strength. Therefore of interest for non-stressed mouldings for interior use where polyester techniques are being utilised
Jute	Polyester	Compression or hand lay moulded into a finished shape	As woven cloth, can be moulded into large radius mouldings, by hand lay process, as bulking medium, provided interlaminar air and tendency to delaminate under stress as a result are taken into account. Also compression moulded at low or high pressures. Useful as a cheaper reinforcement for thickening up (and therefore stiffening) machine guards and similar non-stressed parts
Asbestos paper	Phenolic	—	—
Asbestos felt	Phenolic	Compression moulded into a finished shape	Pre-impregnated material which can be high pressure moulded in a conventional compression moulding press into fairly complex shapes with excellent high temperature performance characteristics, good thermal stability and great resistance to abrasion and wear. Aircraft heater ducting, fan blades, electrical parts are examples of typical uses
Asbestos flock	Phenolic	—	
Asbestos fibre	P.v.c.	Compression moulded into sheet form	Supplied as semi-prepared material; for medium-pressure compression moulding into sheets in flat-bed presses or a finished compressed material for vacuum forming, and for rubber-bed pressing, also available with a coloured surfacing film to give good weathering and attractive surface gloss. Having higher impact strength, greater stability across a wide temperature range and greater stiffness than conventional p.v.c., the material can perform many of the functions of unreinforced p.v.c. at up to 40 per cent cost savings. This material has great potential in building industry applications.
Asbestos fibre	Polyester	Compression moulded into sheet and finished shapes	High stiffness factor with consequent savings on thickness, i.e., materials content. Improved fire performance, and therefore of strong interest in building
Glass fibres	Polyester	Compression, hand lay or otherwise moulded into a finished shape	The widest used reinforced material, moulded by hand lay methods; matched polyester tools; rubber-bag and vacuum; autoclave; continuous low pressure laminating; by using matched metal tools at medium pressure on a compression moulding press; by "pultrusion"; or by filament winding. Highest tensile strength of any plastics material known, weight for weight. Can be translucent. Very versatile in respect of raw material forms and qualities, moulding methods, and finished article complexity
Glass fibres	Epoxide	Compression or hand lay moulded into a finished shape	Hand lay moulded or compression moulded, mainly for high level chemical resistance
Glass fibres	Phenolic	—	—
Glass fibres	Polystyrene	Injection moulded into a finished shape	An injection moulding material combining the cheapness and transparency of polystyrene with the stabilising and tensile properties of glass to give much improved dimensional stability, moderate heat distortion point (220°F.), good stiffness and impact strength. Used for very large injection moulded parts, automotive applications, fan blades, etc.
Glass fibres	Nylon	Injection moulded into a finished shape	Like glass/polystyrene, an injection moulding material of improved heat distortion point (500°F.), lower water absorption; lower elongation, higher tensile and flexural strength than unreinforced nylon, e.g., thermal coefficient of expansion improves from about 60 to about 10; tensile strength from about 11.5 to about 20; compressive strength from about 10 to about 20; and flexural strength from about 10 to about 30
Glass fibres	Melamine	—	—
Glass fibres	Silicone	—	—

6 Properties of reinforced plastics materials.

hazardous that a technique for neutralizing the gas with lime has been evolved.

There seem to be two basic approaches which could largely eliminate the problem of plastics waste. The first obtains in the current situation where many types of plastics waste are so cheap that you actually have to pay people to take it away for you. Here the cure is to have more men around like Herbert Hartley.

He was originally a manufacturer of flexible foams, and was constantly forced to pay to dispose of scrap. Being a northerner this was a constant source of nagging irritation, and he finally hit on a way of sticking the scrap together to form foam with a far higher resilience which was ideal for carpet underlay. He turned all his production over to the reconstitution of scrap, which he brought in from as far afield as the United States, before selling out.

The next stage in the Hartley saga was the manufacture of rigid polyurethane foam, and the same conditions but worse—mounting costs to dispose of offcuts, not from the extrusion plant where waste is minimal, but from the one-shot production of foam blocks. (The foam froths up in a big container, ends up looking like a loaf and has to be cut square.)

The problem here is that low-density rigid polyurethane offcuts are notoriously friable—he tried it as insulation in the roof of a friend's house, which was the end of the friendship—and it is very difficult to find any suitable use for the stuff. However a solution will be found, the necessary non-sequitur being a special feature of British inventiveness as has been shown in the tremendous growth of cannibal industries in plastics. (The scrap merchant's dream of heaven—to be paid to take something away which he can then sell, with the minimum of conversion, to someone else.)

The second line of approach to the problem of plastics waste is to re-use it at source, as is already being done in injection moulding where the sprues are ground up and put straight back in the hopper. This could be done in the case of extrusion, but an extruder has to run for quite a while until its production is just right, and during the preliminaries it is usually a question of getting the stuff out of the way so that it doesn't clog things up. So it ends up on the general scrap pile when with a little care it could be ground up and re-used in the same machine.

Re-use would be a more popular operation if plastics were more expensive, and if current forecasts of the petroleum wells of the world running dry by 1985 prove to be anywhere near correct, then we might at last see this emerge as a viable proposition.

CHAPTER 4 fabrication technology

As a basic understanding of the structure and properties of plastics materials is necessary to the designer, so a knowledge of the principal manufacturing processes is essential if designs are to be produced which are capable of being put into production.

At some stage in their existence plastics materials are malleable, and at that stage they can be moulded into useful form.

Generally speaking, the thermoplastics materials are easier to handle than the thermosets. Thermoplastics can be re-softened by the application of heat, and the curing cycle is therefore not so critical as is the case in the one-way thermoset reaction.

EXTRUSION OF THERMOPLASTICS

The extruder, which produces continuous lengths of sections, tubes and film, is probably the most widely used of all machines in the plastics industry. It consists of a heated barrel with a screw turning inside it. Granular material is fed from a hopper into the screw and is heated not only externally by the heated walls of the cylinder, but also by the friction caused by the screw cutting through the granules.

As the material is forced along the screw it becomes more fluid and is finally forced out through a die, which determines the shape of the extrusion. For example a simple hole will give a continuous rod, a hole with a torpedo suspended in it (fixed at the rear so that the polymer can flow around it) will give a tube, a slit will give a bar and a very wide and thin slit will give a sheet.

The extruded material is cooled when it emerges from the die, but it may also be drawn into an identical but smaller section by emerging onto a belt travelling at higher speed, and with the cooling being delayed. This enables different sizes of profile to be produced from one die.

The speed of extrusion is, of course, determined by the capacity of the barrel and the size of the extrusion. For example, an extruder will produce a small diameter pipe far faster than one of large diameter, this being

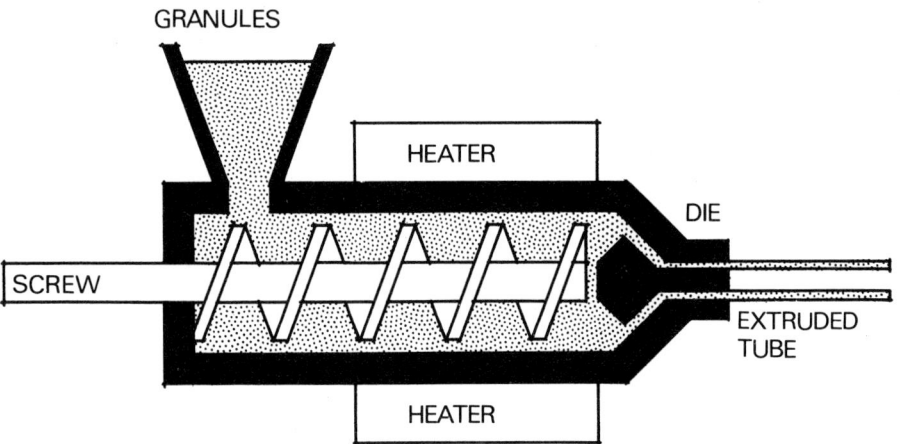

7 Extrusion of thermoplastics.

governed by the volume of material which it can push out. The record extrusion speed would appear to be around 35 m.p.h. for coating telephone wire.

An extruder is a very versatile machine in that the dies can be changed readily and are not unduly expensive (in comparison to injection moulds for example), so that a very wide range of products can be fabricated from one basic machine.

Its versatility is further extended by a technique known as blow moulding, used in the production of plastics bottles. In outline the extruder exudes a length of tube downwards. This tube is gripped by the closing of a two-part mould which nips the top and bottom of the tube into which the air is then blown, forcing the still-plastic tube outwards against the walls of the mould which then parts and drops out a bottle. This is the method which is most commonly used for mouldings up to as large as dustbin size.

A rather similar technique is used in the production of thin film, especially polyethylene film. A tube is extruded which is immediately expanded by being blown out like a balloon. This is then slit, opened and rolled. Film over 30 ft wide can be made in this way.

EXTRUSION OF THE THERMOSETS

This is obviously a more tricky operation than with the thermoplastics. If a thermoset were to go off in the barrel of an extruder, it would be the end of the barrel. So a very different modification of the technique has had to be developed in which the powdered resin is delivered cool to the die, where it is heated up to around 180°C and fully cured only as it emerges. Then if anything goes wrong it is only the die which is lost, and not the whole machine. This paints an unfair picture of what is now a very safe and reliable technique, and one which is beginning to be exploited for the production of window frames, architraves and skirtings.

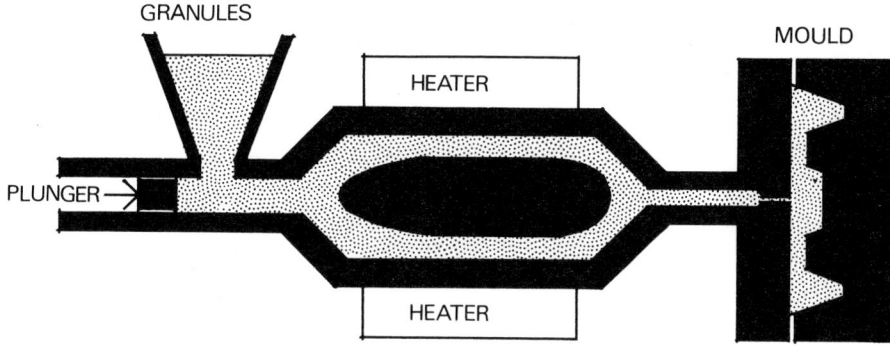

8 Injection moulding in thermoplastics.

INJECTION MOULDING IN THERMOPLASTICS

This is a batch process for the high-speed production of individual objects. A hopper contains granules which are fed into a heated barrel and from which the heated and softened material is forced by a ram through a nozzle at a pressure which can be as high as 40,000 p.s.i. The nozzle leads into the mould, and the material is by now sufficiently plastic to be capable of being forced into the smallest crevices and interstices. The pressure on the material is maintained until it cools and sets when the mould parts and the component is either manually removed or automatically ejected.

The total time taken by this operation varies from a few seconds up to half a minute or more, and numerous variations have been devised to speed up the cycle. Obviously the mould is cooled to speed up the setting process, but multi-cavity moulds are also employed which may produce a hundred or more units per cycle. In addition to this a sort of six-shooter process has been devised whereby one barrel can serve six or more moulds which revolve by stages in front of it. This system is also used for the bottle-blowing technique referred to above.

Moulds have to withstand very high stresses and temperatures for long periods of time (injection moulders normally run 24 hours per day, 365 days per year), are made of beautifully polished or plated high-grade steel, and are consequently extremely expensive.

A mould for the very high-speed production of a small complex unit will have many impressions, and the finished objects will normally emerge connected together by what is known as a sprue, that is a rod or rods which can branch from each other and which are in fact solidified material in the tubes through which the molten material is forced on the way to the various cavities.

The moulded objects are generally stripped from the sprue by hand, but if labour costs are critical a more expensive mould can be constructed with what are known as pin gates—i.e. the mould itself cuts off the moulded objects from the sprue. In each case the sprues are normally thrown into an adjacent grinder, from which the material is put back with the virgin granules in the hopper.

Moulds are objects of great beauty, and mould design is an art form in itself, although hardly recognized as such. The complexities of designing some of the multiple-parting moulds result in some extremely elegant solutions, and the exercise of wrapping one's mind around such a problem would be an interesting subject for architects to study in order to develop their ability to really think in three dimensions.

Injection moulding is, like extrusion, a technique very well suited to thermoplastics materials, and is capable of an incredibly high rate of output. This output is governed by the size and complexity of the object to be moulded, and by the weight of material which the machine can inject per shot. A very typical small scale production run is one recently completed by a local client on a small (16 oz) machine, which produced 2,500,000 curtain runners in ten weeks. The mould had 96 impressions, and the daily output was 35,000.

It was this client who said to me 'Lad'—(from his five years or so head start on me)—'there's chaps in this industry 'ats that clever they can do nowt'. But that's another story.

Giant machines are being produced today, and some super-giants are planned which could mould room-sized units.

It has been calculated that one such machine could produce enough room units to form 100,000 houses or apartments per annum, at a fraction of traditional cost. Unfortunately the operation could only be viable for something approaching that volume of production, and such a standardized demand does not yet exist in any part of the world.

However a possible solution to the problem of harnessing this massive production potential to the production of building components lies in the technique already extensively used in the plastics industry, namely computer-controlled design and production of moulds. If the cost and time of mould production can be drastically reduced, then the cost benefits of enormous production can perhaps be exploited for a far more varied and variable end product.

INJECTION MOULDING IN THERMOSETS

This is a vastly more difficult problem. Injection moulding is ideal for the very high speed production of thermoplastics, but thermoplastic materials are inadequate for many applications, especially applications where a high engineering performance is required.

The challenge to the production engineers was to find some way of modifying the technique to enable the thermosets to be handled at something approaching the speed of the thermoplastics. Tricky, just as with the extrusion of the thermosets; the danger being once again the possibility of the resin curing in the barrel.

The solution, so far, is a combination of compression moulding and injection. Compression moulding is normally carried out in a two-part mould. A quantity of thermoset moulding powder is placed in the hollow

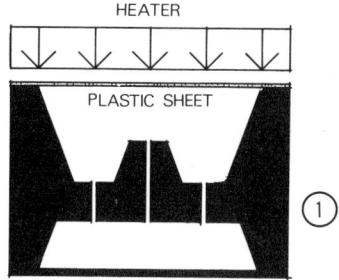

9 Vacuum forming.

or female section of the mould, the plug or male section is closed down into it, and the whole mould is heated until the plastic softens, flows and fills the mould. When the cure is complete the mould is opened and the component is removed.

The pressure involved may be as high as 10,000 p.s.i. and such moulds often require presses with capacities of hundreds or even thousands of tons. It is not a fast process.

However the principle of compression has been applied to injection moulding by substituting a 'transfer pot' for the injection barrel.

The material is carefully prepared in batches, and each batch in turn is placed in the transfer pot where it is heated to the point of plasticity—when it is immediately forced into the mould where it cures. This is faster than compression moulding, but still not up to the speed of the thermoplastics.

However the recently-developed reciprocating screw machine—where the heat build-up is entirely the result of the working of the screw and can be accurately controlled on account of this and the fact that only a small quantity of material is travelling between the screw flights—has made the conventional injection moulding of the thermosets possible. Virtually all plastics materials can now be injected, including phenolics, epoxies, melamines and ureas which could until recently only be handled by slow compression moulding.

VACUUM FORMING

This is a low-cost technique used for moulding thermoplastic sheet materials for relatively small production runs. In its simplest form it consists of an open-topped air-tight box to which a heated and softened sheet of material is clamped. The air is drawn out of the box and the sheet of material is sucked down into a bubble-like form which it retains when cooled, producing an object such as a rooflight.

Very many variations on this technique have been developed, such as sucking the material down over a male former within the box, or plug assisted forming, in which a former is forced down into the heated sheet before the vacuum is applied in order to produce a deeper object without undue thinning out at the corners. Yet another technique consists of draping the sheet of softened material over a male mould prior to the application of a vacuum from within the mould which completes all the fine detail.

These techniques are very interesting to watch in production, and there is just a touch of magic in the sight of a refrigerator lining coming into being by plug-assisted forming. The glossy sheet rises up into a high amorphous shape, and then suddenly all the crisp detail appears for no apparent reason as the vacuum is applied from within.

Vacuum forming is used for relatively short runs. This is because although the moulds are cheap, the technique is slow and labour costs are consequently fairly high. Furthermore production is from sheet material, which is more expensive than granules. If a higher output were required, even for objects as large as the refrigerator lining already mentioned, injection moulding would probably be preferable.

ROTATIONAL CASTING This is an old-established and relatively low-cost technique now being extensively used for the production of large hollow objects in two-piece moulds, normally from p.v.c. paste or polyethylene powder.

The heated metal mould is loaded with the precise amount of material and is then rotated simultaneously around axes at right angles to each other. This ensures the even distribution of the material around the inner face of the mould, and the completed object can be removed from the parted mould after cooling. It is possible to produce a very large and extremely complex hollow object with this technique, and the skin can be as thin as paper if required. The rotational casting of room linings or shells with very complex interiors is a distinct possibility.

CALENDERING Calendering plant consists of a series of mangles for the continuous production of thermoplastics sheet or film at a very high rate. The combination of materials is compounded, pressure and heat are applied, and the subsequent soft mass is automatically carried into a series of rollers mounted in Z or L formation. The rollers control the thickness very accurately and can also apply a texture, and the technique can also be used for coating fabrics. The speed of output can be as high as 400 ft per minute for very thin film and this, coupled with the fact that such simple-sounding equipment is extremely costly, accounts for the limited number of calendering plants.

LOW PRESSURE LAMINATION This is a simple and cheap technique used in the production of glass reinforced polyester laminate, the composite material most commonly used in the construction of plastics structures. This is normally referred to as G.R.P. or R.P. (reinforced plastics), but is also still very commonly called 'Fibreglass' which is fine for the company which uses the name, but no more accurate a description than a trade name such as Twisteel would be for reinforced concrete.

Polyesters (and epoxies) can be moulded without high pressure as they do not form elimination materials which would tend to disrupt the moulding if not firmly contained. Their lamination with fibres which possess a high tensile strength produces a material which can range from highly translucent to opaque, with a higher strength/weight ratio than aluminium or mild steel, an impact resistance greater (weight for weight) than most metals, a dimensional stability range from the equivalent of aluminium to better than steel, excellent chemical and weather resistance and, if required, an inability to support combustion.

Polyester resin can be formulated to set or cure at room temperatures without any outside assistance, although the cure can be speeded up by the application of heat and/or pressure. The normal formulation is, simply, resin plus catalyst (which generates the reaction) plus accelerator (which governs the speed of hardening).

A wide range of reinforcing materials can be used in conjunction with polyester, but the one in predominant use is glass fibre.

Glass develops incredible tensile strength when drawn out into fibres thinner than human hair (this high fibre strength is not peculiar to glass—fibres of nylon or polypropylene possess tremendous strength as a consequence of the alignment of the molecules when the materials are drawn out into fibre form).

Under laboratory conditions, the tensile strength of glass fibre may be well over one million p.s.i., and allowing for all the normal difficulties and accidents which arise in practice, it can be developed to 250,000 p.s.i. on the job. It was, weight for weight, the strongest constructional material by far—until relatively recently.

Glass fibres do not creep, have good resistance to most forms of chemicals, and have the fairly good Young's modulus of 10.5 million p.s.i. They are dimensionally stable and resist temperatures of up to 600°C. Considerable development work has resulted in 'textured' fibres which give an almost ideal bond to the resin.

The material is commonly available in the form of chopped strand mat (2" fibres distributed in random fashion and lightly bonded together for handling, the resultant mat being normally a little thicker and heavier than a handkerchief), rovings (continuous filament for very high unidirectional strength) and woven cloth (for very high two-way strength).

The mould for a simple low-pressure lamination may be male or female (depending upon whether the surface finish from the mould is required on the inside or the outside of the finished object), and only needs to be strong enough to carry the weight of the lamination. So it can be made of timber or plaster or light metal, although commonly a 'dolly' (or model of the finished object) is made from which the production mould is taken in g.r.p.

The mould is coated with a release agent, and then the first coat of liquid resin is applied by spray or brush (hence the derogatory term 'bucket and brush' used by operators of more sophisticated moulding equipment). Into this a mat of glass fibres is laid and compacted with a hand-roller.

fabrication technology /37

Then another coating of resin follows another layer of glass. This process is continued until the required thickness is built up. A structural shell will normally be around $\frac{3}{16}''$ thick, and at that thickness will contain 4 oz of glass fibres (2 to 4 mats) and 10 oz of resin per square foot.

The laminate is stronger with better compaction, and this is sometimes achieved by sucking a sheet of Cellophane onto the moulding by a vacuum. This is effective in eliminating the air bubbles which can be trapped and which can disturb the even performance of the material.

The weathering properties of the laminate can be severely impaired by glass-fibres protruding through the surface and creating a capillary path for moisture penetration. Glass-fibre surfacing tissues are used together with a 'gel coat' or resin-rich final coating to eliminate this possibility.

The cure of the laminate may take from a few hours to a day, and is often accelerated by the application of heat. Nevertheless this is still a slow process compared to those previously outlined—although not when one is considering an object such as the 153 ft long research minesweeper with a one-piece translucent g.r.p. hull recently completed for the Royal Navy.

Some of the labour content may be taken out of the hand-layup process by spraying chopped glass roving and resin simultaneously onto a mould, although compaction still has to be carried out carefully.

FILAMENT WINDING   A technique evolved for small or large components which have to carry high stress. A collapsible mould is rotated on an axle, and continuous rovings of glass fibre are passed through a bath of resin and wound around the mould under tension. The winding may move back and forth along the length of the mould in order to align the fibres in the direction required for maximum strength. Tanks and high pressure pipes are made by this technique, also boat hulls up to about 70 ft long and room units.

Pre-impregnated glass mat or 'pre-preg' consists of a glass mat loaded with a precise amount of resin which is partially catalysed. The cure is completed by the heat and pressure of compression moulding between matched metal moulds. This is a general-purpose material which may be moulded into deep-draw forms, and is very consistent in performance as the batching is entirely reliable. The surface finish of both sides is excellent, and large wall panels are being increasingly made thus.

Dough moulding compound consists of random glass fibres, polyester, catalyst and filler, and is used in compression moulding, pultrusion (a modification of extrusion) and some injection moulding. Its particular qualities are low cost, good weathering and impact resistance, and the ability to be moulded in thick sections without the stress cracking which creates problems with other plastics materials used in this way.

Sandwich construction. Sandwich panels or shells are composites in which layers of different materials are used in conjunction with each other in order to build up the desired physical properties of the finished unit. A typical sandwich consists of an inner and an outer face of thin, stiff material

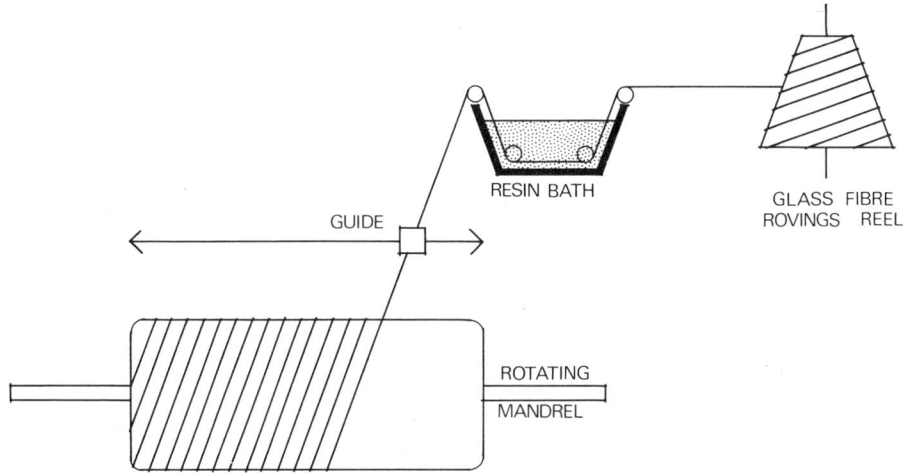

10 Filament winding.

with a core of lighter, weaker material. The skins act rather like the flanges of a R.S.J. and withstand the bending stress, while the core transmits stresses from one face to the other, takes up the shear, prevents the thin skins from buckling and often provides excellent insulation.

The production of a very basic sandwich shell would consist first of all of the hand or spray application of polyester and glass on a female mould (to give a good outer finish). Then, while the inner coat of resin was still tacky, cut panels of polyurethane foam, perhaps $\frac{3}{4}''$ thick, would be pressed into place, and the inner skin would be completed on top of the layer of foam. Alternatively polyurethane could be sprayed onto the outer skin, but as its thickness cannot be accurately controlled in such an application, it would form a rather lumpy base for the inner skin. So in each case the inner finish, lacking mould control, tends to be rather rough.

It has been known for many years—I heard of it in France in 1959—that certain foams of the polyurethane family can be introduced into heated, hollow metal moulds where they can be induced to cure solid when in contact with the heated mould, while remaining in the foam state internally. Thus a sandwich panel or shell can be produced in one operation. This technique is now fairly widely used for furniture and decorative products on neoprene moulds, although it has not yet been applied to general building products.

A more recent development lies in the injection moulding of thermoplastic foams. Here two different polymers are fed into the mould from two separate barrels—the first one being the solid skin material which travels part way into the mould and is then forced home (and effectively lines all mould faces) by the injection of the foam which fills the cavity between the skins. This process is making tremendous advances in furniture and vehicle building (it can 'look like wood' only too easily), and may well cause many of us to re-assess the structural potential of unreinforced thermoplastics in building, if only because the resulting sandwich has from three to five times the stiffness of a solid moulding, and it is already cheaper to use than timber.

fabrication technology /39

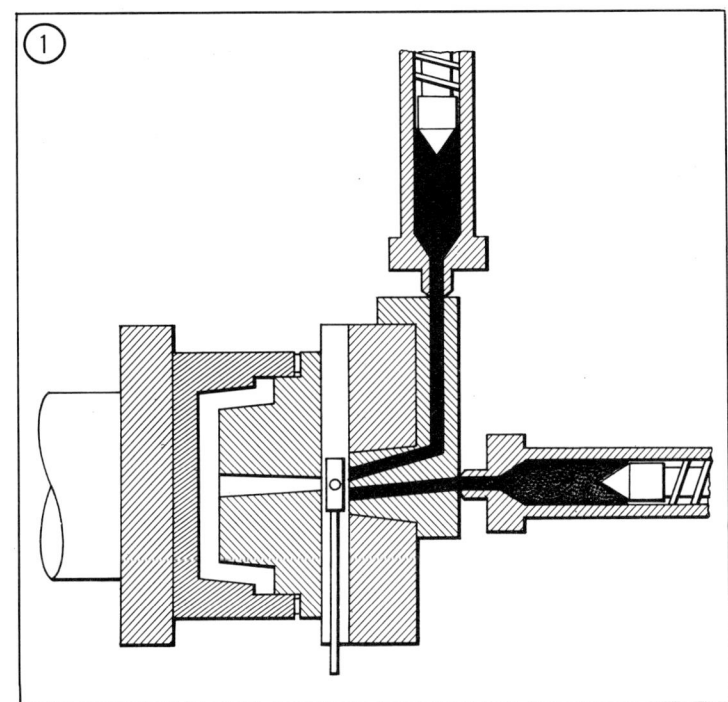

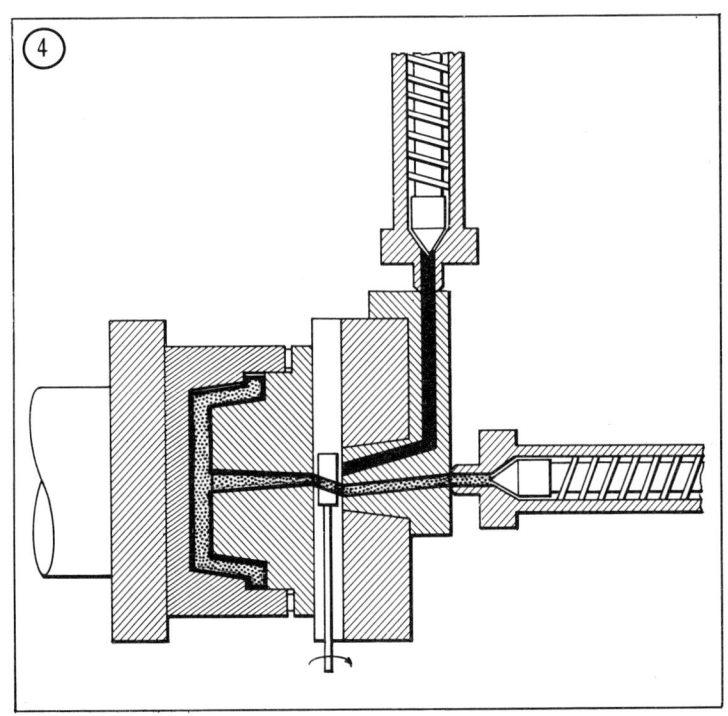

11 Sandwich injection moulding.

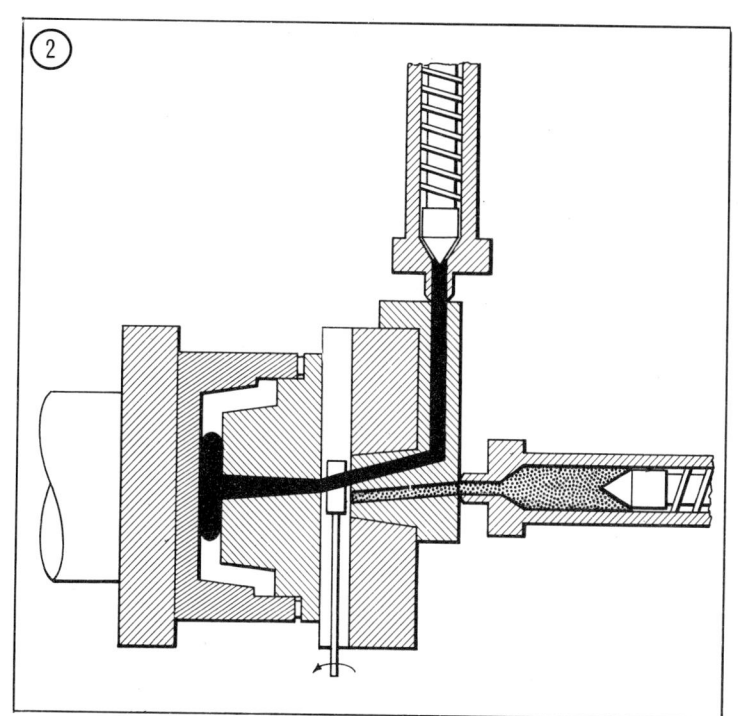
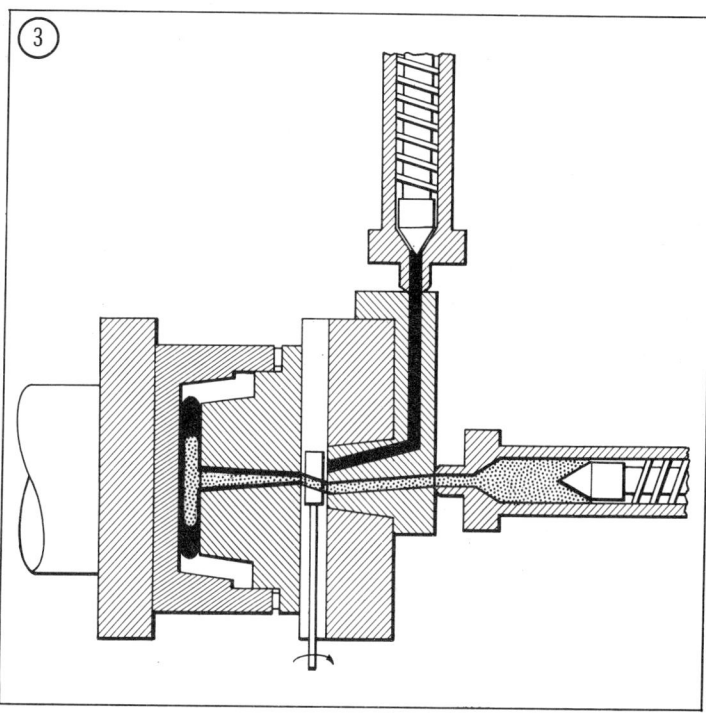
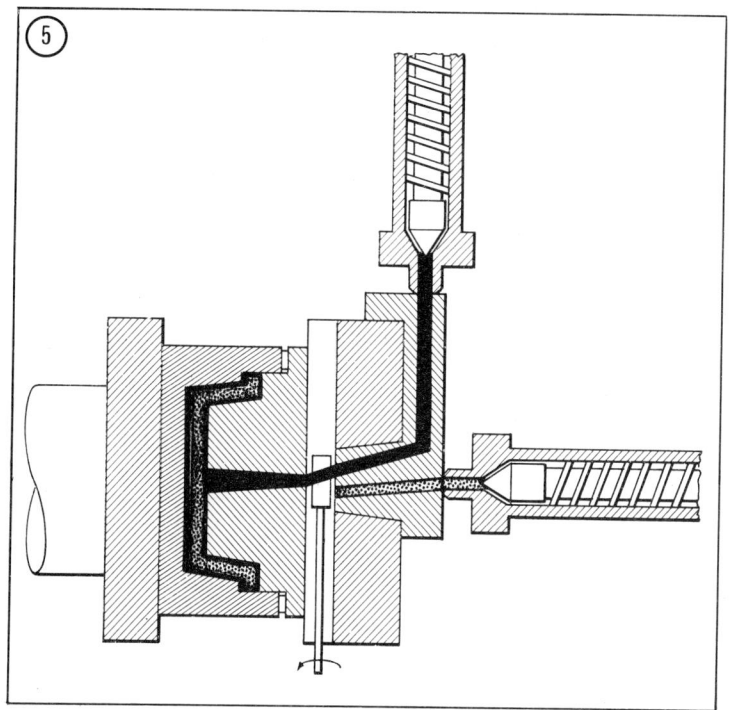
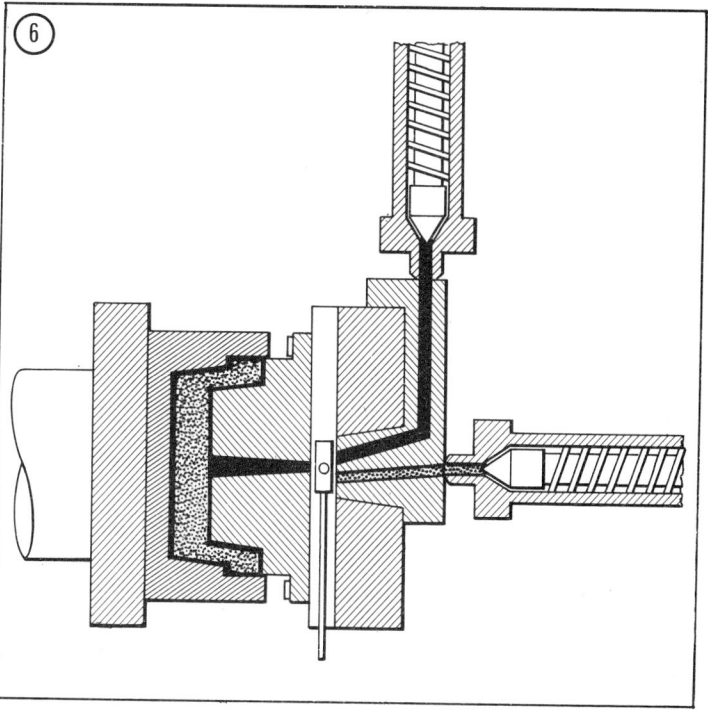

REINFORCEMENT	ROVING ROD UNI-DIRECTIONAL	UNI-DIRECTIONAL CLOTH S1/225/450/E†	SATIN WEAVE CLOTH S2/225/E†	PLAIN WEAVE CLOTH P6/225/E†	WOVEN ROVING FABRIC	CHOPPED STRAND MAT, PREFORM AND NEEDLED MAT	POLYESTER RESIN (UN-REINFORCED)	ALUMINIUM	STRUCTURAL STEEL
Specific gravity	2·0	1·9	1·8	1·8	1·8	1·6	1·3	2·7	7·8
Glass content % by weight	75	68	65	65	62	35	—	—	—
Tensile strength 1000 p.s.i.‡	150	90	55	40	50	24	6	10–35	60–70
Specific tensile strength 1000 p.s.i.	75	47·4	30·5	22·2	27·8	15	4·6	3·7–13	7·7–9·0
Tensile modulus p.s.i.	$6·0 \times 10^6$	$4·5 \times 10^6$	$3·0 \times 10^6$	$2·8 \times 10^6$	$2·3 \times 10^6$	$1·5 \times 10^6$	$0·3 \times 10^6$	10×10^6	30×10^6
Specific tensile Modulus p.s.i.	$3·0 \times 10^6$	$2·4 \times 10^6$	$1·7 \times 10^6$	$1·6 \times 10^6$	$1·3 \times 10^6$	$0·9 \times 10^6$	$0·2 \times 10^6$	$3·7 \times 10^6$	$3·8 \times 10^6$
Compressive strength 1000 p.s.i.	70	45	50	38	16	27	21	10–15	50–60
Flexural strength 1000 p.s.i.§	157	95	75	60	42	34	13	10–25	60–63
Shear strength 1000 p.s.i.	22	19	21	18	22	12	—	12–20	45–50
Impact strength ft. lb. Izod	35	25	12	8–10	8–10	6–10	0·2	up to 18	up to 50
Moisture Absorption % (24 hours immersed)	0·15	0·2–0·5	0·2–0·5	0·2–0·5	0·2–0·5	0·2–0·5	0·2–0·6	—	—
Linear coefficient of expansion/degF	5×10^{-6}	$5–6 \times 10^{-6}$	$5–6 \times 10^{-6}$	$6–8 \times 10^{-6}$	$7–9 \times 10^{-6}$	$10–18 \times 10^{-6}$	$50–60 \times 10^{-6}$	$12–13 \times 10^{-6}$	$6–7 \times 10^{-6}$
Thermal conductivity B.t.u. in/ft² h degF.	3·0	2–3	1·5–2·5	1·5–2·0	1·5–2·0	1·4–1·9	1·2	1,400	300

† From DTD 5518 Aircraft Material Specification.
‡ Laminates tested to B.S. 2782, paragraph 3 method 301B.
§ Laminates tested to B.S. 2782, paragraph 3 method 304B (using ⅛″ radius blocks).

* Values for Fibreglass reinforced epoxide and phenolic resin laminates are of the same order of magnitude.

12 Properties of typical g.r.p. laminates.

MATERIAL	SG	ULTIMATE TENSILE STRENGTH	YOUNG'S MODULUS	SPECIFIC STRENGTH	SPECIFIC STIFFNESS
		lbf/in^2	lbf/in$^2 \times 10^{-6}$	lbf/in^2	lbf/in$^2 \times 10^{-6}$
Steel (S97)	7·87	145 500	30·0	18 500	3·8
Al alloy (L65)	2·8	67 200	10·5	24 000	3·75
Ti alloy (DTD 5173)	4·5	134 300	16·0	29 900	3·55
Mg alloy (DTD 88C)	1·8	40 300	6·3	22 400	3·5
Aircraft spruce	0·5	10 000	1·9	20 000	3·8
Glass fibre	2·54	250 000	10·0	98 400	3·94
RAE carbon fibre	2·0	275 000	55·0	137 500	22·5
CFR plastics	1·54	105 000	22·0	68 000	14·0

13 Carbon fibre reinforced plastics: specific strength and stiffness of various aircraft materials.

CARBON FIBRE REINFORCEMENT

Over the past few years, considerable research has been carried out into the development of materials with strengths exceeding those of glass fibres, particularly as a result of demands from the aircraft and aerospace industries. Crystalline whisker growths on aluminium first showed promise, but in the early sixties work in Britain switched to carbon fibres, in view of the intriguing gap between the strength of existing carbon cloth (Young's modulus 6 to 9×10^{-6}) and graphite whiskers (100×10^{-6}).

The development and patenting of carbon fibres was completed by the mid-sixties, and resulted in a material which possessed engineering properties far in excess of anything previously available, and capable of being combined with thermosetting resins to produce laminates with a far greater stiffness than the metals. Indeed the stiffness is so great that normal engineering assembly methods have to be re-thought. For example, in fixing a metal shell to a rigid frame, it is possible to bolt one end up and then pull the other end slightly into alignment to allow the bolt to be inserted. With a carbon fibre laminate this simply cannot be done.

It is not an exaggeration to say that carbon fibre laminates open up a whole new phase in plastics developments—or will do when their price drops to a figure at which they can be used in conventional engineering applications. The high cost of production has discouraged several companies from licensing the process from the British government who are the patent holders. However the demand exists and will grow, so inevitably the price will come down. Few people nowadays would dare to take the attitude of the radio engineering lecturer who shortly after World War II showed his students a transistor valve. 'Very ingenious' he said, 'but far too costly ever to come into general use.'

There will, of course, be other developments to equal or exceed the performance of carbon fibres, so if these are to be fully exploited the cost problem will have to be solved fairly quickly.

historical applications

CHAPTER 5

The history of the development of plastics in architecture starts not with materials but with individuals, and not with technology but with aesthetics.

One might almost commence with Gaudi, although the real impact of his work was hardly felt on an international scale until the 1950s. Perhaps it would be better to suggest that the purity of the modern movement in the first two decades of its development was not found to be entirely satisfying by all sympathetically-minded architects at the time, and that some were compelled to rebel against the right angle, the post and lintel, blocks, slabs of flat walling and panels of glazing.

Notable amongst these rebels was, of course, Eric Mendelsohn whose work on the Einstein tower at Potsdam (conceived as an exercise in the sculptural use of concrete although constructed finally in brickwork and then rendered) and earlier sketches for Labour Hall projects, while lying dormant for many years, nevertheless had an appreciable if subconscious effect on the minds of many younger architects. And when finally a range of materials came along which made such sculptural structures a practical possibility the subconscious awoke and affected many of the early prototypes of plastics structures.

John Johannsen is a designer very much in the Mendelsohn tradition, even to the extent of experiencing great difficulty in actually constructing some of his fluid concrete projects (double curvature shells tend to end up as single-curved sections of cylinders), and his work received considerable publicity in the few years immediately prior to the sudden development of plastics structures in the mid-fifties.

However, perhaps the biggest single influence upon the first generation of plastics architects was Frank Lloyd Wright, who came to be known especially through the writings and interpretations of his disciple Bruno Zevi. Those of us who started our careers in the middle years of this century could not fail to be influenced by Wright's thinking, by his breaking up of previously-rigid architectural forms by the involvement of a structure in its setting, the blend of interior with exterior, and also by his City by the Sea project (1912), Larkin Building (1904–06) and the houses for his two sons (1952 and 1953), Johnson Wax structures (1938 and 1950), and especially the Millard house at Pasadena of 1921. In this latter example, we have an illustration of a simple textured structure which still holds many lessons for us in how we might use a plastics material to achieve the richness which is so lacking in most of our projects to date.

The first real plastics structure was Ionel Schein's house, shown at the Paris Exhibition of 1956 but designed and constructed in 1955. However, considerable development work on the structural applications of plastics in building had been carried out before this date, both in Europe and the United States, indeed from the late thirties onwards. This was true of Britain perhaps more than elsewhere, for Britain was starved of constructional materials during the war, and a number of organizations were set up to investigate possible solutions to the problem.

This problem was only too often seen then, as now, as one of substitution, and most of the developments carried out were concerned with cladding panels, building blocks, window frames, light structural members, complete staircases and small items such as roller shutter laths.

These experiments were hampered by the limited range of plastics materials which were available in 1940 and 1941, and especially by the fact that only ureaformaldehyde and phenolformaldehyde were commonly available from the family of thermosetting resins.

However this did not prevent a number of architects—notably Sam Bunton and T. Warnett Kennedy of the Building Plastics Research Corporation of Glasgow—from putting forward proposals for the development of an industry for the prefabrication of plastics housing, realizing as they did not only that such organization was necessary for the proper exploitation of the materials, but also that the post-war years would bring with them an international explosion in the demand for housing.

Proposals for a range of rapidly-erected flexible house types based upon the use of a standard plastics panel were drawn up by the Building Plastics Research Corporation of Glasgow as early as 1941, and included precise jointing techniques and permanent internal and external finishes. In the following year they called upon the plastics industry to set up house prefabrication companies to co-ordinate the products of the various plastics companies and to undertake or supervise site assembly.

Unfortunately the immediate post-war years in virtually all countries turned out to be a time of political upheaval in which such proposals as these were forgotten or rejected, with the emphasis lying on rejection. Even the Churchill house, the only real attempt ever made in Britain to bring manufacturing technology to bear on a mass housing market, was rejected and is still scorned, quite undeservedly, as the 'prefab'. It was a time of return to the supposedly solid virtues of the past; return despite the problem of rationed building materials in an impoverished country.

Demonstration houses were built of plastics materials in a number of countries, notably Sweden, Germany and the United States, from as early as 1933, but these were all limited exercises in the obvious use of currently-available plastics materials, and were often merely publicity vehicles for a certain manufacturer's product range. This type of house still goes on, and still makes as little contribution to plastics in architecture as it ever did.

And so we come to 1955 and that great landmark in the development of plastics structures, the first all-plastics house, designed by the team of Ionel Schein, Yves Magnant and R. A. Coulon, and with Antoine Fasani as colour consultant. This was a remarkable tour-de-force of design and construction within a very short period of time, particularly as Schein acknowledges no precedents and no especial influences.

The concept of the house was based upon the growth of a snail's shell, so that the house consists of a basic circular living space with cooking area, sanitary block and warm-air heater, to which a number of bedroom units may be attached at will. As the shell grows to accommodate the snail, so this house grows to accommodate the family.

The planning was advanced for its time, although perhaps not outstandingly so, and the rather thin and flat curvature of the exterior was rapidly superseded in the designers' later work. However the successful reconsideration of the elements of housing—clip-on heating, moulded sculptural doors, moulded-in equipment in bedrooms and kitchen, the evolution of a true structural skin, and above all a most revolutionary bathroom core—were the features which made the house the remarkable and truly worthy foundation of the evolution of plastics in architecture. So remarkable that it is still a very potent influence today, and projects are still being designed which echo its form in the most direct manner.

The fabrication of the prototype must have been chaotic—this was a time when architects were hardly aware of g.r.p. boats and few had dreamed of g.r.p. housing—certainly the progress photographs look like a Laurel and Hardy comedy, with the finished shells coming off in such a state, that they needed a tremendous amount of hand-finishing and final trimming with a hacksaw to an exact fit.

Nevertheless go together it did, and its chequered subsequent career has included three years on the roof of a storage depot, and a grand total of fifteen assemblies and demountings. Now it has reached what may be its final resting place; it was reassembled in 1969 at Douai and is inhabited, in the grounds of Charbonnages de France, the company which originally sponsored its development way back in 1955.

However one feature of its conception has not yet had its full impact (and in this respect the black-and-white architectural press has much to answer for), and that is its colour. This was a true polychromatic exercise, and had it been publicized as such we might not today be groping around for a vocabulary by which to exploit the colour potential of plastics materials.

The period immediately after 1955 was one of intense creative activity for Schein, Coulon and Magnant. They had established themselves as leaders in a new field in architecture, and proceeded to design a wide range of buildings and building components. Unfortunately they did not

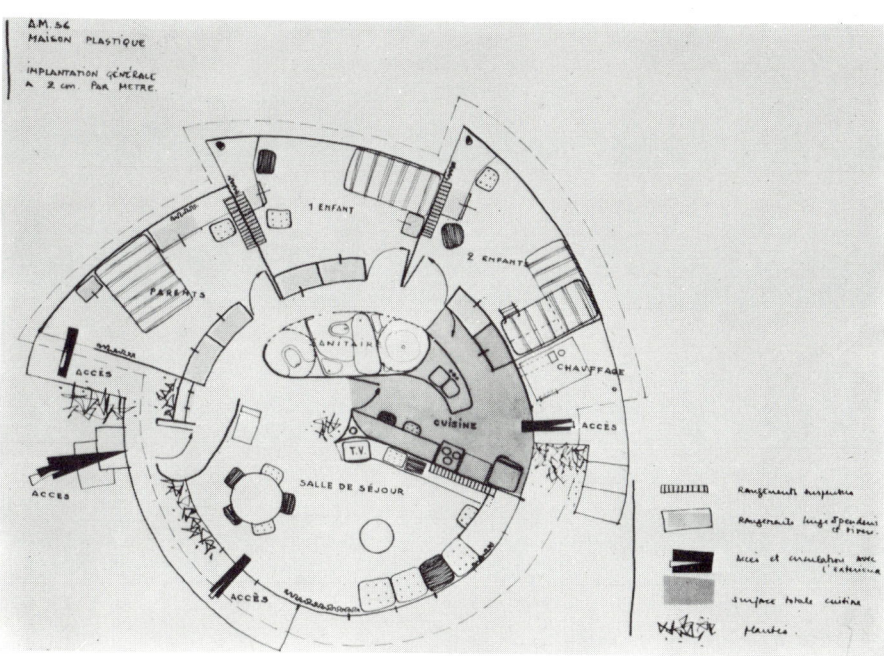

14–16 The first all-plastics house, Paris Exhibition of 1955. Ionel Schein, with R. A. Coulon and Yves Magnant. Top, exterior; centre, sketch plan and below, bathroom unit.

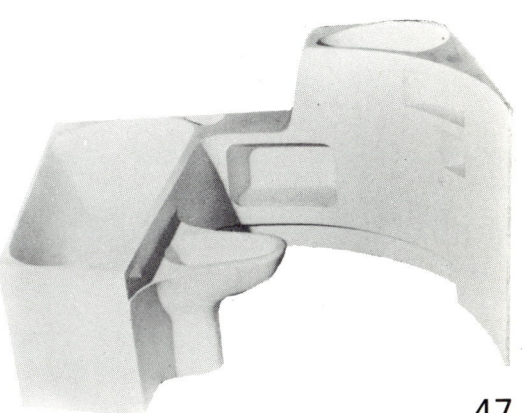

17 Motel cabin by Ionel Schein, with R. A. Coulon and Yves Magnant.

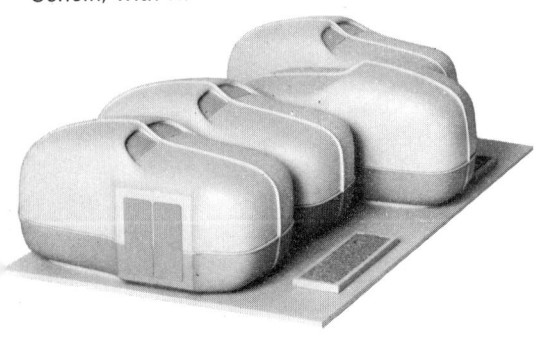

18 Mobile library exhibition units by Ionel Schein, with R. A. Coulon and Yves Magnant.

receive the encouragement and financial backing which they deserved and it is difficult to say why, unless it was that the plastics companies of France expected the building market to become theirs on the strength of one or two experimental structures, and then lost interest when it became evident that this most conservative of markets was not going to change overnight.

Whether this was the reason or not, the fact remains that Coulon, Schein and Magnant suffered the embittering experience of neglect in their own country, and saw other architects in other countries profit from their work and from opportunities which should so rightfully have been theirs. Nevertheless their work in the period 1956–8 was quite remarkable, and it is as fresh now as the day it was designed.

The motel cabin is an excellent example—conceived in September 1956, constructed October–November, and exhibited in December. And that is quite a timetable. One wonders where Schein would have led us by now if only the necessary backing had been forthcoming.

The cabin itself is a brilliant exercise in the development of a living capsule to cater for ten hours of night and eight hours of daytime. It includes twin beds which convert for daytime use into a couch and a table, and a splendidly compact top-lit bathroom with W.C., shower and washbasin. The g.r.p. moulding and the manipulation of the double-curvature forms were both greatly advanced from the design of the house, and the whole lightweight unit was designed for transportation by truck and grouped assembly on site.

The comment in *Techniques et Architecture* for December 1959 is very much to the point: *Il est dommage que ce prototype n'ait pas reçu d'authentique production architecturale.* ('It is regrettable that this prototype should not have been put into proper architectural production.')

This was followed by a development of the motel cabin in the units designed for a mobile library exhibition, by a range of heavily sculptured cladding panels with all equipment moulded in place, by shell units of construction, and by a most delightful acrylic window, all in 1957–8.

The window is a remarkable example of radical thinking and of the inventive use of easily-moulded materials to achieve the total elimination of the subframe. One example only is still in use, namely in the concierge's house at the office of the Caisse des Depots at Arcueil, near Paris.

In 1956 a plastics house designed by Alison and Peter Smithson was exhibited at the Ideal Home Exhibition in London. This house, although largely a mock-up and containing a rather large number of space-age gadgets and fashions, demonstrated some of the first examples of g.r.p. shell chairs, in both saddle and petal form, and also 'Pogo' fold-flat chairs in transparent acrylic.

The construction was never intended to be fully industrialized, as the design was an examination of the way in which we might live rather than of the means whereby that end might be attained. This also was a most under-rated design which might well have generated further exercises into ways of living.

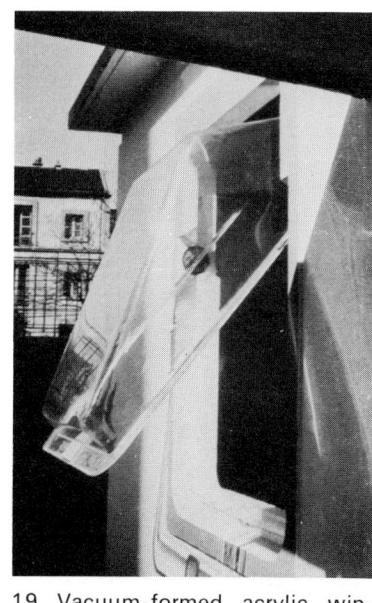

19 Vacuum-formed acrylic window for Sahara research structure. Schein, Coulon, Magnant.

20, 21 House of the Future by Alison and Peter Smithson. Bedroom and dining area.

The Monsanto House of the Future was designed by Hamilton and Goody, and built in 1957, one year after the Smithson house. This is still probably the best known plastics structure in the world, yet its contribution was chiefly significant from a structural point of view, and it made little addition to the development either of industrialized housing or to innovation in living conditions.

However it was without doubt brilliantly engineered. G.r.p. shells with multiple honeycomb cores cantilevered from a concrete core with windows in the flank of each arm—a demonstration of how plastics can overcome some of the most difficult stress conditions and combinations.

The house was visited by around 20 million people during its ten-years life in Disneyland, and successfully withstood earthquakes and ninety m.p.h. winds. When its demolition was planned the wreckers arranged to have it down in one day. However their 3,000 lb steel balls bounced off the g.r.p. walls, chain saw blades broke and the demolition crane which tried to tear it loose only succeeded in pulling itself off its mountings. Finally, after two weeks, the house was successfully crushed with choker

22–24 Monsanto House of the Future by Hamilton and Goody. Plan, assembly and completed exterior.

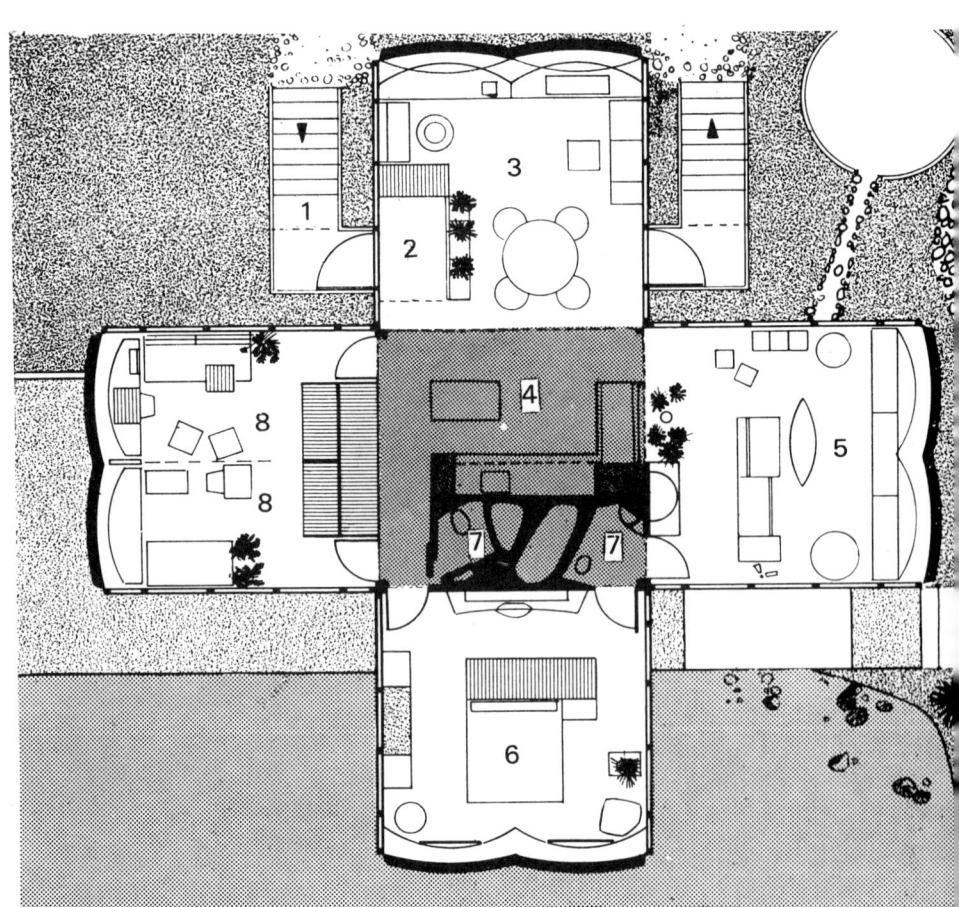

50/ historical applications

25–27 Left, component housing system by Cesare Pea. Facing page, vaults by Roberto Menghi. XIth Milan Triennale. Aerial shot of model and below, two units assembled at the exhibition.

cables. Perhaps future demolition should be a serious factor in the design of plastics structures?

Cesare Pea developed a g.r.p. housing system in Italy in 1957 based on the use of four standard folded forms, plus variable end panels, and at the same time Roberto Menghi designed an elegant single-curvature vault (of translucent g.r.p. with a paper honeycomb core) which could be assembled with other identical shells to enclose a varied range of spaces. Two shells were fabricated, and were exhibited at the XIth Triennale at Milan.

The first German plastics house was produced in 1959 by Rudolf Doernach, and consisted of four identical g.r.p. shell roof/wall elements. The vertical units incorporated a translucent plastic-skinned honeycomb core filled with a fluid which reacted to the sun by evaporation, giving off a light- and heat-controlling veil. The house was inhabited, initially, for four years.

In the same year the first British shell structure was designed by a group working in the architect's research and development section, British Railways (Eastern Region). The group was concerned with industrial design and had already taken out several patents when they were set the problem of a range of structures of standard height, three spans and variable length, to contain signal relaying equipment and to be used throughout the eastern part of the country.

Three shells were designed which could be put together in a variety of ways to meet these conditions, being constructed of an inner and outer skin of $\frac{1}{8}''$ g.r.p. and a $\frac{3}{4}''$ core of expanded phenolic, all on a female g.r.p. mould.

The first structure was assembled at Thameshaven Junction in Essex in 1961 and over three hundred were subsequently produced including variations on the design, and were used as far afield as the Antarctic. This is undoubtedly the most successful g.r.p. structure yet to go into production. It is perhaps a pity that other designs produced in the group at the time

52/ historical applications

28 Plastics house by Rudolf Doernach.

29 Relay Room system for British Railways by Arthur Quarmby, with David Appleby, 1959. Roof plan, smallest version.

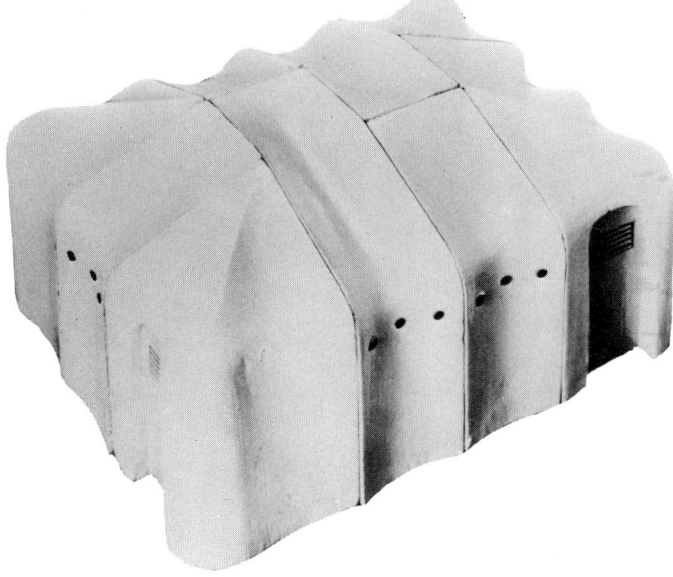

30 Relay Room system for British Railways, architect's models: above, small span (14' 0") structure; centre, intermediate span (18' 9") structure; and below, full span (23' 6") structure.

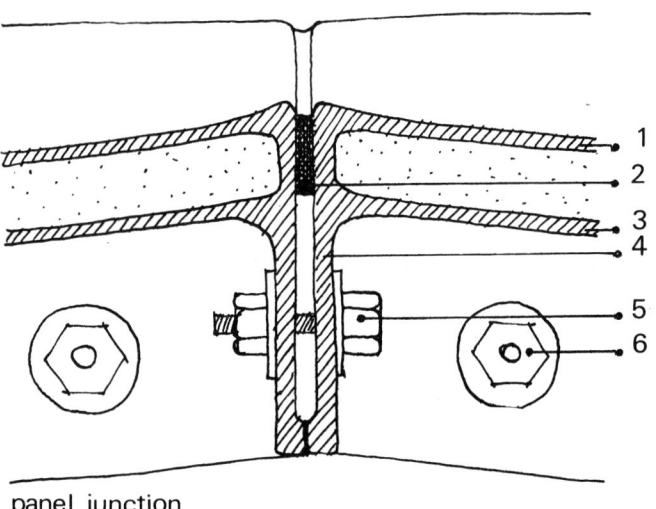
panel junction

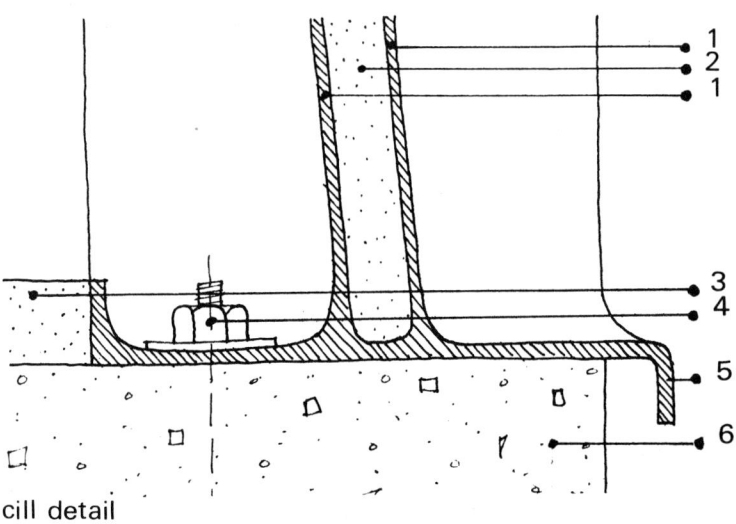
cill detail

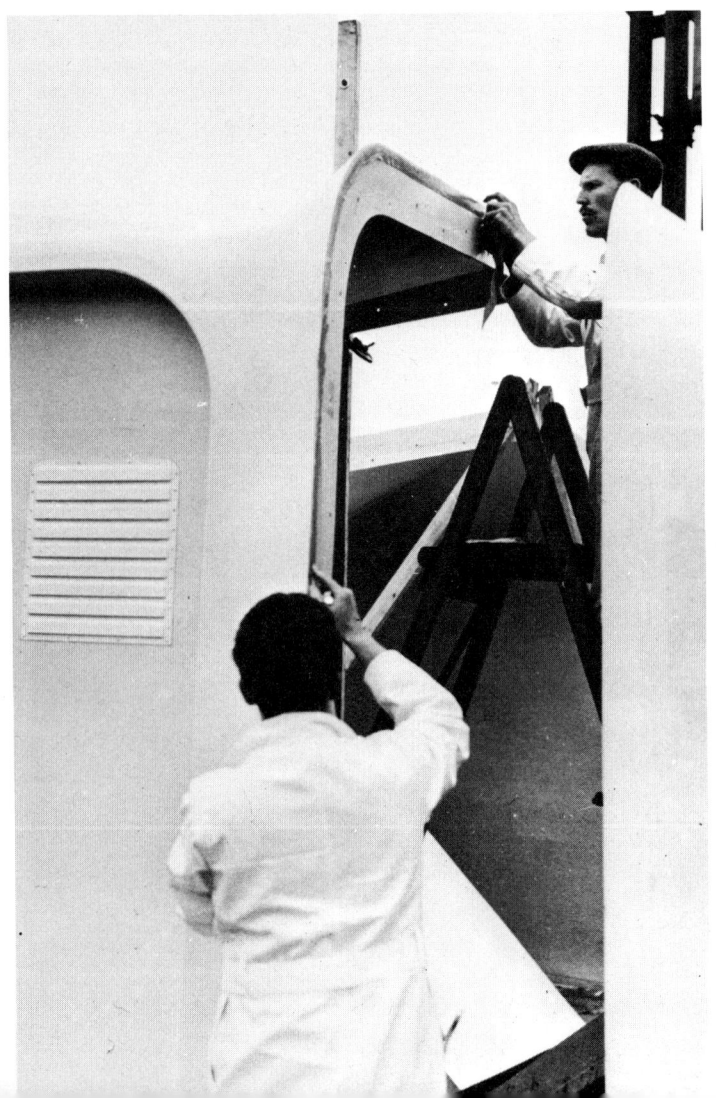

31–34 Above: constructional details of British Railways Relay Room system. Left: 1 and 3, $\frac{1}{8}''$ g.r.p. skins; 2, Polysulphide rubber sealant strips; 4, $\frac{1}{4}''$ g.r.p. flange; 5, Assembly bolt; 6, Holding-down bolt. Right: 1, $\frac{1}{8}''$ g.r.p. shells; 2, $\frac{3}{4}''$ expanded phenolic core; 3, Screed; 4, Holding-down bolt; 5, $\frac{1}{4}''$ base flange; 6, Concrete base. Below: Relay Room at Thameshaven Junction in Essex. Fixing the polysulphide rubber sealant strip. Fabrication and assembly by Mickleover of London Ltd. Facing, above: assembling the shells and below, the completed structure.

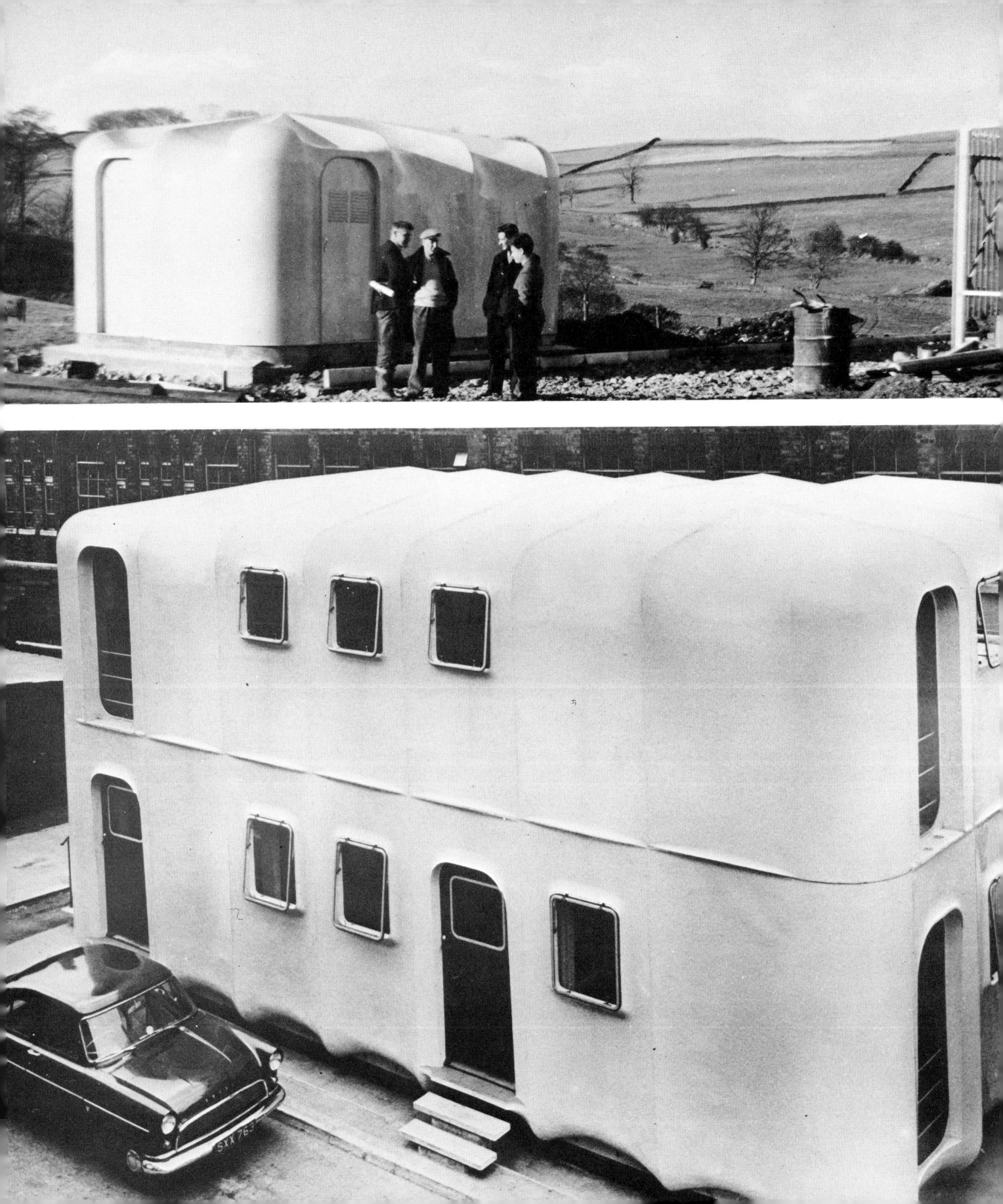

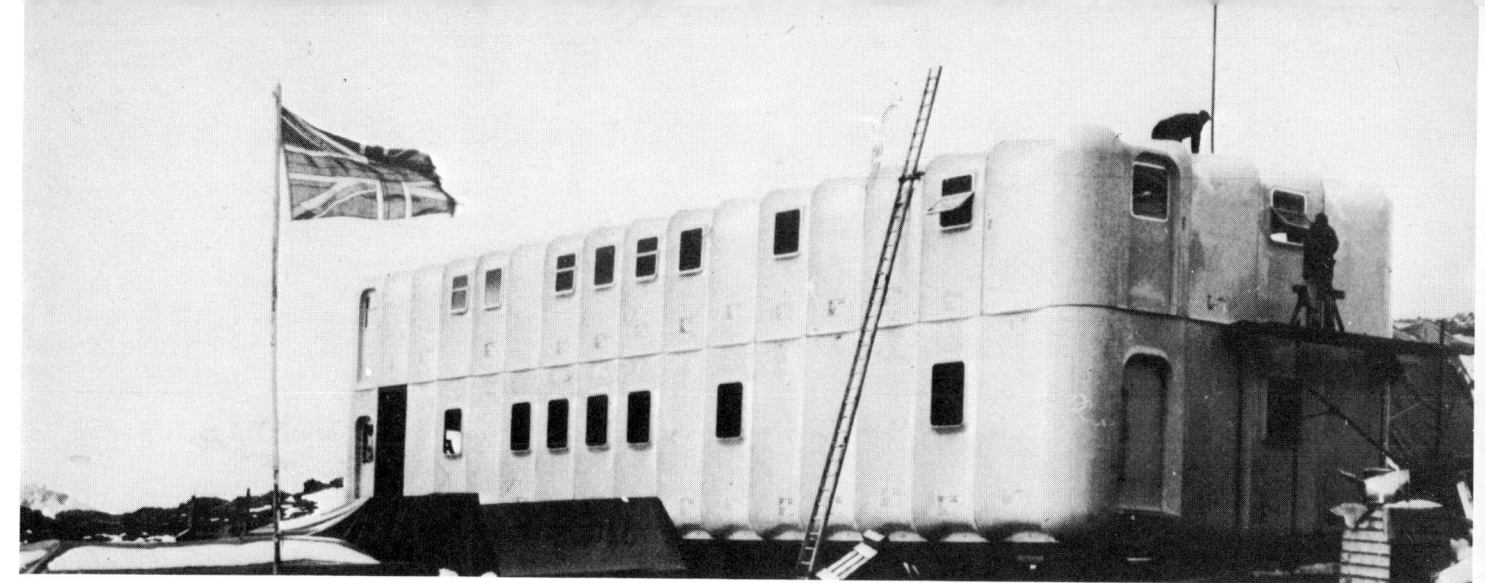

35–38 Facing, above: Relay Room units used as electricity substation in Scotland, by Mickleover of London Ltd. Facing, below: modification of Relay Room system as telephone exchange for Bakelite Ltd at Birmingham, Costain Ltd with Mickleover of London Ltd. Steel-edge beam carries full-span shells, with half-shells slung below and bolted back to concrete base. Above: Biological Research Laboratory, Signey Island, 1963, by Mickleover of London Ltd for the British Antarctic Survey. Similar to the telephone exchange, but core increased from $\frac{3}{4}''$ to $1\frac{1}{4}''$ for extreme climate. Below: single-skin modification of Relay Room system as vehicle washing bay for Schweppes; $\frac{3}{16}''$ translucent shells, intermediate span, mould inserts for increased height. Mickleover of London Ltd.

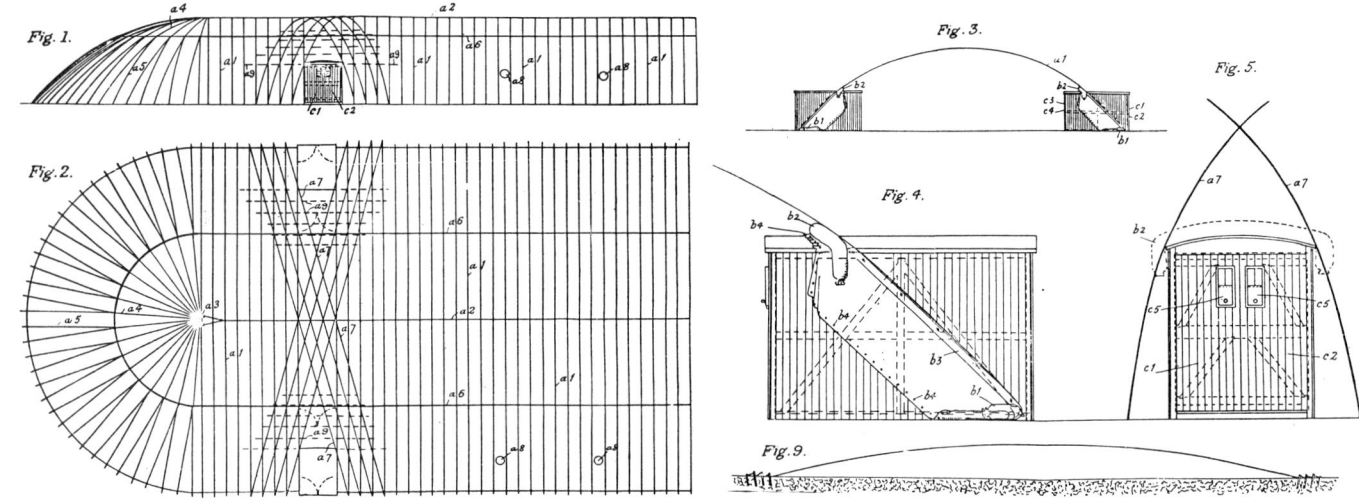

39 Drawings from patent No. 119,339 by F. W. Lanchester for a cable-restrained pneumatic construction.

were not carried out, and that the Region has not maintained this early standard of experiment.

It is impossible to outline the history of plastics structures without reference to the very odd development of pneumatic structures. This could quite reasonably be taken back to around 800 B.C. when Assyrian troops used inflated skins to help them in swimming across rivers However, the story really starts in twentieth-century terms with the remarkable series of patents taken out by F. W. Lanchester in 1917.

These patents contain almost all the ingredients of present-day low-pressure pneumatic construction—spans of over 100 ft, air-lock doors, inflation fans, inwards-turned flap skirtings, anchorage points, nets or cables to carry major stresses for large-scale enclosures—everything except the skin material, which at the time was an impervious balloon fabric with oiled silk for localized translucency.

Indeed in some respects we have yet to match Lanchester's proposals. For example, he used mobile railway vans (similar to the containers of today) in dual form—both as air-lock doors, and also to contain the packed-up structure with its nets and cables, for transport. Also he was well aware of the need to increase internal air pressure to counteract the load applied by high wind, and proposed to use wind cowls—designed to face into the wind—so that when pressure increased externally the internal pressure was also raised.

The influences which governed Lanchester's inventiveness may also be deduced from the patents, which refer on numerous occasions to certain constructional features identical to those used to make non-rigid balloons.

Unfortunately these patents were not exploited at the time, and it was thought until recently that all the real work was carried out by Walter Bird at Cornell University in the immediate post-war years. Indeed Irving Skeist in his book *Plastics in Building* credits Bird with the invention of pneumatic construction.

60/ historical applications

However low-pressure pneumatic domes were in production in Britain in the mid-thirties (R.F.D. Company of Godalming), and were in extensive use by 1938–9 as gunnery training enclosures, with films of attacking aircraft projected onto the inner surface. These domes contained airlocks, and were 20 ft to 30 ft in diameter.

The inflated rib Igloo tent was developed even earlier than this by the Pneumatic Tent Company of Dorking. Designed in 1934, it was brought into commercial production in 1936 and continues in use to this day. Its success led to the extensive use of inflated rib structures for aircraft enclosure during the early years of the war in Britain.

There were at this time one or two individuals whose imaginations were stimulated by the possibilities of plastics materials, and of these Walter Neumark is outstanding.

Otto Walter Neumark was born a British subject in Brünn, Czechoslovakia in 1921. He abandoned a course at Leeds University to fight with a British volunteer force for the Finns against Russia in 1939, started to study architecture at Helsinki but was subsequently interned in Sweden, finally being released to work on flight control for the R.A.F. throughout the remainder of the war.

His inventiveness started to manifest itself back in 1939, when he designed a flexible kayak which drove itself through the water, like a fish, by undulations generated by pressure from each foot in turn. The design was modified in later years to inflated construction, and incorporated a chemical engine 'muscle' as a byproduct of reverse osmosis, or membrane desalination.

This was followed by a considerable amount of work on subterranean architecture—an elevating bed which rose through the roof and was contained by a transparent plastic dome which could split open or close as required; explosions to form underground craters for living, with central courtyard and garden and a bomb-proof lid which could be raised as a sunlight mirror, and imaginative proposals for underground industry.

At the same time—1940–2—Neumark was engaged on the design of spray plastic housing, and also on inflatable enclosures for caves and fissures on the moon, to be covered with moon dust which would give thermal insulation and also act as a visible leak-detector.

In 1947 he was rejected by Cambridge University as his proposed course of study was Geology, with especial relation to the physical exploration of the moon and nearer planets. As he says 'a misunderstood motive in those days'.

However by 1945 he had started swimming with the porpoises in the Middle East, and was fascinated by the efficiency of these creatures. He rescaled their design for himself, produced a plastics porpoise suit, and by 1953 had mastered the body undulation technique which enabled him to do a steady eight knots submerged, without abnormal effort. A patent was taken out in 1955 for the porpoise suit in which arms and breathing gear were enclosed, the driving force being confined to the undulation of the streamlined form and the thrust of the highly efficient fluke into which the swimmer's feet were fitted.

40 Porpoise suit patent drawings (No. 795,477) by Walter Neumark.

41 Walter Neumark testing his 360 sq. ft. self-inflating Para-foil.

Neumark's activities in the 1950s included ascending parachutes, the design of an inflated glider (which he still flies), inflated aircraft, Daedalus sky-diving wings and flying inflated Delta wings.

In 1955 he joined the plastics sheet fabrication firm of Frankenstein & Sons Ltd. of Manchester, and quickly introduced them to and subsequently produced a wide range of inflated structures, spray polyurethane buildings, inflated ships and boats, liquid beds, radar domes and suspension structures.

One of the most commercially successful of these is the suspension structure designed as an air-portable hangar. This structure, which is in the form of a truncated triangle, has a span of 110 ft between each of the three masts, and encloses an area of over 11,000 sq ft. It can shelter up to eleven fighter aircraft and is extensively used by N.A.T.O.

Walter Neumark has more recently designed and patented a range of modifications to the principles of pneumatic construction, notably a technique for controlling form over vast areas not by nets or cables, but by an internal catenary selvedge hanging down from the fabric seam which may be restrained by weights, ground anchors or simply by tailoring.

However one of his most startling designs, produced in 1961–2 and subsequently constructed as a very large working model, is for an articulated caterpillar structure. This is a combination of inflated enclosure and hovercraft, which can walk itself up and down slopes, across rivers, around or over obstacles, carrying a load such as three 60 ft long sections of steel box-girder bridge suspended within itself.

One can only say of Neumark, as of Schein, that it is regrettable that our society seems incapable of harnessing and exploiting to the full the dynamic inventiveness of such men whose work is so often used by other men of lesser imagination but greater business acumen, and who profit from the work of their predecessors both financially and by reputation.

42 Mobile, articulated caterpillar structure, 240 ft. long × 65 ft. wide, shown carrying bridge sections within. Walter Neumark.

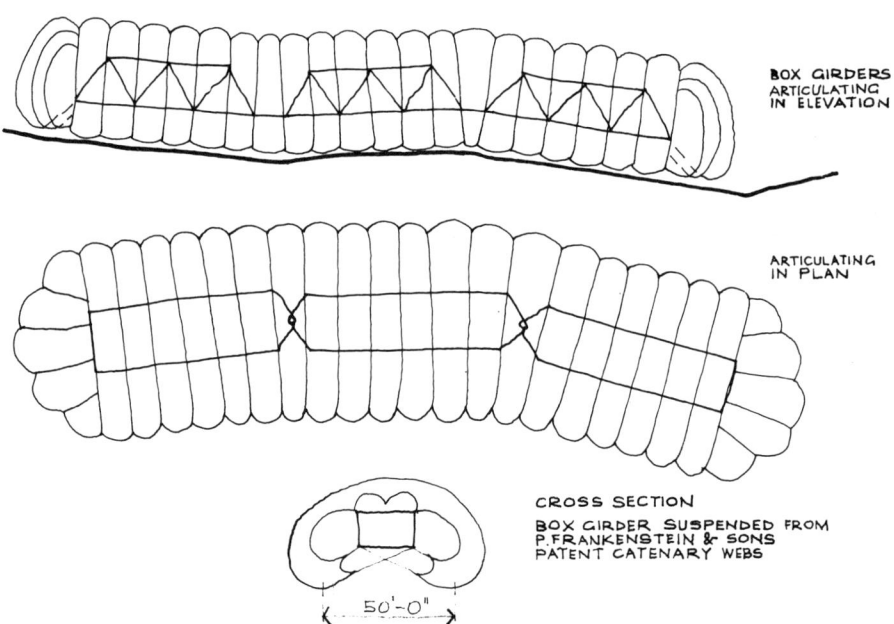

62/ historical applications

CHAPTER 6 spatial enclosures

This chapter covers designs where the enclosure of space is the sole or the prime objective, and other work where a multiplicity of functions is performed by the structure is therefore excluded.

This chapter is subdivided into sections as follows:
1. Shell assemblies.
   - (a) Pure shells.
   - (b) Trussed shells.
   - (c) Frames with shell infill.
2. On-site enclosures.
3. Folding structures.
4. Suspension structures.
5. Pneumatics.
   - (a) Low-pressure enclosures.
   - (b) High-pressure structures.

INTRODUCTION

There are two things which plastics can do really well in building—they can be employed to produce units of great complexity at high speed and low cost on extremely expensive equipment where the high capital outlay can be amortized over a bulk market, or alternatively they can be used to manufacture simple, large forms relatively slowly, at moderate cost, and with very low tooling overheads.

In the absence of any organized bulk market in building it has been this latter aspect which, so far, has been exploited most extensively. However, despite the fact that the use of low-cost equipment gives a unit cost which is higher than would otherwise be the case, it is still possible to span further and cheaper with plastics than with any other material.

SHELL ASSEMBLIES
PURE SHELLS

Much of the early work in this field was concerned with the design of a simple shell which could be put together with other identical shells to form an enclosure which was variable in length, and sometimes also in span and/or height. Examples of this include the g.r.p./polyurethane sandwich

43 G.r.p. stores building for Scott Bader Limited, by Scott Bader Services Ltd.

44 Early single-skin scalloped dome by William R. Orr, at Fort Worth in Texas. The shells carried a 2-ton internal crane.

vault designed under the direction of Professor Z. S. Makowski at Battersea College of Technology in 1965, the sulphur warehouse which Renzo Piano built in 1966, and the recent developments by the firm of Anmac Ltd. of Nottingham, England, with the John West Design group.

It is quite easy to design a folded or hyperboid lozenge shell which will generate hexagonal-based or octagonal-based structures, and the length of enclosures can be extended at will. However, varying the span can only be achieved within very small limits, and alternative heights tend to give some fairly unusable interiors. The evolution of a single shell which will alone give genuine three-dimensional flexibility has not yet been solved, and while a delightful mental exercise, is one which many brains will only stand for a limited period of time.

Most of us, in moving on, have comforted ourselves with the thought that with mould costs so low for what were in most cases single-skin g.r.p. applications, we were justified in using a number of panels to achieve flexibility (g.r.p. laminate $\frac{1}{8}''$ thick, 40p per sq ft. Female mould three or four times this cost, plus the 'dolly' or master mould).

Despite the low cost of the production mould, the master mould can be an expensive item. For this type of g.r.p. work, it is commonly made by hand from timber and plaster, and can be a complicated construction for double-curvature forms. Consequently the recent research of John Zerning into master mould construction is important. Having analysed the geometry involved in double-curvature construction, he has evolved an economical form of mould which makes use of a p.v.c. cocooning spray over any reticulated network for the production of highly-warped hyperbolic paraboidal forms. The cocooning skin shrinks on curing and forms a leather-like minimum-surface form which can be used for the formation of the female production mould.

This cocoon-spray technique has been used structurally for several years, certainly since the late 1950s when a couple of tubular steel structures with

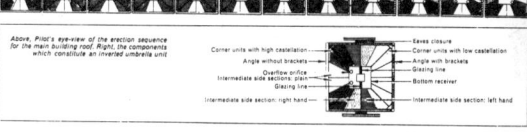

45, 46 G.r.p. shells at Dubai Airport by Page and Broughton, with Costain Civil Engineering and Mickleover of London Ltd. Side elevation, and roof plan and shell detail.

spatial enclosures /65

47, 48 Sulphur factory in Rome, by Renzo Piano. Opaque and translucent g.r.p. shells. Above, exterior and below, interior.

49, 50 (Facing page) Motorway service area bridge in g.r.p. by Mickleover of London Ltd.

51 Translucent single-skin g.r.p. swimming pool enclosure by Anmac Limited. Designed by Scott Bader Services Limited.

52 $\frac{1}{4}''$ translucent g.r.p. warped folded plate vault for the M62 motorway on the Pennines. 120 ft. propped span; shells nest together for delivery. Arthur Quarmby.

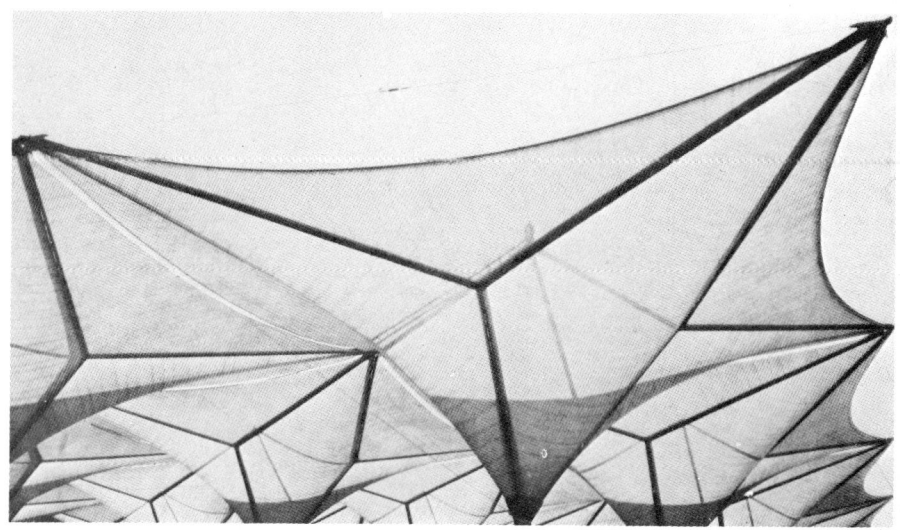

53 G.r.p. sail forms, restrained with wires. Swiss National Exhibition, Lausanne. Florian Vischer.

cloth tapes and a sprayed skin were erected at the Illinois Institute of Technology under Richard Baringer. It is also used for the skins of suspension structures, and will be referred to in this context later in the chapter. (See figures 104–110 below.)

One might wonder why more experiments have not been carried out into variable shell enclosures in recent years—these researches seem to have been neglected in favour of the simpler single unit repetition of geodesic dome construction and the vault work of Yves Chaperot. However it may be that much of the effort has been channelled into the closely related subject of folding structures, which will be dealt with later.

TRUSSED SHELL ASSEMBLIES

Geometrically, it is easier to link standard shells together with all joints in one plane and then to brace the whole assembly with tension or compression members from the high or low points of the panels, than it is to design three-dimensional shells which in themselves give the effective depth necessary for an adequate structural performance. It is perhaps for this reason that very many structures using this technique of braced shells have been built since the early experiments of Professor Makowski and Kenneth Turner and the constructions of William R. Orr.

Very many experiments have been made, but even more have not. With the very low development costs involved it really is surprising that every architect does not take the opportunity to have a few linkable shells made to his design, or to try to devise a new type of grid using braced panels. Few of us appreciate how fortunate we are in still being able to realize our individual creations, and the irony is that for much of the time we simulate machine-made repetitive units in our work. When we are compelled to use such units as a general rule, we shall no doubt rebel and try to achieve an impression of individuality.

Let us seize this lingering moment, while the building industry still hesitates on the brink of industrialization, and give free rein to our

spatial enclosures /69

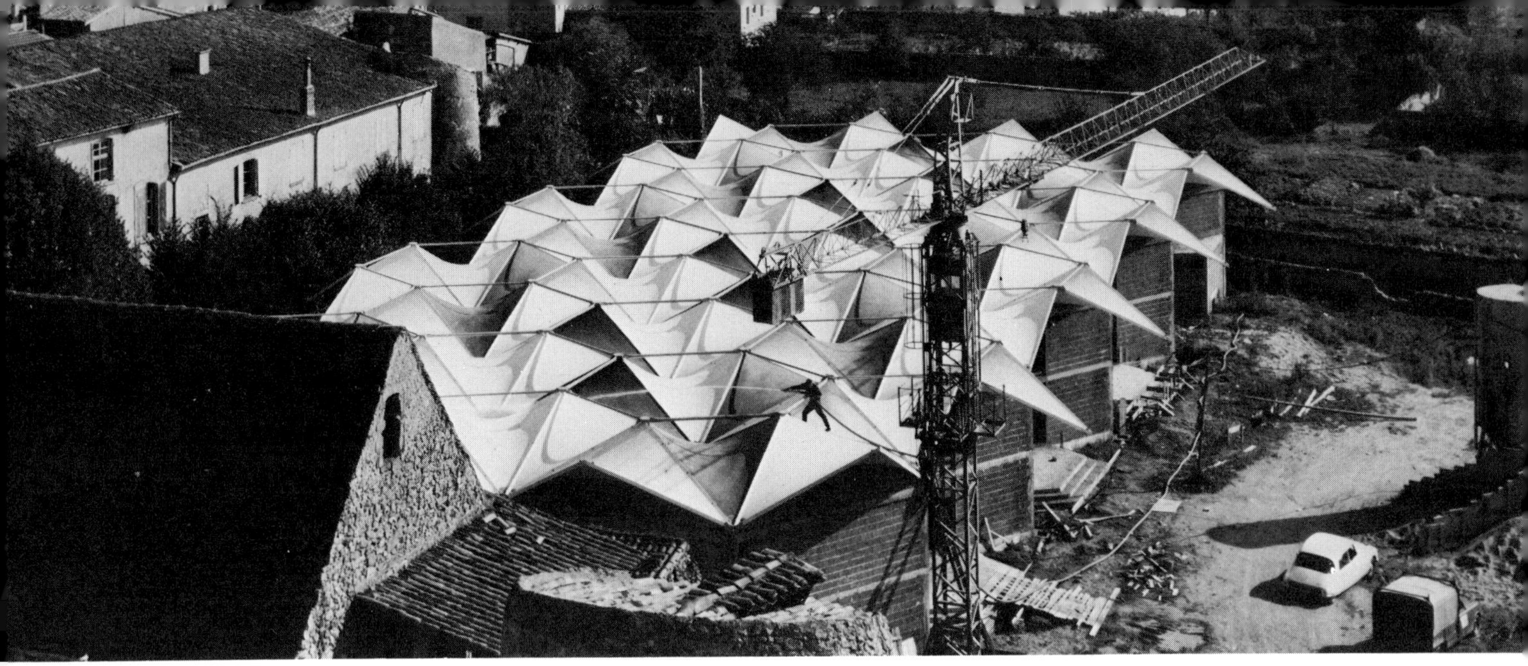

54, 55 Above: covered market at Lezoux, by Yves Chaperot. Below, left: interior.

56 Factory roof of trussed pyramids, by Renzo Piano.

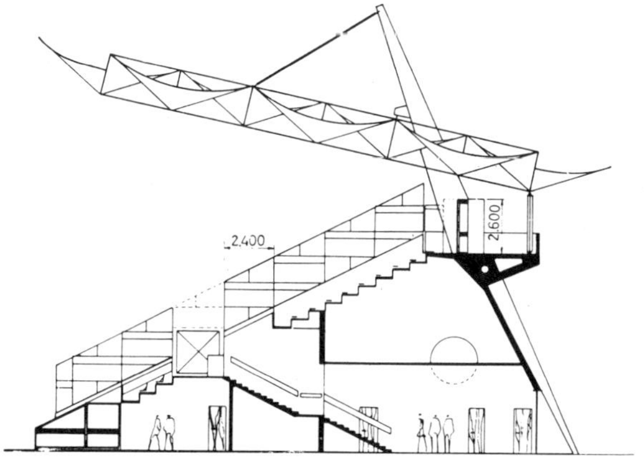

57 Municipal sports stadium at Laval, by Saint-Arroman and du Château, using shells by Yves Chaperot. Section and completed structure.

58–60 Early trussed shell factory in Fort Worth, Texas, by William R. Orr. Exterior and (below), interior during construction. A line of shells is bolted together for the full length of the factory, one edge is jacked up and another line added to it. Assembly continues and the arch slowly takes shape without framework or scaffolding. Below (right), detail of hyperboid and rod assembly.

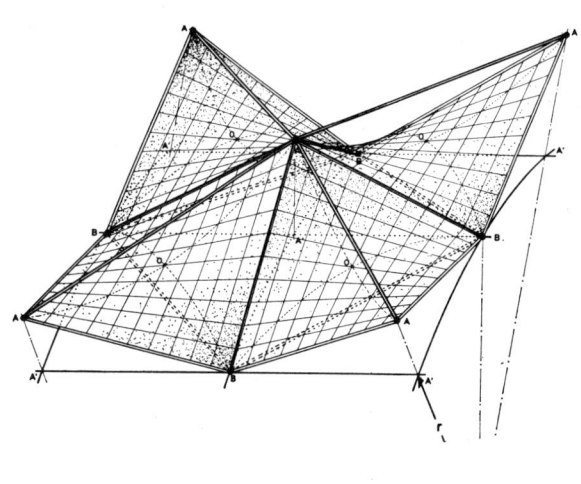

61, 62 Model of trussed shell roof using inflated forms and below, factory roof in Genoa, by Renzo Piano. The g.r.p. shells are tensioned with rods and ties below. Detail of final site-sealing of joints.

imaginations—it could be that in so doing we might favourably affect the form of changes to come. A reaction against plain panels and flat roofs has been gathering momentum for some time; already one can say that the output of real industrialized building will be quite different from what we imagined was required ten years ago, and plastics projects and structures have been in the van of this swing.

63, 64 Italian Pavilion at Osaka, by Renzo Piano. Development—indeed a reversal—of the roof illustrated in fig. 62.

FRAMES WITH SHELL INFILL

These may be defined as skeleton frameworks where the plastics shell components do not fulfill a primary, but merely a secondary structural role. The frame would stand up quite adequately without the panels. Into this category fit the Fuller dome from the Montreal Expo '67, du Chateau's beautiful bubble domes and the Douglas holiday centre by Gillinson, Barnett & Partners. In virtually every case in this category, it is the structural transparency or translucency of plastics materials, whether acrylic, g.r.p. or p.v.c., which engenders their use.

Quite simply, no other material could do it. And yet this is, in every case, a rather modest and even hesitant way of exploiting the real structural potential of plastics. On a really large scale, some difficulties could and do arise with frames with shell infill and trussed shell assemblies on account of the different rates of thermal expansion between the shells and the ties or struts, but this does not apply, of course, to pure shell assemblies, and is one more reason why they deserve to have far more attention paid to them.

JOINTING TECHNIQUES

The jointing of pure shell assemblies is normally carried out by flanging the panel edges downwards and bolting them together from within with a sealant between. Many different sealants are, of course, on the market, but one very popular type is polysulphide rubber. This is available in tape form, or may be gun-applied and is pressure-sensitive—in other words when the panels are bolted together and the material is squeezed, it sticks,

65, 66 Derby Castle Solarium, Isle of Man. Gillinson, Barnett and Partners, with J. Phillips, Lomas and Partners.

67, 68 Below and facing page, acrylic heating plant domes, Stéphane du Château.

69 U.S. Pavilion, Expo '67, Montreal. Buckminster Fuller.

70 Bloedel Conservatory, Vancouver. 140 ft. diameter, with triangular acrylic panels.

creating something like a soft weld. This can transmit a fair proportion of load through itself, thus enabling the numbers of bolts to be reduced and making their design less critical; but it can also be cut through with a sharp blade if the necessity arises for the panels to be taken apart for re-assembly or extension.

Upstand flanges are occasionally used, especially where the internal appearance is more important than the external, and a push-on capping strip can be used as a sealant if very careful measures are taken to overcome the special problem of the four-, six- or eight-way joint at the node.

It is also possible to design a more sophisticated weatherproof joint where the water is accepted into the flange and channelled round to emerge elsewhere, but this can lead to considerable complications where the same panel may be used in positions ranging from the vertical to the horizontal. Theoretically the easy solution is to weld on site—see R. Piano's factory in Genoa, 1966. However this is rarely practicable because the cure of the resin is sensitive to changes in temperature and humidity.

Perhaps one day it will be possible to make more extensive use of the special characteristics possessed by a material known as polyisobutylene (p.i.b.). This was employed back in the thirties on the Siegfried Line, but is only now coming into general use. It is a single-layer flexible material used for skinning roofing panels, and the weatherproof joint is in the form of a tape which is in effect the material itself in suspension. The tape is pressed home, lapping adjacent skins, and gradually sinks into and blends with them.

The long-term weathering of translucent g.r.p. panels is still open to some criticism, although this depends not so much on the materials themselves as the way in which they are used by the fabricators. Several unfortunate experiments in the early days have made us more cautious—I have seen twenty-year-old corrugated g.r.p. rooflights in Switzerland which have completely 'strawed'—(i.e. at the time of manufacture some of the glass fibres protruded through the final coat of resin, creating a capillary path for moisture, and over the succeeding years this allowed frost to embed itself so that the whole surface was lifted).

Precautions are normally taken against this happening nowadays—a surface tissue of very fine glass fibres is used and this is covered with a 'gel coat' or resin-rich surfacing from the mould. Often, too, a later coat of polyurethane is applied for added protection. Even better is a final coating of transparent polyvinylfluoride (p.v.f.) which not only adds a further fifteen years or thereabouts of life to the outer surface, but may also improve the appearance of a translucent laminate.

ON-SITE ENCLOSURES

Many architects share a latent desire to create on site rather than on paper, and some have used plastics materials to achieve this end.

One of the first examples was the Smithson plastics house of 1956 (20, 21) which was intended to have massive soil/resin external walls which were to be cast on the ground and then lifted up into place. Work which may perhaps be classed under the old title of 'bowellist' falls even more clearly

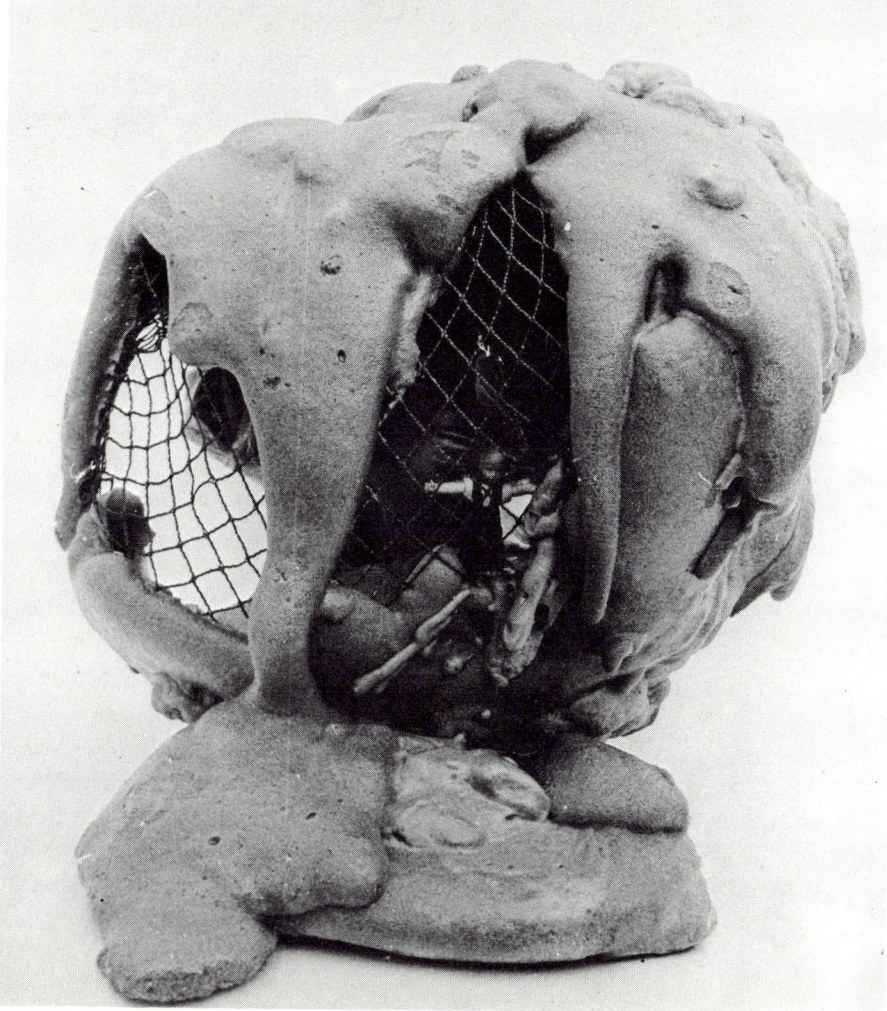

71 Children's gloop house project by Rudolf Doernach.

spatial enclosures /77

72 Emergency housing in Peru. Spiral generated polyurethane foam on re-usable pneumatic formers, by Bayer Chemicals.

into this category—cave-like forms which consist of spray or plaster technique on thin wire mesh which can be pulled around and into shape while the work is actually going on.

Some of Hausermann's work is of this type—shell forms which he happily sprays on site either with plastics or 'gunite' concrete (146, 148, 149). My own House and Garden project is in a similar vein—a curving sprayed wall with platforms and shells inside, and with an on-site steam-blown rigid double-walled dome over the top (see 212–14).

All these examples really form part of the back-to-nature movement in that they tend to deny the machine, and are more properly classed as do-it-yourself sculpture than architecture. Not that I would entirely dismiss them—such projects are splendid for stretching the imagination in a way which is free from constrictions of cost and construction. And indeed who knows—it is just possible that the portable spray kit may be a big factor in the future environment (imagine a filament spray so light that, on a still day, one could create gossamer patterns in the air strong enough to support themselves and subsequent coatings. Like candy floss. And why not like candy floss, for then we could eat it? We already have synthetic proteins from plastics byproducts, and the possibility of edible enclosures for emergency applications is not to be entirely rejected).

73 Spiral generated 'Styrodome' at Michigan, by Dow Chemicals. 87 ft. diameter, 6" thick.

Techniques of spiral generation are perhaps a compromise in this matter. The structure is formed entirely on the site but its form is substantially predetermined and regular. A typical unit consists of a truck with a boom mounted above, which contains an extruder producing a continuous plank of polyurethane foam. The boom travels round at ground level and gradually rises and closes, forming a foam dome. As the plank is normally about 8" thick, the final structure has incredible insulation and is not cheap. The alternative system, using an inflated former inside or outside on which a much thinner skin of foam is sprayed, is far cheaper if more rigid in form, and less mechanized.

FOLDING STRUCTURES

The folded plate is an elegant and well-known technique for producing a rigid structure from thin panel or sheet material. In autumn 1965, I read a book on structures which showed how to make a folded plate barrel vault from one sheet of card, with no cutting or jointing. This led to the chance discovery that the structure could fold up into itself and into a flat, compact form. The geometrical relationship of panel shape to structural form and foldability was then analysed and a basic range of structures developed and patented.

We were not the first in the field with this work—several others (notably the International Structures Corporation in the United States) had developed structures along similar lines—but our work demonstrated the virtually unlimited range of structural forms which can be fabricated from cheap, lightweight panels, and which will fold flat for delivery and storage.

The first prototypes to be built were hexagonal- and octagonal-based barrel vaults, and were constructed in order to prove that the rigidity of the structure was not dependent upon the strength of the joint at all, but was a result of the overall geometry.

For example, our engineers said that as each joint had a degree of flexibility, the total flexing of the vault from end to end would be the sum of the flexings of each joint. It seemed to us from model experiments that this was not so, and prototypes proved that the joint flexings were absorbed by the diagonal cross-arching of the structure, and that a flexible joint could be used.

The shelters developed for migrant agricultural workers in California by the International Structures Corporation were based on polyethylene-skinned paper-faced polyurethane foam panels, and the folds were impressed into the material. This led to some cracking, and it is not yet economically possible to fabricate from one large sheet of rigid p.v.c. with localized flexibility along the fold lines. Nor is it yet possible to use the second best approach, individual panels of self-skinned polyurethane foam, taped together.

Incidentally tape is a terribly neglected and unduly-despised building material. The range of tapes nowadays is very extensive, and grab and cure characteristics can be quite outstanding. And yet we continue to drill and plug for fixings which could be achieved with a tape which could provide perfectly adequate performance in tension and shear.

Lacking either ideal solution one is left with a compromise. Expanded polyurethane board is produced by continuous extrusion at a very low cost, and its skinned strength-to-weight ratio is of a very high order. Unfortunately it is normally extruded between Kraft paper, the weathering of which is always suspect despite doctor-blade coatings of polyethylene or p.v.c.

A better solution would be to extrude the foam between skins of polished aluminium foil, and experiments are in hand at the moment which appear to offer a good chance of success. The foam can nowadays have a fairly high fire rating, the surface spread of flame on aluminium is negligible and the finished board, $\frac{1}{2}''$ thick, should cost around 5p to 6p ($0.12 to $0.15)

spatial enclosures

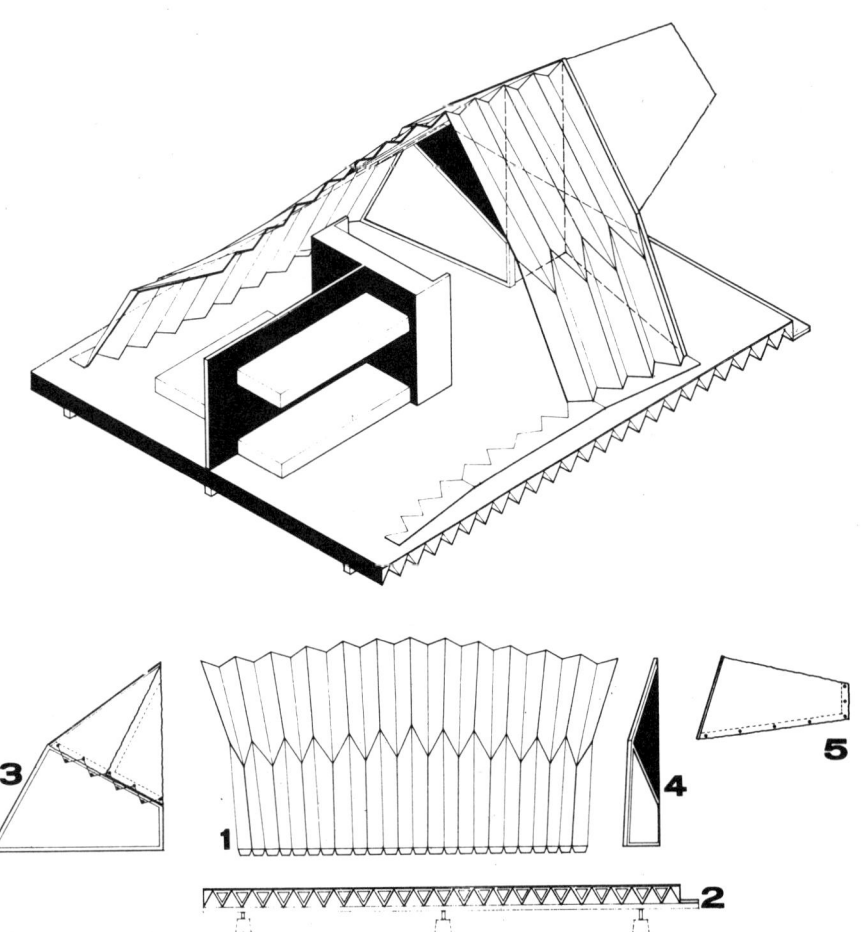

74 Plydom housing for migrant agricultural workers, California, by Herbert Yates for the International Structures Corporation. **1** Polyethylene-coated, paper-faced polyurethane panels with impressed, folded joints. Aluminium junction piece at ridge. **2** Chipboard floor on jacks. **3** G.r.p. end screens. **4** Aluminium door. **5** Canvas canopy.

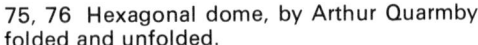

75, 76 Hexagonal dome, by Arthur Quarmby, folded and unfolded.

77, 78 Above, unfolded square dome, below, unfolded octagonal vault, inset folded. Arthur Quarmby with students of Bradford Regional College of Art.

79–81 Left, square vault, folded and unfolded, using 45° triangles. Centre, square dome, folded and unfolded. Below, vault with half-dome. Arthur Quarmby.

82, 83 (Facing page) Design details: square vault (fig. 79) and square dome (fig. 80).

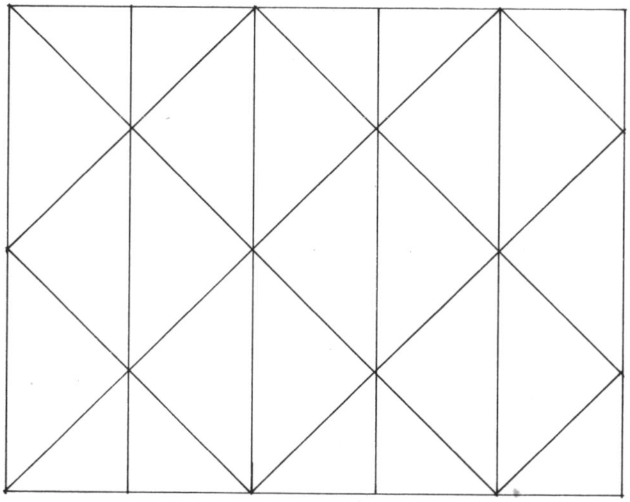

Assembly

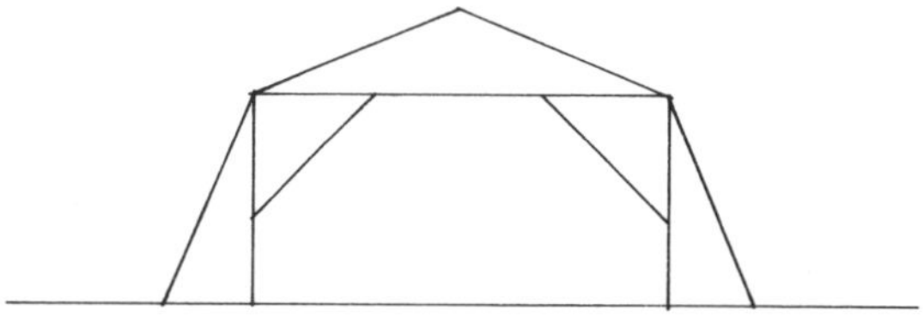

Erected

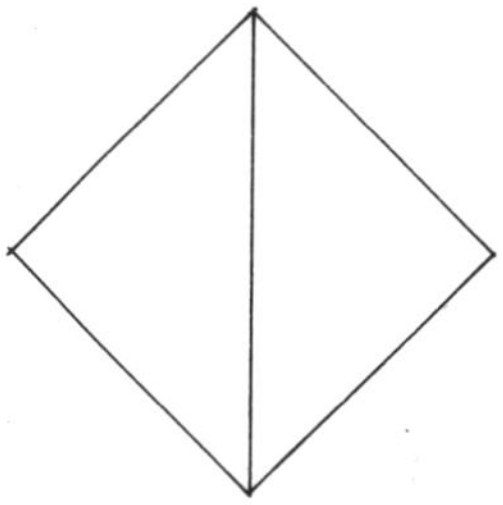

Folded

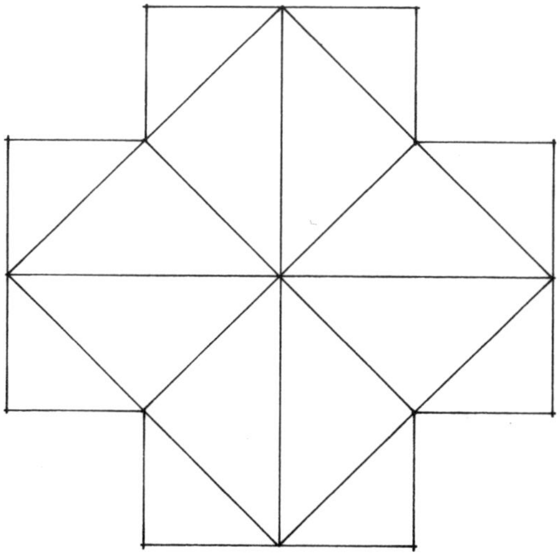

Assembly

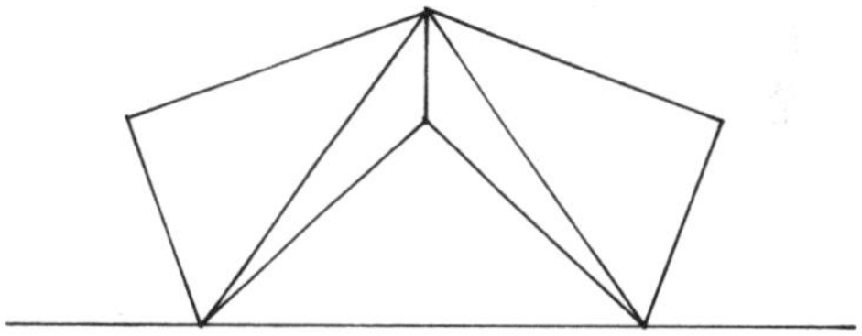

Erected

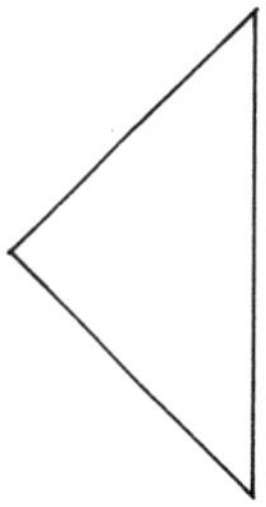

Folded

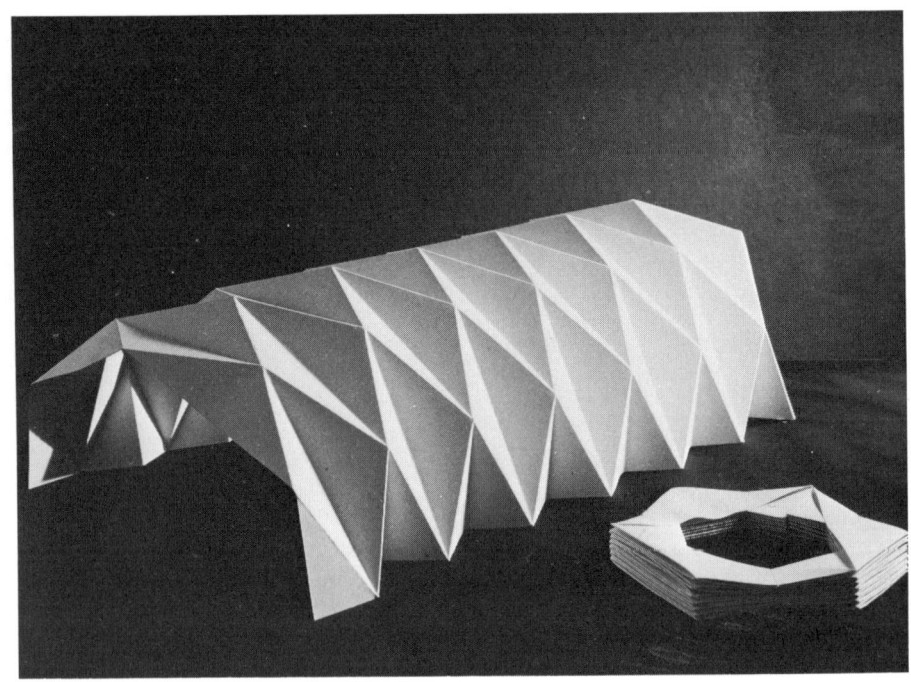

84–87 Above, hexagonal vault, folded and unfolded, using 30° triangles. Below, hexagonal dome, folded and unfolded. Facing, above: design details, hexagonal vault and below, hexagonal dome. Arthur Quarmby.

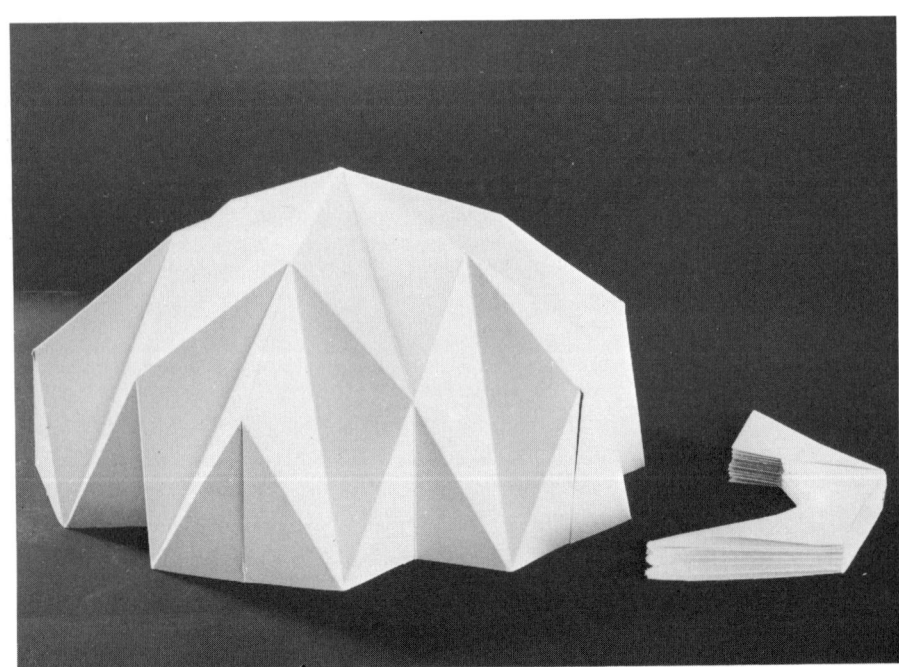

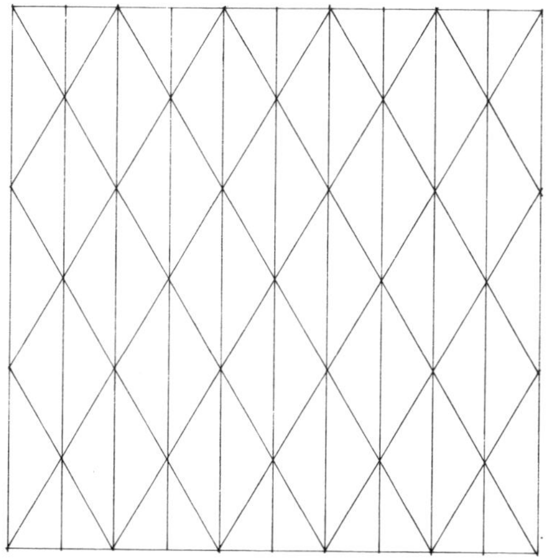

Assembly

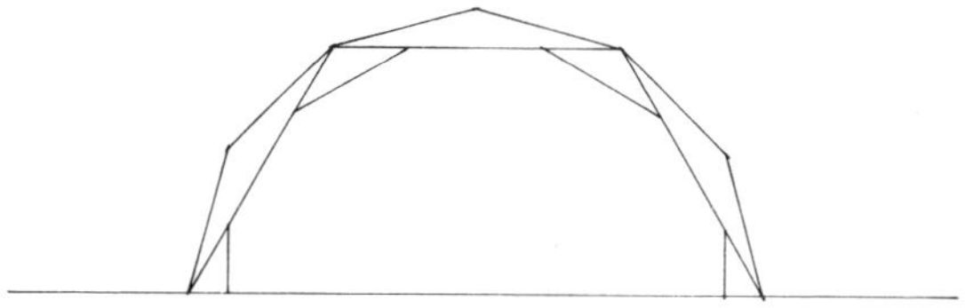

Erected

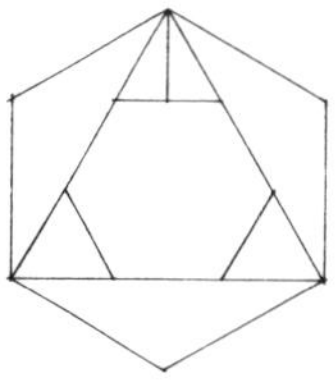

Folded

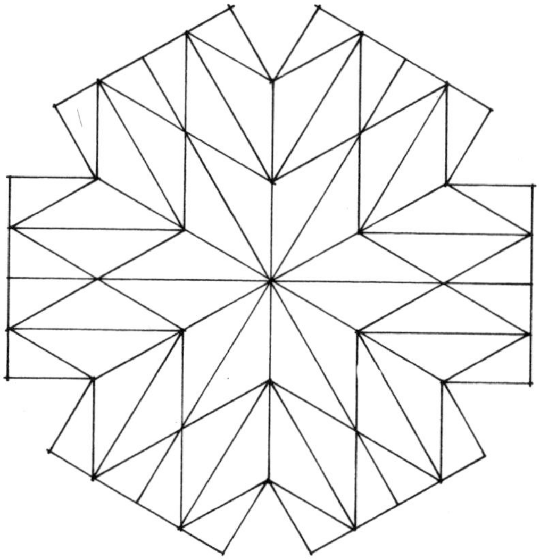

Assembly

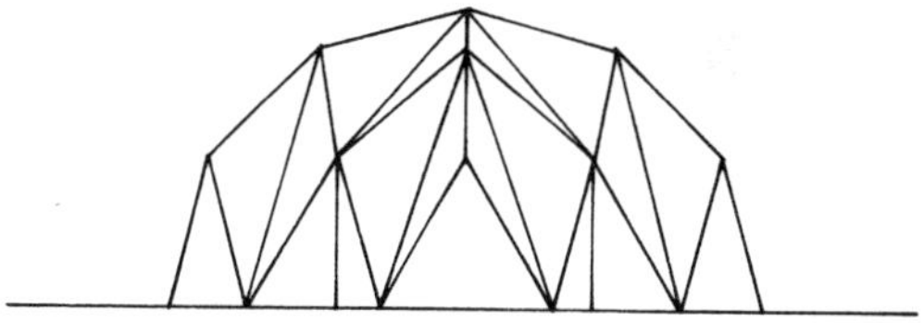

Erected

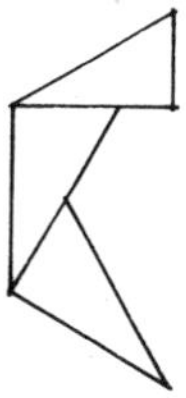

Folded

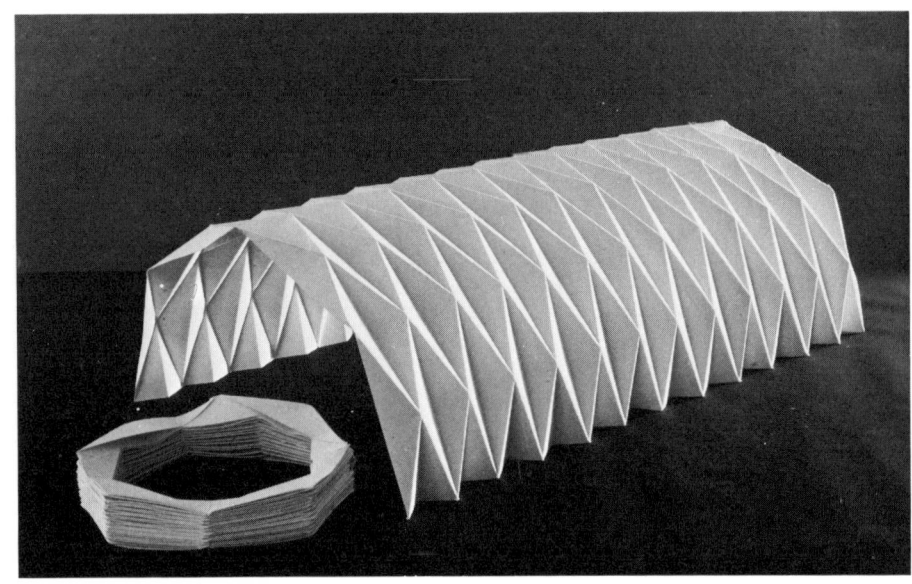

88–91 Above, octagonal vault, folded and unfolded, using 22½° triangles. Below, octagonal dome. Note that in all cases a half-dome may be used to close off the end of the appropriate vault (as in fig. 81) and will fold in with it. Facing above: design details octagonal vault and below, octagonal dome. Arthur Quarmby.

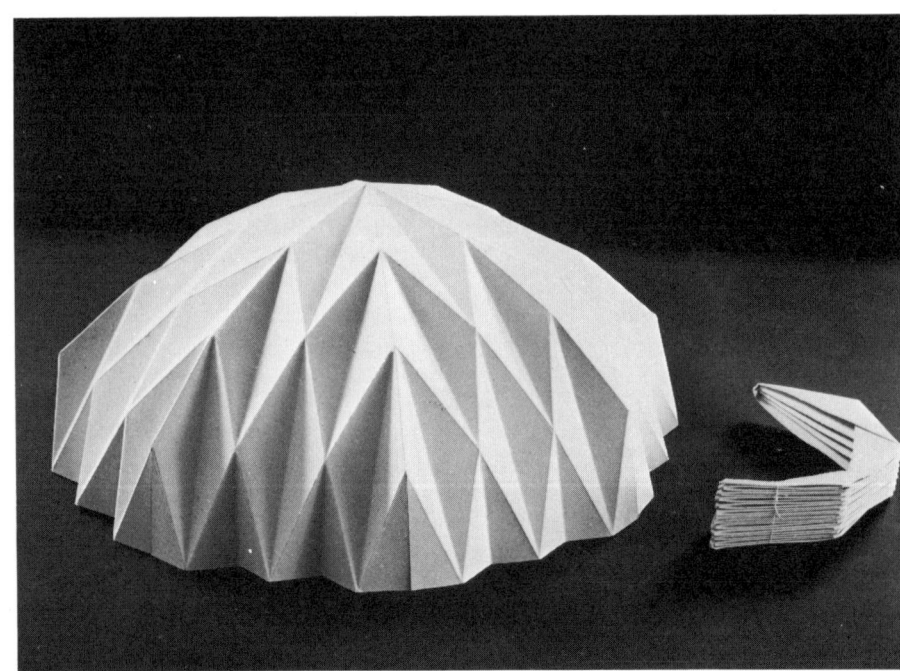

Assembly

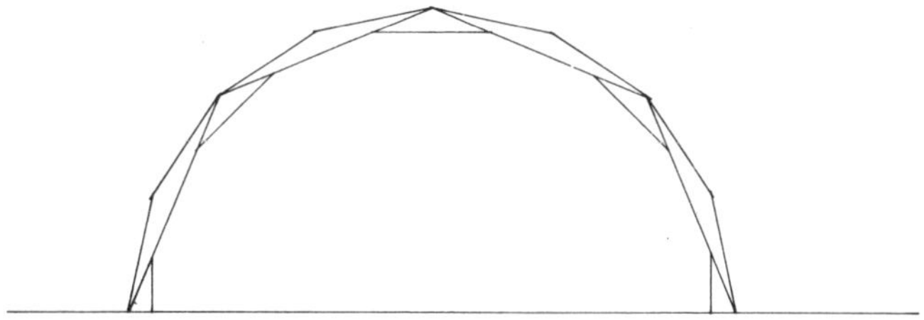

Erected

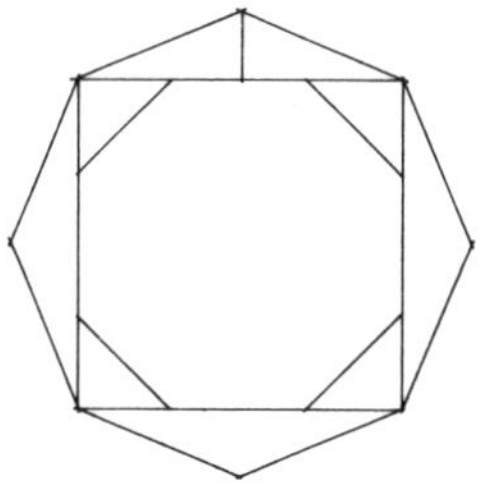

Folded

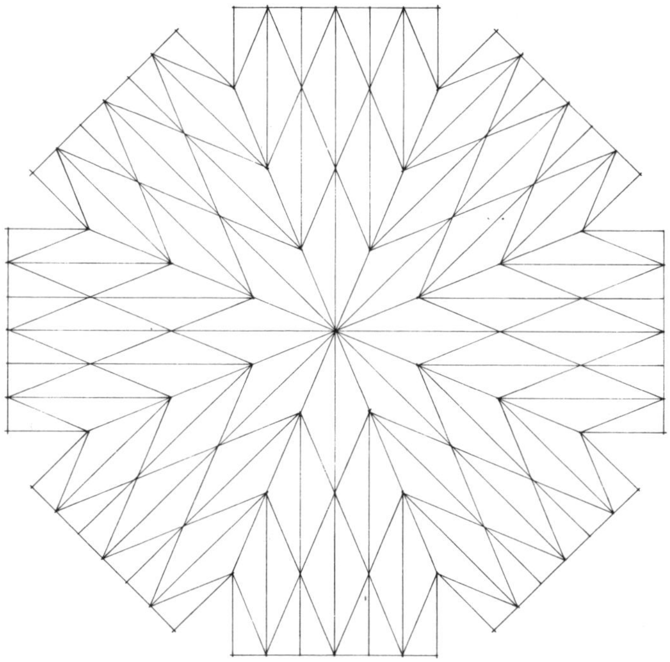

Assembly

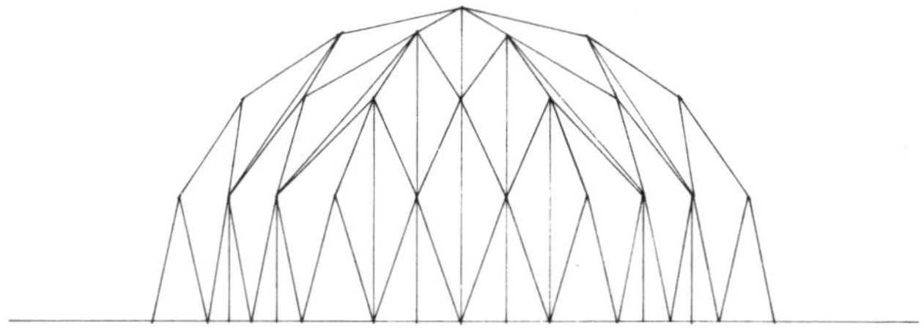

Erected

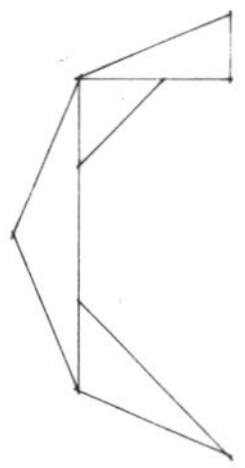

Folded

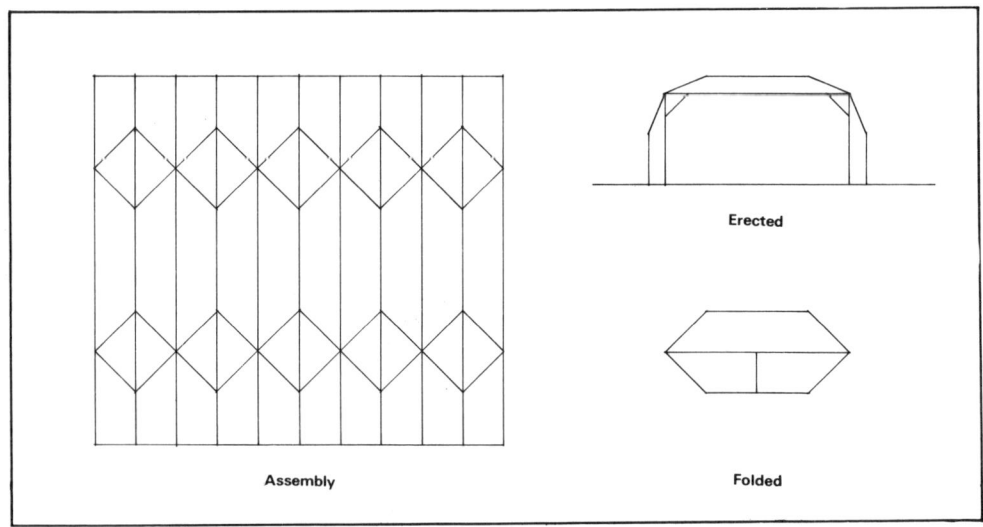
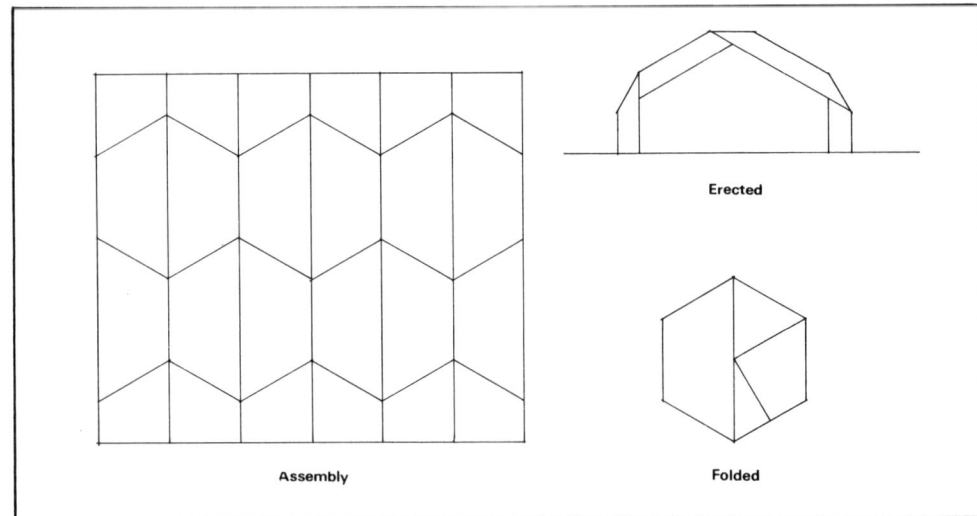
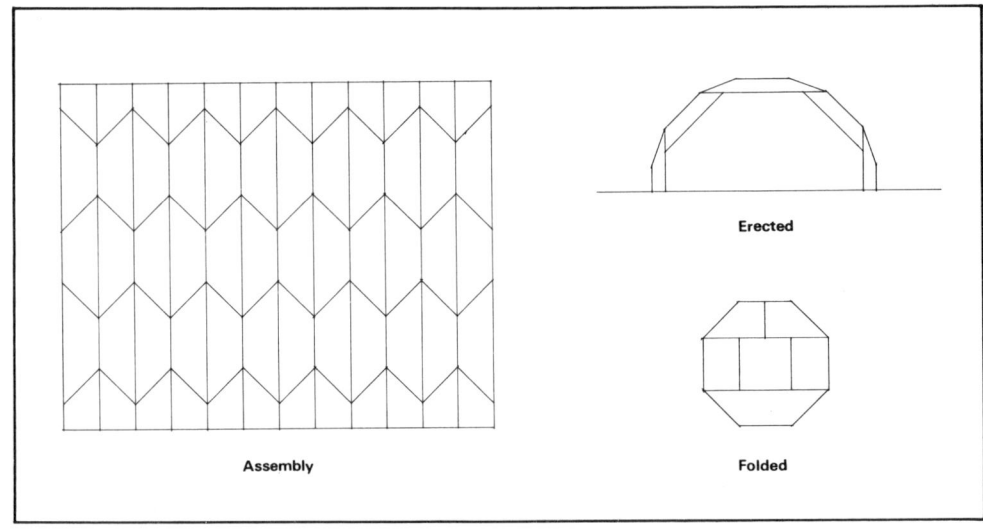

92–94 Design details of (above), linear square vault; centre, linear hexagonal vault and below, linear octagonal vault, all second range. Note that all forms may also be folded in ways other than those shown. For instance, a joint capable of flexing in both directions permits all vaults to be folded into a long, thin, rectangular form, and all domes into the same form, but with a taper at one end. Arthur Quarmby.

95 Early suspension hangar for NATO by Walter Neumark.

per square foot. However this is still a laminated board, and the edges must be protected in order to avoid delamination or moisture penetration. Nevertheless, it is possible to span at least 40 ft with a $\frac{1}{2}''$ board at a cost equivalent to tentage, with a very high degree of insulation and with speedy assembly and demounting.

There would appear to be a great deal of scope for the use of folding structures for a wide range of enclosure and storage applications, and at a price far below that of the cheapest form of conventional construction. However the movement at the node from flat to erected to fully folded is complex and requires a thorough mathematical analysis.

SUSPENSION STRUCTURES

This subject has been covered very effectively and thoroughly in recent years, and is therefore approached from the purely plastics and architectural points of view.

To me, the tensile structures not only of Frei Otto and Gernot Minke, but also of their students and other students throughout the world include some of the most elegant and graceful forms ever produced in engineering and architecture.

One might go further and say that it is really very difficult to produce an ugly suspension structure. Even when a manufacturer puts a standard form on the market it is beautiful.

However one tends to notice that the structure is often much more attractive before the enclosing membrane is fitted, and that this is a result of the recent tendency towards separation of the main cables and secondary network from the membrane.

Otto used single membranes on much of his early work, but as the scale of his structures grew, so did the problems of stress concentration and variation, and this led first to the use of cables in sleeves within the membrane (Swiss National Exhibition at Lausanne) and then (this being considered not entirely satisfactory), to complete separation. The separation

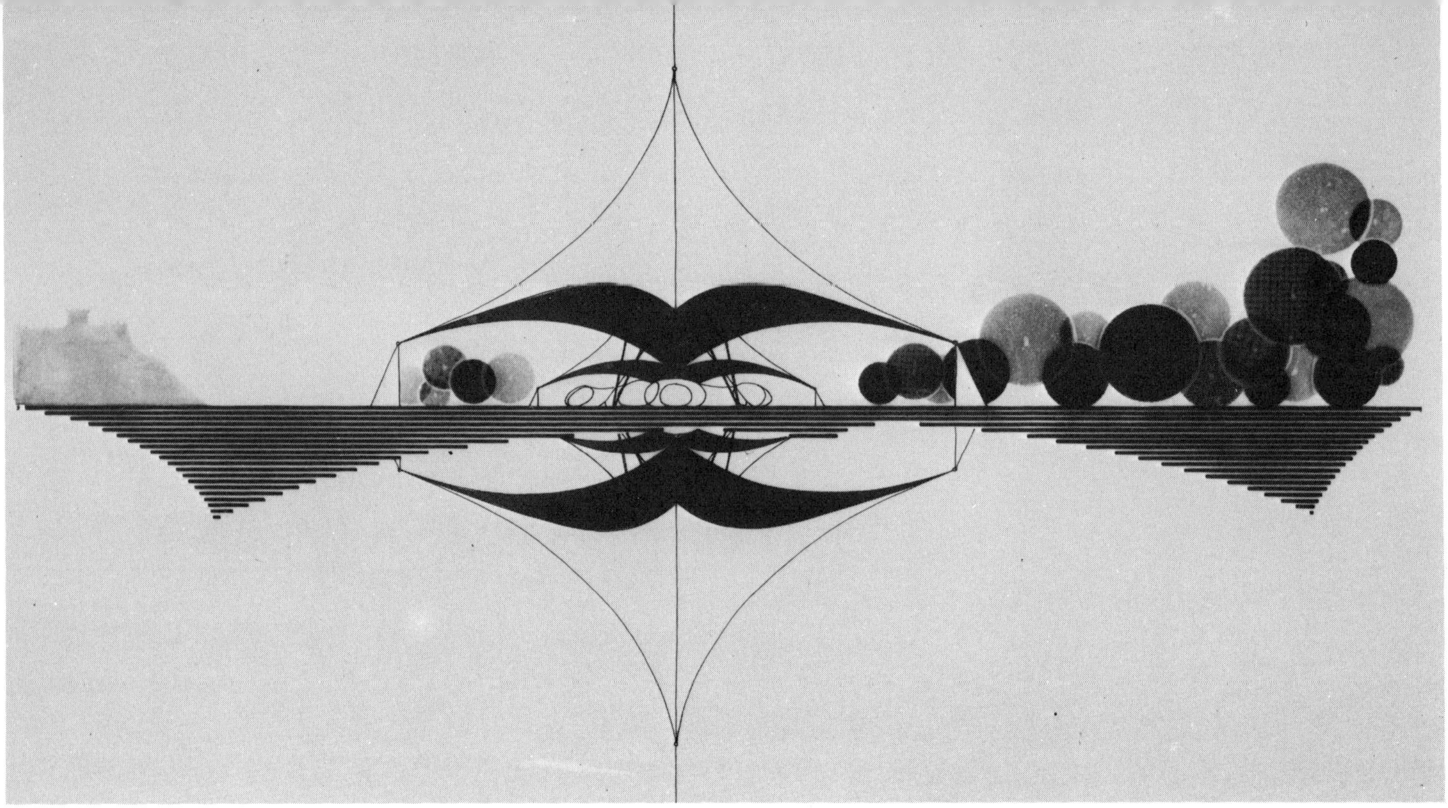

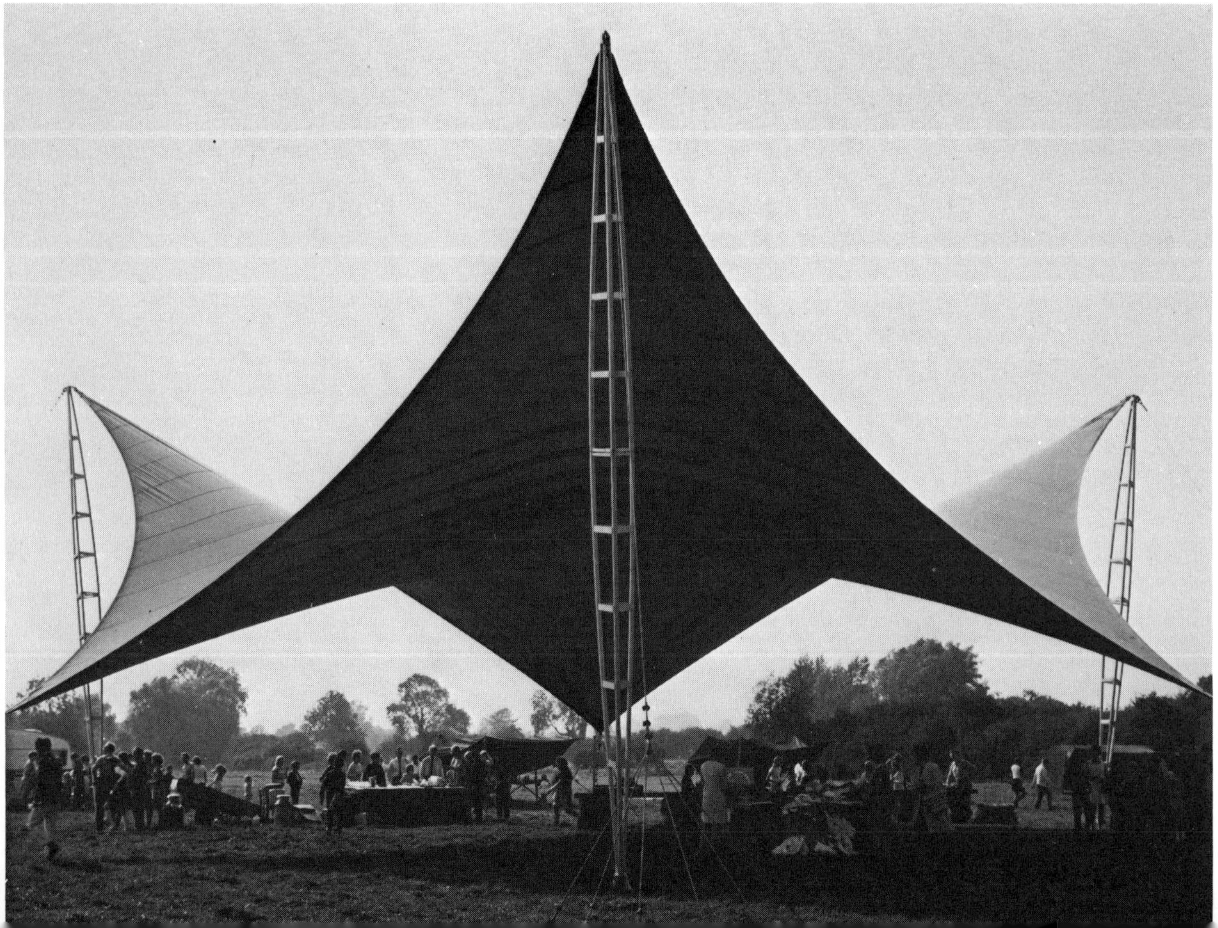

96–99 Facing, above: service station at Lancaster for Shell-Mex and B.P. by Arthur Quarmby. Translucent suspension sails (mirrored in tidal pool) with spray polyurethane on mesh service module beneath. Below, 'Trisail' standard suspension structure, by the Irving Air Chute Company. This page, views of Kuwait stadium model, by Otto, Tange and Kamiya.

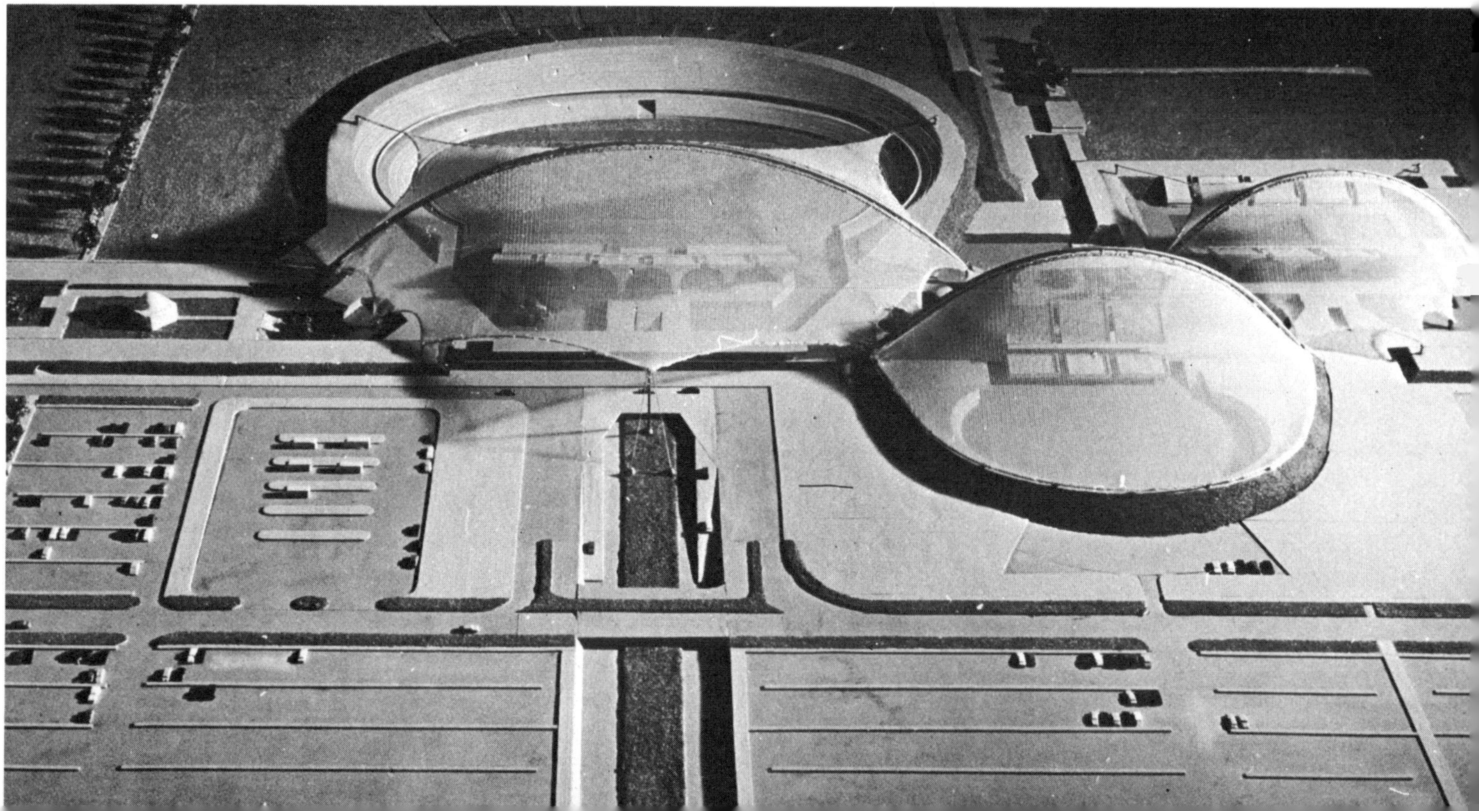

of the cable net from the membrane simplifies the design of a suspension structure. Soap bubble experiments can set the general form of the minimum surface area, but subsequent membrane analysis is incredibly complicated, and the design of a cable net is very much more straightforward. The membrane can be slung from the net and its form is then not quite so critical.

However, this simplification brings about a consequent complication—that of fixing the membrane to the cable net—which is what tends to ruin the sleek, light finish of the structure.

The difficulty of calculating the exact form of the minimum-surface membrane is only part of the problem. In addition to this, it is extremely hard to achieve a reliable and completely even performance from a woven fabric which may have varying fibres at various levels of stress. Then if we add stress concentrations at certain points, the picture is nearly complete. On a relatively small scale these problems are unimportant or can be overcome. On a large scale they become critical, and in consequence we have to settle for separation of membrane and cable network.

There would appear to be two lines of research which could usefully be followed up here. One is more work on the development of high-stress membranes to give even performance under load, and also to evolve a more economical technique for withstanding local stress concentration by varying the fibre content and pattern. This would also involve far more sophisticated stress analysis techniques than are currently in general use for suspension structures, and may well make use of the photo-elastic analysis technique based on the use of the reflection polariscope being carried out at Salford University in Britain under Dr J. B. McNicholas.

However a more simple and direct solution would be to accept the fact that a cable net is very much simpler and quicker to design than a membrane, and look for a technique which enables a membrane to be applied direct to the network.

100–102 Facing, separation of cable net and membrane. West German Pavilion, Montreal, by Frei Otto. Right, cables in sleeves: Swiss National Exhibition at Lausanne. Below, retractable awning over open-air concert hall in West Germany, by Frei Otto.

103 Folding umbrellas over an open-air concert hall, by Frei Otto.

104–106 Facing page, double-curvature shell roof developed by John Zerning, using his cocoon-spray mould-forming technique.

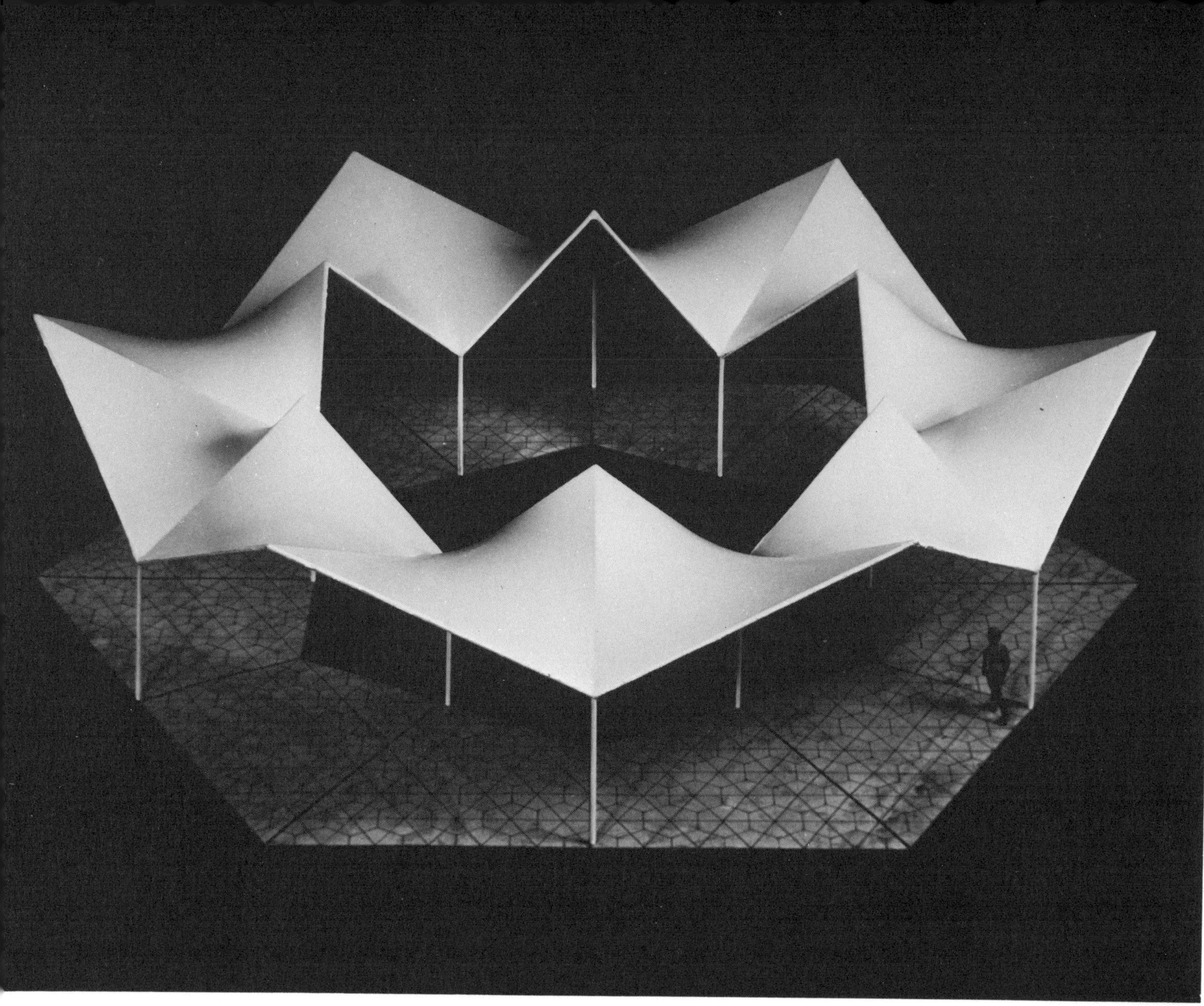

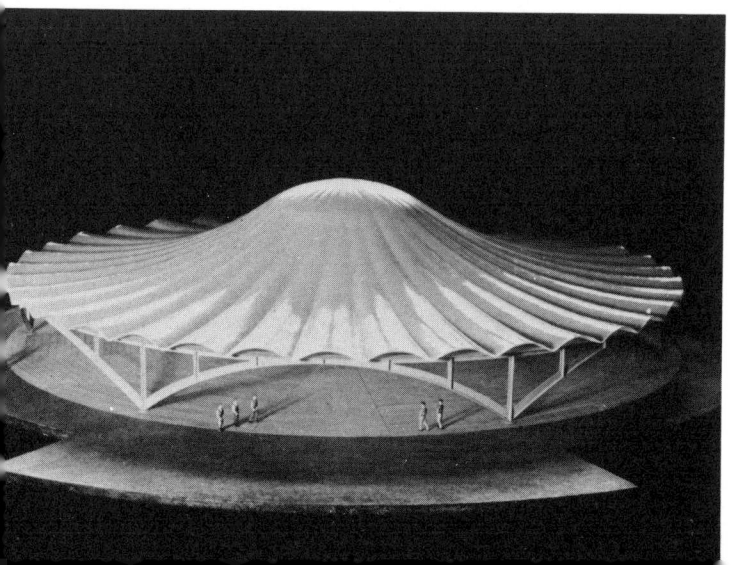

107–10 Left, early tension structure—p.v.c. cocoon-spray on cloth tapes at 2 ft. centres on tubular steel framework, by students at Illinois Institute of Technology under Dr Richard Baringer. Below, demonstration of John Zerning's cocoon-spray technique and on facing page, models by John Zerning using this technique.

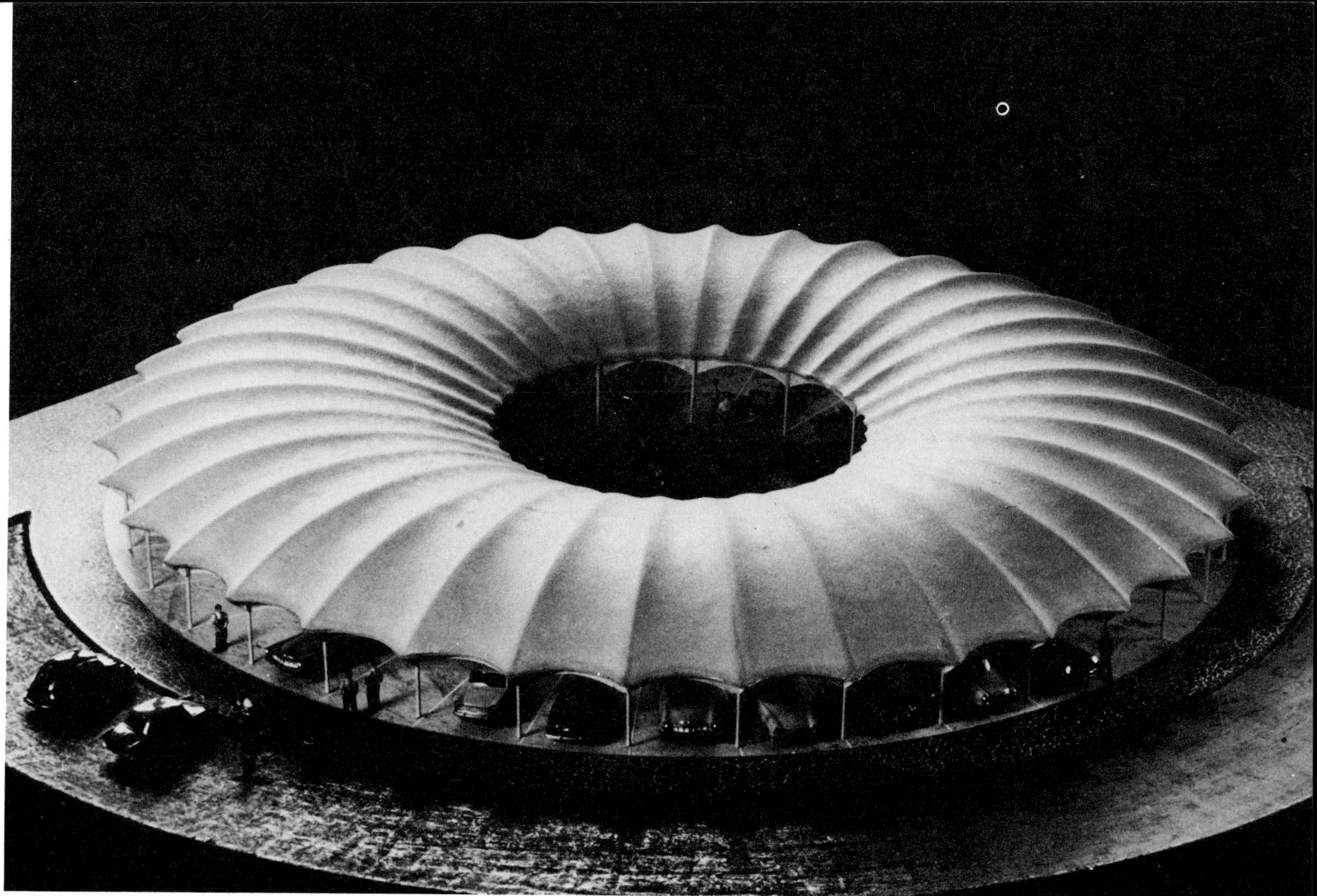

Any normal sheet membrane close to the net would have to go through the involved calculations outlined above and to be fixed to the net in the current cumbersome way. However the cocooning technique of p.v.c. spray described earlier has been used on several suspension structures and its further development would seem to be called for.

P.v.c. may be sprayed onto a net up to two feet in size. The spray is applied diagonally and cobwebby filaments float across from cable to cable and build up a skin. The cables would normally be sprayed from both sides, resulting in their encasement in a leather-like skin. Several layers are commonly applied, and surfacing techniques such as the incorporation of heat-reflecting aluminium granules are often used.

This system would perform in a similar way to a net-enclosed low pressure pneumatic form, where the net carries all the main loadings and the membrane only has to cope with the stresses between.

There are a number of aspects of this spray technique which require considerable improvement before it can be used on a large scale. Cost is one (around 50p ($1·20) per square foot, although this may be a consequence of the currently small demand—we seem to have run out of battleships to wrap up), and another is strength; I suspect that we really ought to be looking into a fibre-reinforced spray technique. In addition to this I, in common with many architects, would like to be able to use a highly translucent or even transparent sprayed skin. Unpigmented, plasticized p.v.c. tends to degrade under sunlight, so it may well be that a variation or even a different polymer is required.

None of these is impossible, but their development does depend upon a demand being created by architects and engineers.

PNEUMATIC STRUCTURES
LOW PRESSURE PNEUMATICS

Is it true that the history of architecture is the history of the longer span? That the Romans could span farther than the Greeks, that the Gothic builders could in many cases go farther than the Romans, and that since the Iron Bridge in the Midlands we have developed a continuous and accelerating ability to span wider spaces? If this is so then the most remarkable development has gone largely unremarked.

It is often claimed that there is no theoretical limit to the space which a low-pressure pneumatic form can enclose, and in certain circumstances this claim can be substantiated. Certainly it is now (and has been for several years) a practical proposition to enclose areas many square miles in extent by using a technique which is unique in that its cost rate falls as the span increases. How is it that this matchless technique has so far failed to revolutionize architecture?

Perhaps my own chapter of accidents with three pneumatic structures may explain some of the reasons for this phenomenon. The empiric method of testing pneumatics is very fast and rather dramatic.

The first was a 26 ft high parabolic dome built by architectural students at Bradford College of Art in 1963. We used transparent polyethylene film with a T joint (which the fan tended to pull into pinholes) and a water-filled base tube. Or rather partly filled, for at 15" diameter it would have held over three tons of water. So it was partially filled and up went the dome—only to fall over right on its face. The ground was not quite level and all the water had run down to the low point, leaving the remainder understrained. A simple case of momentary mindlessness, corrected by the choice of a flat site (though not without red faces all round).

The second case was a 30 ft high onion dome built of black polyethylene by students at Leeds School of Architecture in 1965. I had wanted to turn the skirt inwards and shovel it full of sand, but was persuaded out of this by the students with their idea for sausage-shaped tubes of polyethylene stuffed with sand, slipped through loops welded to the skin.

Having had this on internal display for a fortnight, we took it outside. By now two of the three fans had been sent back, so inflation was very slow; there were gusts of wind too. The wind whipped the structure about and tore off all the loops, and half a dozen of us were left hanging on as we were intermittently lifted into the air and dumped down again. Finally tired hands released their grip, the wind got right under the skin, and carried it away like a vast black bat. Of the several lessons learned, the two major ones were never take any risks with perimeter fixing, and when designing an onion dome to make the chimney exaggeratedly long and dramatic. Otherwise when seen from anything like close range it will look like a pea on a drum.

Both of these domes ran at about 3 lbs/sq ft pressure above atmospheric, but the third accident was with one inflated to around 13 lbs/sq ft.

This was a dome for the 20th Century Fox feature film 'The Touchables'. A story about four girls who lived in a pleasure dome on the edge of a lake, and who captured a pretty boy and played competitive games for his services. We were called in as advisers at the stage when the director had already decided he wanted an 80 ft diameter transparent three-quarter sphere.

Now a three-quarter sphere is a pretty dodgy form pneumatically—pressure and uplift conditions vary around it and a difficult concentration of stresses develops at the crown. Added to this, it is not possible to get a really transparent coated fabric, and fabrication difficulties ruled out such materials as Melinex. Having examined various possibilities, we finally settled on 8 thou. clear p.v.c. film with a nylon net over the top to carry all the major stresses.

When all the research and fabrication was complete, the producer went ahead alone and put it up. A tubular steel podium covered with canvas and sprayed to look like concrete, a mirror floor of polished aluminium panels, entrance from a sprung door below and a completely silent fan.

Unfortunately the fan inlet was constricted during the laying of the floor, and was then further reduced by a grid over the top. 'We thought', I was told later, 'that the same amount of air would come through, but it would come through more quickly.' It did not. Less air was blown in and the structure softened. A wind came down from the hills, hit the dome and the crown blew out. However this was not all loss despite a very worrying few weeks for all concerned, as the bursting was so effective that it was done again, deliberately, at the climax of the film.

111, 112 Scene from the Twentieth Century Fox film 'The Touchables', shot inside a transparent pneumatic dome, an 80 ft. diameter three-quarter sphere in transparent p.v.c. with nylon net.

Also as soon as proper precautions were taken, the dome behaved beautifully as the largest transparent pneumatic dome in the world, and gave the opportunity for some simply magnificent photography from the director, Robert Freeman.

Until recently most pneumatic structures were designed on the basis of experience. Certain manufacturers had developed a number of standard forms which they knew worked, and these were and are available on the open market. However if anything out-of-the-ordinary was required, this created something of a problem as no design team existed, and indeed the basis of the design process for pneumatics was not generally understood. This situation perhaps goes some way towards explaining the very slow development of pneumatics in Europe, and especially in Britain.

But now, things are changing. Reference books are available which set out the calculation process for a wide range of membrane forms, and more and more engineers are taking an interest in the subject. However, the calculations involved on checking the performance of a pneumatic form are very complicated and time-consuming, and must stem from a design which is the result of a sensible if intuitive approach to the subject by the designer.

A low-pressure pneumatic structure will hold up if the increase in the internal air pressure equals and slightly exceeds the weight of the skin. If the fabric weighs one half oz per square foot, a pressure rise of a touch over one half oz per square foot is needed. This is for simple support in still air conditions and unfortunately is the least of the stress problems.

Wind causes most of the difficulties, and the internal pressure must at all times, or by adjustment when required, be able to match and slightly exceed the pressure exerted on the exterior by the wind. Curvature must also be sufficiently strong to prevent any tendency to flutter developing as, if unrestrained, this could build up, like the Tacoma bridge incident, to dangerous proportions.

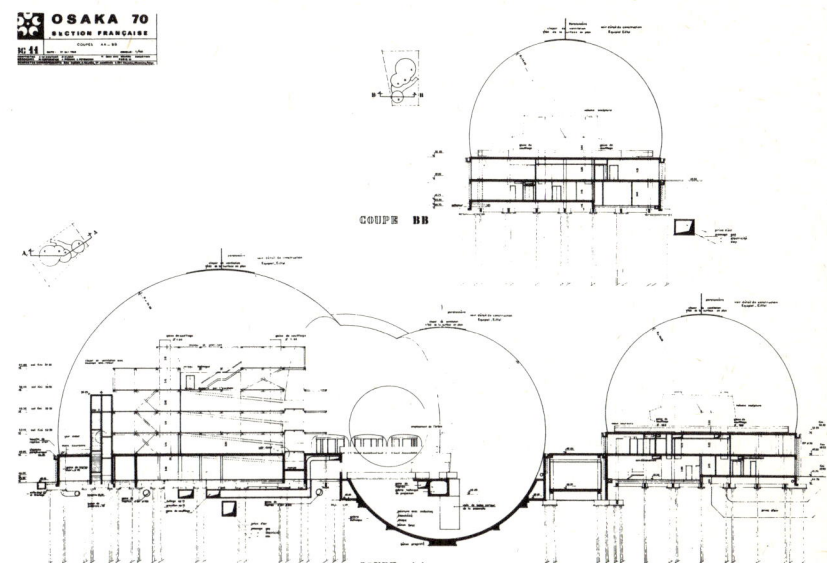

113–15 Facing, above, inflated project for the French pavilion at Expo '70, by Le Couteur and Sloan. Four linked forms covering 60,000 sq. ft. Below, the project is tested in a wind tunnel. Right, sections of the pavilion.

The internal pressure must also be capable of withstanding the weight of snow which may accumulate on horizontal or near horizontal surfaces.

As the internal pressure of this type of structure is exerted evenly over the whole internal surface, one has to define the worst possible external stress which may be applied and design to cater for it throughout. This is in general terms and must be modified in certain cases—for example, if it is necessary for a man to walk on a structure for maintenance or cleaning, one would not conclude that it was necessary to counteract his load of perhaps 400 lbs/square foot throughout the structure. One would decide that temporary localized deformation under his weight was acceptable.

The choice of skin should, one would think, be governed by the general level of stress which the envelope has to withstand, but in fact stress concentrations, very severe in some cases, can develop which will themselves dictate the strength required of the membrane. Once more on the principle that the whole envelope must be capable of resisting the highest stress which may be applied at any part of it—but this time because the 'tailoring' of the skin to give a higher performance in certain localized positions while possible is not yet a financially-viable proposition except in very crude terms.

Finally the uplift load, a resultant of the pressure per square foot over the total ground area related to the perimeter on the perimeter fixings, should be evaluated. This again is often assumed to be even around the perimeter, but is in fact capable of being varied to some degree by gusts of wind.

Form is dictated by the tendency towards minimum area, but may be adjusted by tailoring. For example, if one were to inflate a cube envelope, it would do its utmost to turn itself into a sphere. Nevertheless, excrescence-like addenda may be formed in the skin, and these will stand up rather like fancy balloons with horns or noses.

Balloons lead to bubbles, because it is on the study of the form of bubbles that the sympathetic and therefore logical design of low-pressure pneumatics should be based.

spatial enclosures /103

116 Black and white hexagonal inflated p.v.c. church at Montigny-les-Cormeilles, by Hans-Walter Müller. Seven-minute inflation time; seating capacity 200 persons.

117 Wembley stadium enclosure project by Arthur Quarmby for Polyplan Ltd. Length 750×400×200 ft. high. Weight 7·65 tons, pressure rise 0·065 lbs./sq. ft.

118 Early U.S. inflated 'Atoms for Peace' mobile exhibition to South America, by Victor Lundy, with Birdair Structures Inc. Two linked double-skin domes, with high-pressure tube arched entrances at each end. Length 300×120×54 ft. high. Probably the first sculptural use of inflatables.

119–21 Boston Arts Center Theatre at Woods Hole, Mass., by Carl Koch and Margaret Ross, with Paul Weidhinger and Birdair Structures Inc. Below, section and elevation of double saucer inflated roof, restrained with perimeter compression ring. Right, above: interior of completed structure and below, exterior.

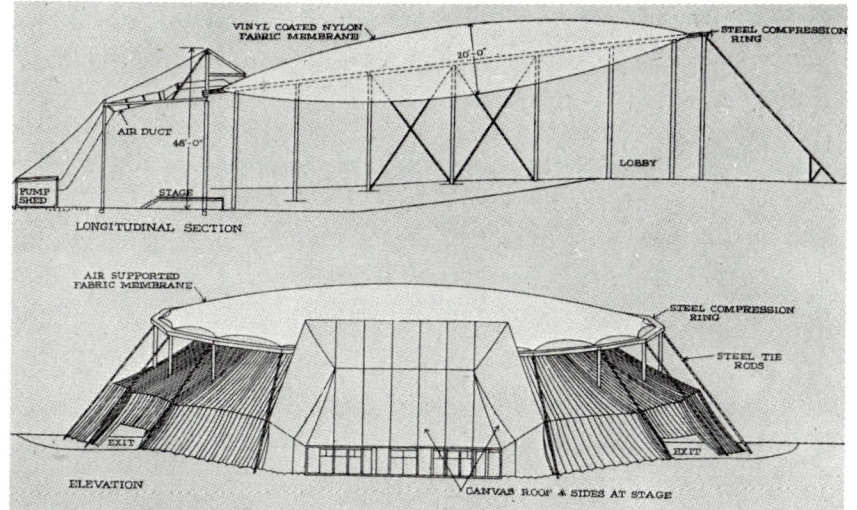

122 (Below) large-span indented pneumatic landscape enclosure project, by Frei Otto.

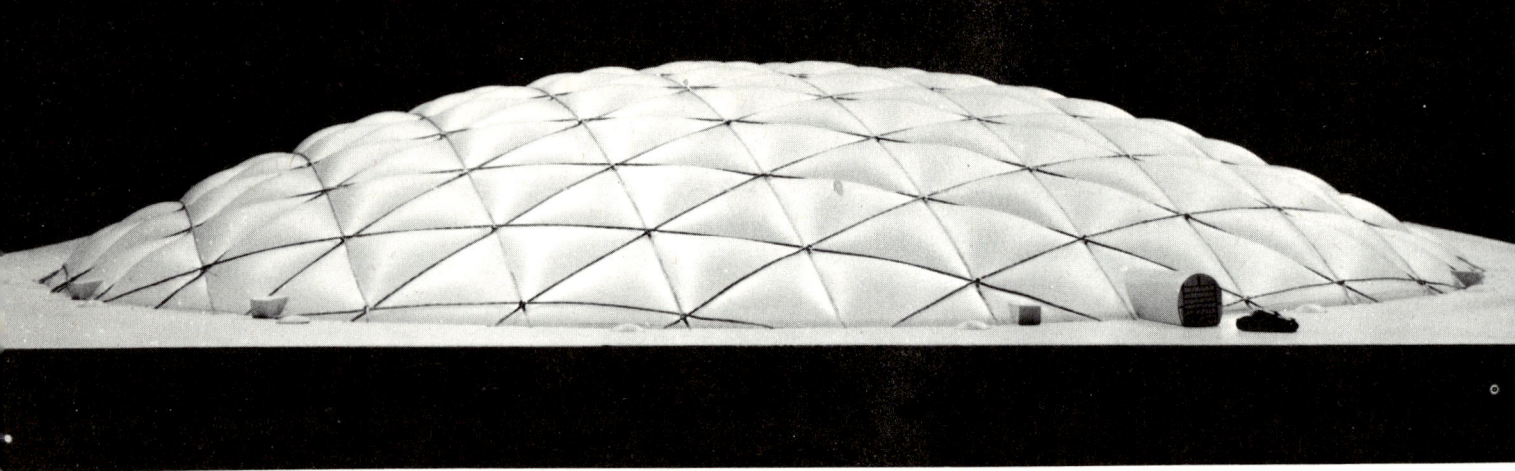

123 Cable-restrained stadium roof project, 600 ft. diameter, by Birdair Structures Inc. Triangular cable system results in minimum distortion, and spans of up to 1,000 ft. are feasible with costs of around $2 per sq. ft. of floor area.

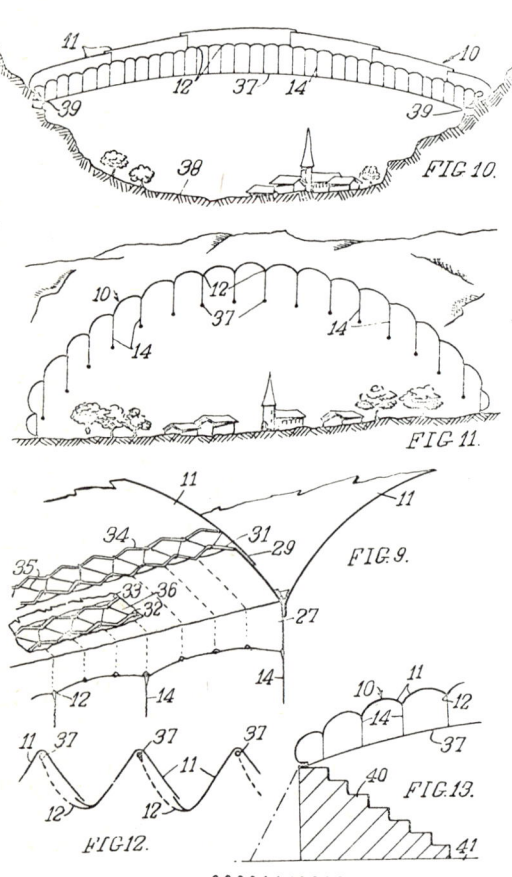

124 Patent drawings for very large span pneumatics by Walter Neumark, illustrating variations on the suspension seam technique which he also employed in the perambulating caterpillar structure (fig. 42).

A bubble, like any low-pressure pneumatic form, consists of a skin enclosing a volume of air at slightly increased pressure (on account of the weight of the skin), and a bubble will always enclose a given volume with the minimum surface area.

Leaving aside the obvious case of the plain soap bubble, one could perhaps consider a wire ring in one plane where, no matter how complicated the shape of the wire, it will be spanned by a planar bubble film. However if the ring is bent, then the film 'will become curved into a surface which may be extremely complicated, but is still the smallest possible surface which can be drawn continuously across the uneven boundary'.

And here I am quoting the daddy of them all on bubbles—and not only bubbles but on the physical structures of all living things, of elements, of drops of moisture, of ink drops in liquids—D'Arcy Wentworth Thompson who in 1917 published a magnificent work called *On Growth and Form*, which no designer can afford to be without.

I wonder how many of us have been surprised by this book, and by the odd facts which he reveals from time to time. For instance, when discussing the silica skeleton of a member of the sponge family called a Radiolaria, he casually announces that '... no system of hexagons can enclose space; whether the hexagons be equal or unequal, regular or irregular, it is still under all circumstances mathematically impossible'.

So the basic design could well start from this source, before moving on to the recent outstanding publications on the work of Frei Otto. It should always be borne in mind that very complicated calculations are required to check the performance of the form produced by the designer. Get that form right in the first place and it will save a lot of time and money.

Some of my own work on bubbles has led me to conclusions at variance with those currently accepted. For example, it is suggested that the form of a soap bubble at rest on a flat surface is an ideal one for a low-pressure pneumatic form. This is correct for conditions where it is only necessary to balance the weight of the skin by the internal pressure, but in all practical cases a better comparison would be a bubble which is being blown by air introduced from beneath, and this type of demonstration can sometimes give rather dissimilar results.

This applies especially in cases such as a bubble blown over an irregular plan form—a star shape for example. Here the bubble lifts off from the perimeter by means of a series of what might be termed tensile pendentives, in which the membrane tapers down to the ground rather than dropping down at or near a right angle.

There is a great deal of work still to be done on low-pressure pneumatic structures, and I impatiently await the day when we control the climate over really large areas. Why are our sports stadia still open when the best games in every sport are played in ideal conditions? Why do our holiday resorts in Britain not realize that it is already a viable proposition to enclose a large area of land and sea and provide guaranteed (if artificial) sunlight, thus beating the resorts of the Mediterranean coasts at their own game? Why do we still build new towns and cities in the open and create thousands of little micro-climates when the whole job could be done under one enclosure? How should we wish to live if this were done, and what of architecture then?

HIGH PRESSURE PNEUMATICS

High pressure pneumatic structures normally consist of a compartmentalized envelope, which is inflated into a structural form—for example an airbed—or tubes inflated to a moderately high pressure, which then carry an enclosing membrane.

The first examples of this work for structures were of the latter type, and many are still being made. However, on a large scale, the size of tube grows tremendously and the resultant form may be composed entirely of tubes adjacent to each other.

Some of the more surprising features of h.p. pneumatics, which point to further future developments, are illustrated by the work of the Military Engineering and Experimental Establishment at Christchurch and the R.A.F. research establishment at Cardington, both in Britain. Imagine a bridge packed in the back of a small truck, which may be inflated by the exhaust to enable the truck to drive across a ravine; a hose with close-fitting rollers by means of which a man can be lifted, in a harness suspended from the rollers, by the pressure of air from behind; a pad which can be exhaust-inflated to jack a vehicle back onto its wheels; an inflated enclosure (low pressure this time) which can be used to float a tank across a river. Inflated chimneys, inflated dams, inflated compression members for space deck structures—limitless possibilities and yet I believe that the real future for h.p. pneumatics lies in specialized applications such as these rather than in large spatial enclosures.

The fact of the matter is that I have never been happy about the safety aspect of h.p. structures. With a really large l.p. enclosure it is almost possible to fly a light aeroplane in through one side and out through the other without the membrane collapsing around your ears. For example in the project for the l.p. enclosure of Wembley Stadium, England, it was

128 (Facing page) inflated tube radome by Birdair Structures Inc. Stability is unaffected by the deflation of one section.

125 Articulated tube structure by Walter Neumark for the Frankenstein Group Limited. 100 p.s.i. inflation pressure.

126 Clamshell pivoting articulated shelter by Walter Neumark for the Frankenstein Group Limited. 32 ft. diameter, Terylene fabric coated with white Hypalon for Arctic use. Opens or closes fully within seconds.

127 High-pressure rib radome erecting device by Walter Neumark for the Frankenstein Group Limited.

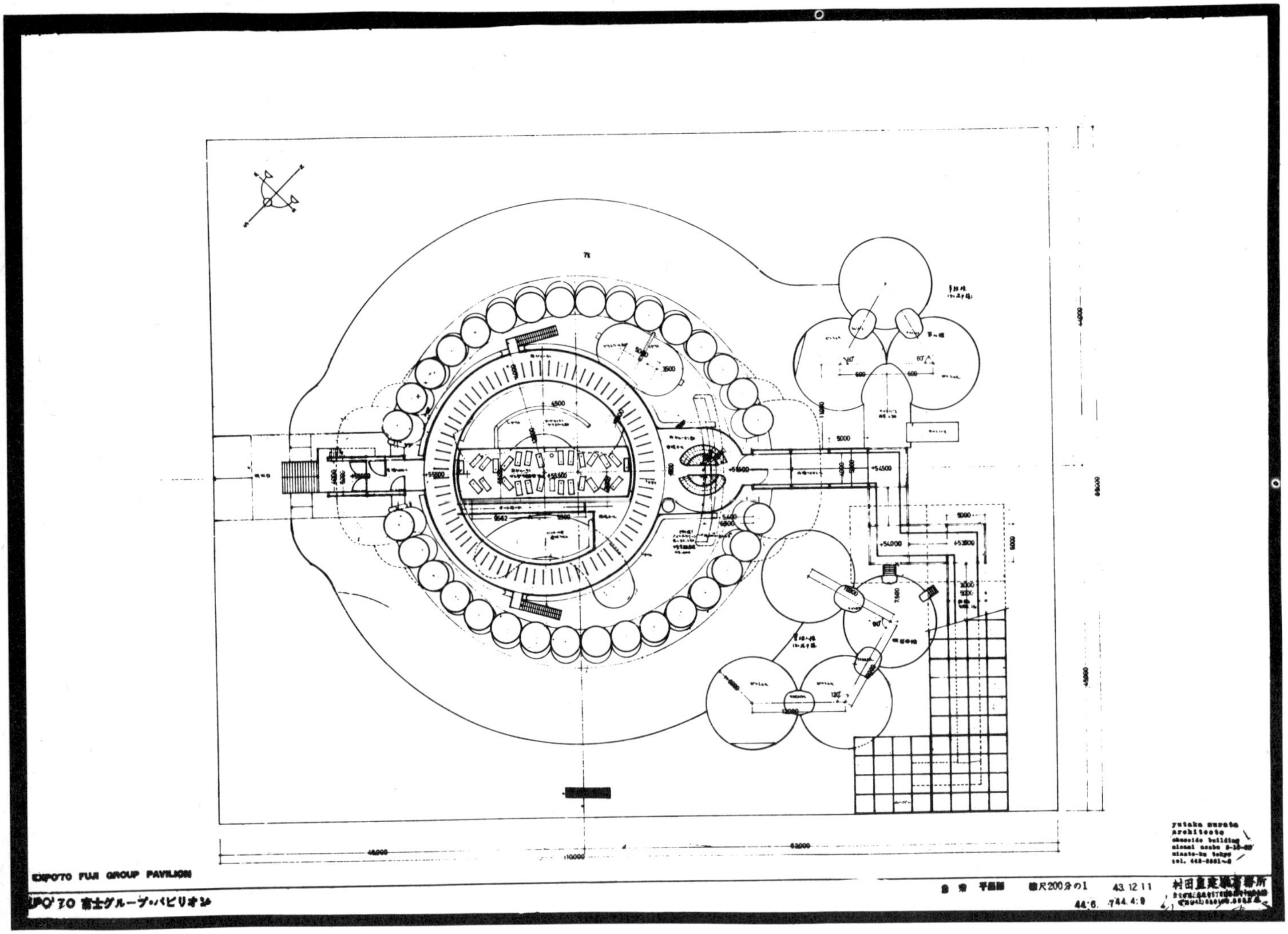

129–31 Fuji Pavilion, Expo '70, by Yutaka Murata. Plan, side view and entrance of the tensioned, high-pressure tube structure.

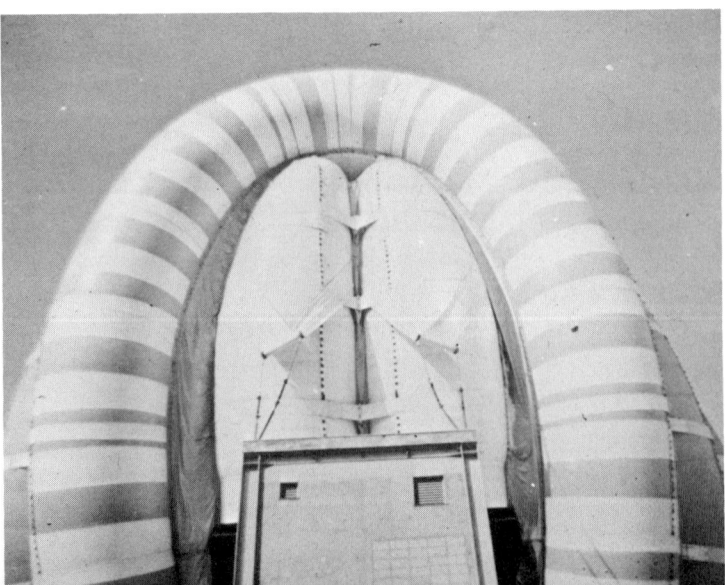

132, 133 Above, panel inflated structure by M.L. Aviation Company Limited. Each panel consists of two skins of coated fabric linked with a multitude of threads, and each can, if required, be inflated independently. Below, U.S. Atomic Energy Commission mobile exhibition by Joseph Eldredge and Birdair Structures Inc. Inflated compartments give free perimeter.

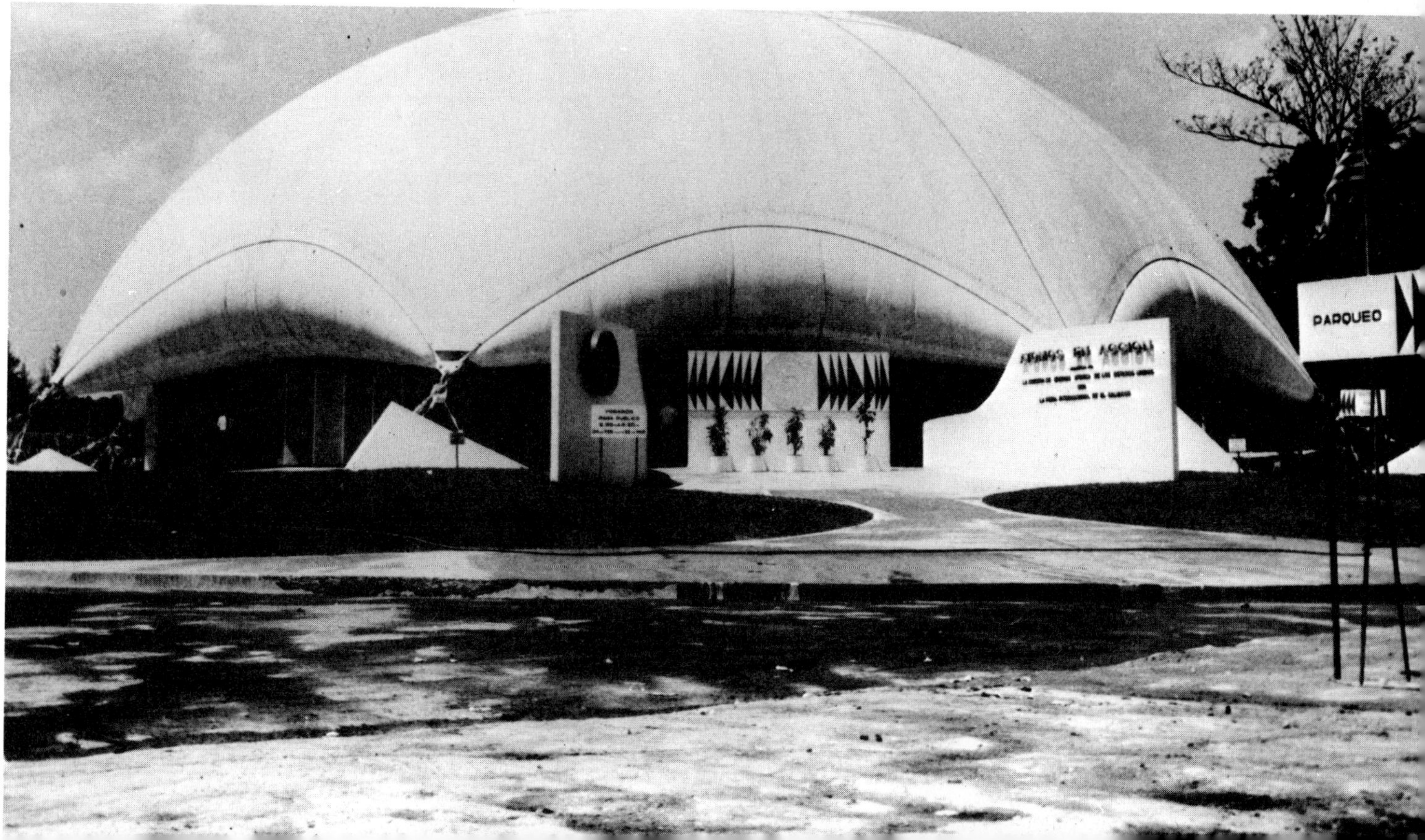

134 Taipo River 'Fabridam', Hong Kong. Nylon fabric coated with neoprene and 'Hypalon'. Partially filled with water, it controls the flow of the river for the Plover Cove Water Scheme, and can be walked upon when the river is low.

135 Compression tube structure by Aubert, Jungmann and Stinco of the Beaux-Arts School, Paris, under David Georges Emmerich.

136–38 General-purpose enclosure for 5,000 persons, by J. Aubert, Beaux-Arts School, Paris, under D. G. Emmerich. Right, detail of component panel and tubes, below top, section and bottom, exterior.

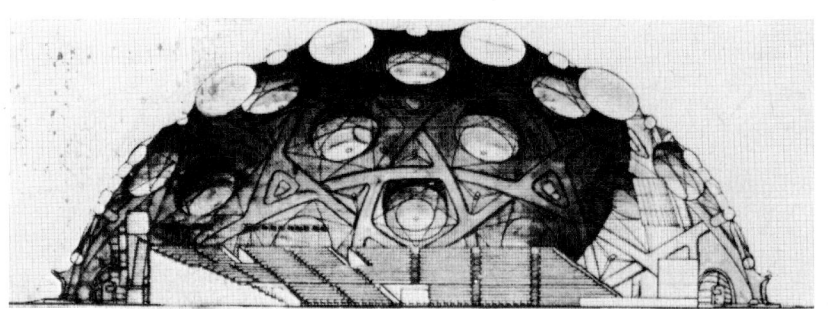

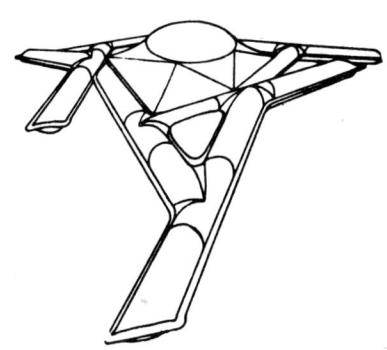

139 Gas-lifted roof project for Wembley Stadium, by Arthur Quarmby.

140 Inflated tube apartment block project, by Pohl and Smith. Internal pressure lifts the roof, from which the internal floors are suspended on rods. External diagonal bracing prevents deformation.

calculated that if all the fans were turned off and all of the 79 doors, each 7′ 6″ square were opened, deflation would take about four hours. The pressure inside is so slight, that air does not rush out—it drifts out like a gentle breeze.

Now with a h.p. form one small puncture creates a danger of immediate collapse. It is possible to duplicate the structure or compartmentalize it to localize the failure or to have fans to replace the leaking air, but until we have a lightweight self-sealing skin this criticism will remain valid.

I had this trouble myself on another project for Wembley stadium—one which was never put forward—which consisted of a compartmentalized envelope filled with helium lifting a translucent tension skin which was in turn tied back to the perimeter of the existing structure. Research revealed that while fabrics were available to withstand birds' claws, and while bullet holes were of small significance, a true self-sealing skin for a lightweight flexible envelope was not available. Nevertheless the project was practical both constructionally and economically, and designers could well start to look at the support potential of the cheap helium which is being produced by certain oil and natural gas fields.

I believe that pneumatics are the most important discovery ever made in architecture; that they can free the living environment from the constraints which have bound it since history began and that they can in consequence play an immeasurable part in the development of our society.

CHAPTER 7 component construction

Component construction starts inevitably with housing and progresses through panel construction to bathroom units and functioning cores. Applications such as these where a multiplicity of functions is performed and where the components are complex in form are far more ideal for the full exploitation of the properties of plastics than the simple enclosures of the previous chapter.

For instance, a section of a room can be created with much of the equipment moulded in, as one operation. Examples of this are limited because although this can so easily be done in plastics and although the final product can be both very sophisticated and extremely cheap, the tooling cost will be very high, and therefore a vast repetitive market is required, and this does not yet exist in building.

Far more work has been done along these lines in the automobile industry. The bonnet of a small popular saloon is now press-moulded in d.m.c. (dough moulding compound, a blend of polyester and short glass fibres; high strength and good surface finish). This is complete in one operation, whereas 32 different assembly stages were involved when it was fabricated from traditional materials. The application of the self-skinning technique using polyurethane foam (which the building industry uses for mock-antique beams and reproduction porticos) is being used for its strength/weight properties in the production of amphibious army vehicles in Germany.

Although applications are limited, component construction is dominated by housing. The real development of plastics structures started with the Schein plastics house (see 14–16) and was followed by the Monsanto house (see 22–24), and as the work started so it continues.

All over the world houses are needed most desperately—and by and large and making due allowances for differences in the customs and living standards of the peoples involved and the climates in which they live, a house is a house.

HOUSING

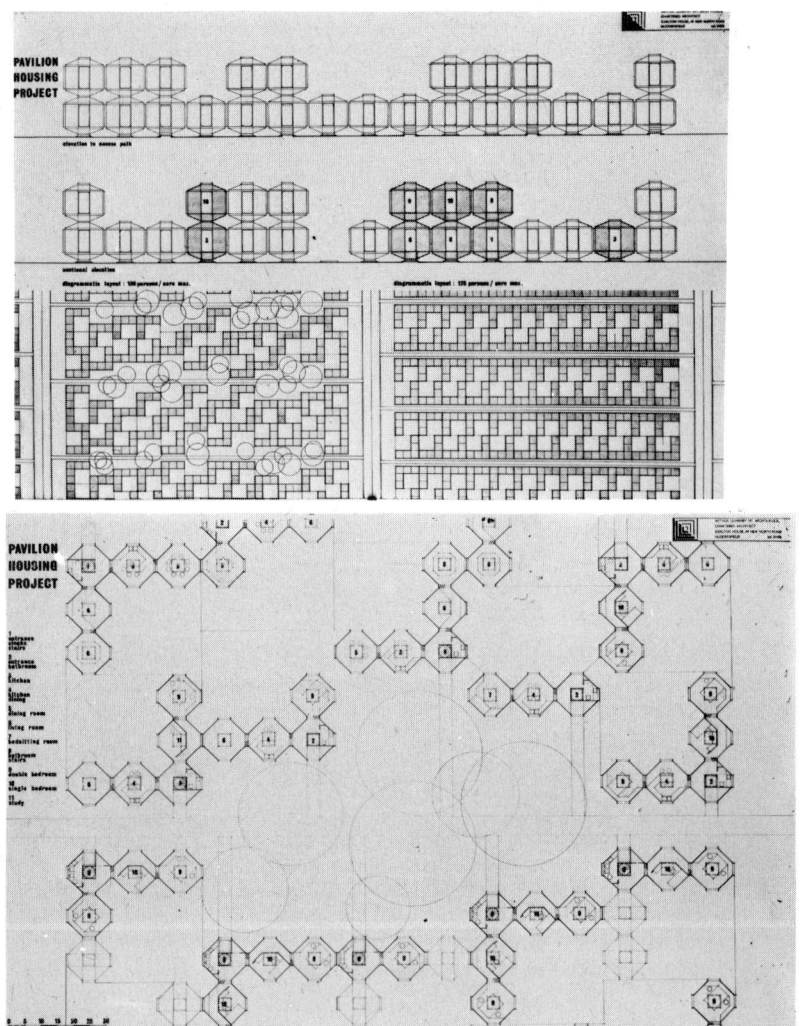

141, 142 Pavilion housing project, Arthur Quarmby. G.r.p. sandwich room units of the same general form, designed to be assembled together on all four sides, above and below, contain within themselves a complex, rotationally-cast lining. There is a choice of eleven basic room types, with luxury variations of each. House can grow from a minimum of three to a maximum of ten units, and can also shrink. There would be direct sales from manufacturer to public—plan your own house from the catalogue—with a trade-in scheme for the latest models. (Old units are refitted: old thermoplastic lining is ground up for reuse.) Below: view of the model.

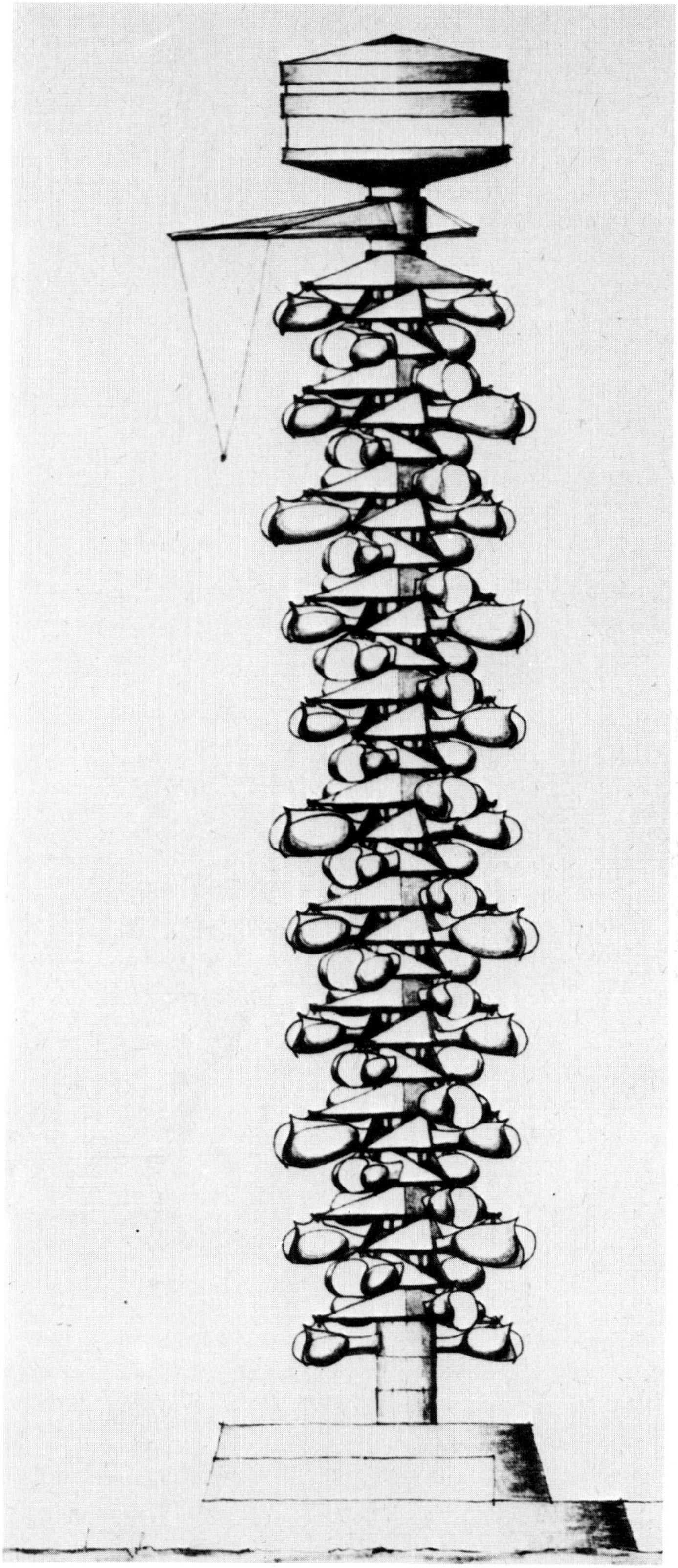

143, 144 'Corn on the Cob' suspended apartments project, by Arthur Quarmby. Pre-stressed concrete lozenges assembled on top of each other with radiating arms, post-tensioned from top to bottom. Three types of g.r.p. living units with walk-out-upon blister windows, translucent walls for bedrooms, etc., units delivered by truck, and hung on arms by twin-jib crane. Services top and bottom. Living units bought—and mobile. Hanging space rented. Elevation and left, typical plan.

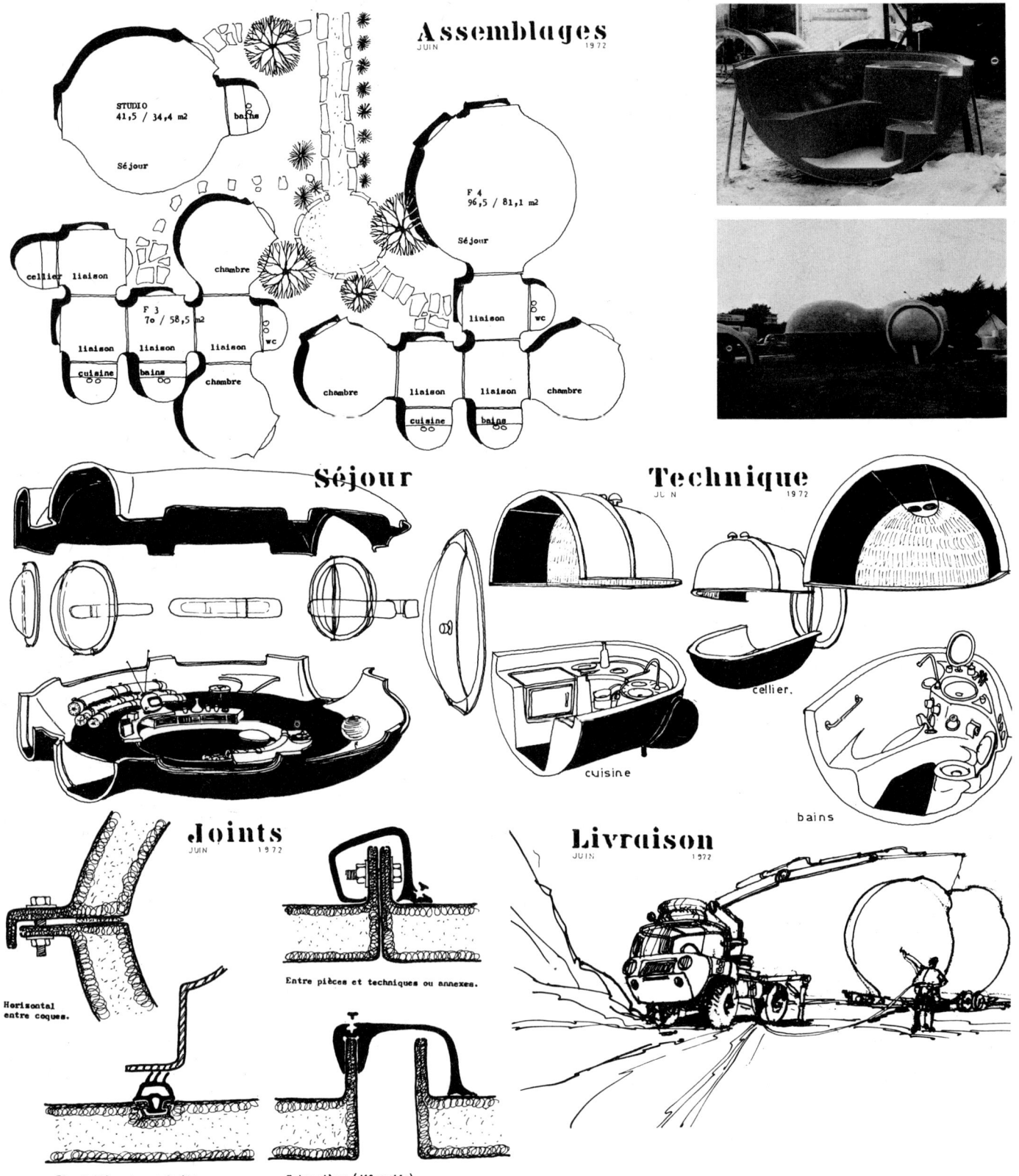

146 Above, left, industrialized housing, series 'bulles', version 2, by Pascal and Claude Hausermann. Cocoon-spray p.v.c. models on wire framework.

145 (Opposite) variable g.r.p. housing system by Pascal and Claude Hausermann. A recent development of a most consistent range of work carried out over a ten-year period, latterly with Governmental backing.

147 Above, right, 'Hotel Mobile' project by Gernot Nalbach. 80-bedroom hotel erected in one day by mobile crane, with one-way transparent room enclosure.

148, 149 Below, left and right, variable g.r.p. housing. Model. Pascal and Claude Hausermann.

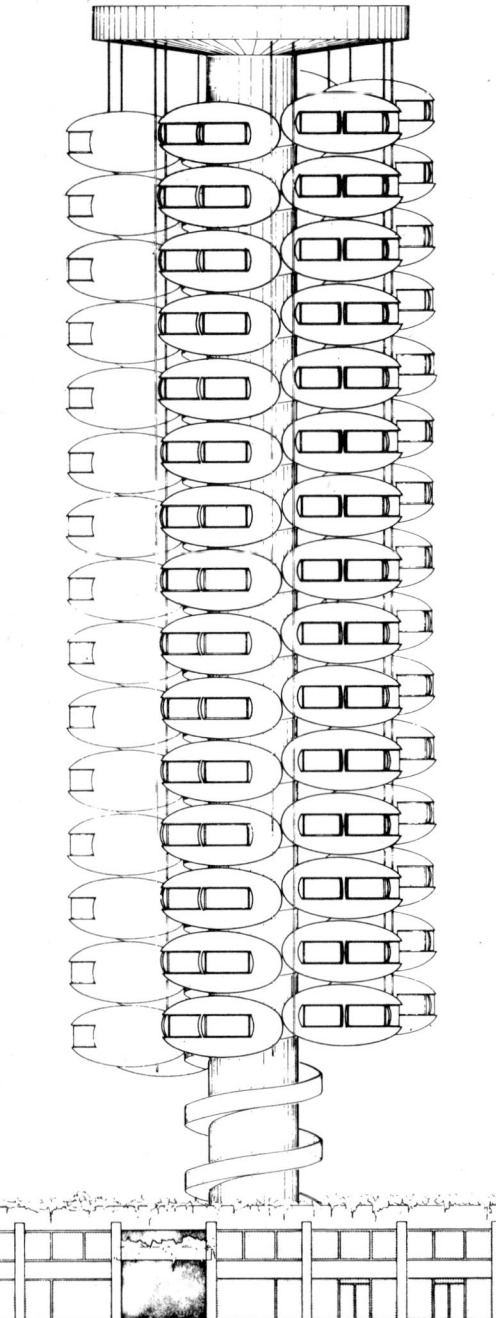

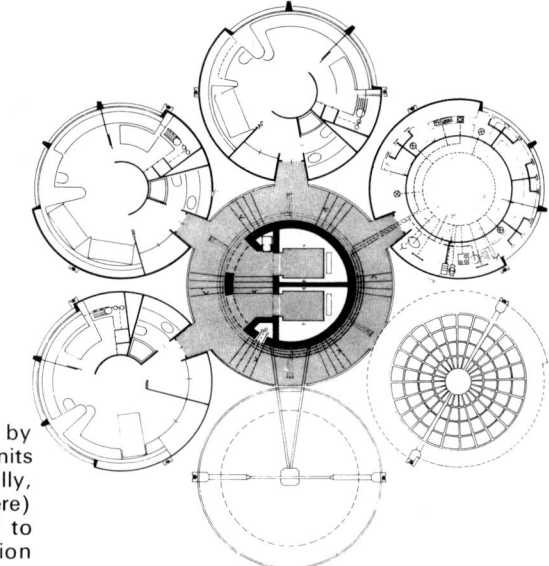

150 'Rondo' housing project by Casoni and Casoni. Housing units capable of being used individually, assembled into blocks, or (as here) suspended from a structural roof to form an apartment tower. Elevation and plan.

The majority of people would I believe accept as basic requirements a place to prepare food, a place for excretion, a place for cleaning oneself, a place for sleeping and a place for eating and/or living. We can make do with less, we can demand far more, and if we think about it carefully enough we may be able to redefine these requirements quite differently. Nevertheless in the present state of the world and for what may perhaps be considered to be a majority of its peoples, these basic requirements would apply.

This enormous basic market has always tended to dominate the thoughts of designers in plastics—despite the fact that the bulk of the demand comes from people with an annual income so low that they can afford nothing. Nevertheless inability to buy the product does not indicate any lack of demand, and many of us remain convinced that we could develop a range of components which could be used to form sophisticated, self-contained housing (possibly with the exception only of a power supply) in a price bracket from the most basic right through to the luxury category.

However, when the houses of the native townships in South Africa are produced at a cost of around £350 ($732), then even the shipping costs of any sophisticated product would tend to put it out of court.

To counter this problem we might well consider the development of a project in the United States where a number of old naval vessels are being converted into floating factories for housing production. Even using conventional building construction, such factories, based on converted Essex aircraft carriers, are capable of producing 5,000 dwellings per annum. Plastics production could increase this figure to at least 125,000 per annum—and imagine these sailing up the rivers of the underdeveloped countries of the world.

One always tends to say 'yes—but' to this sort of proposition. Yes—but one would be imposing an alien way of life on the inhabitants, who would only keep goats in them anyway. And yet the failure of so many similar

component construction

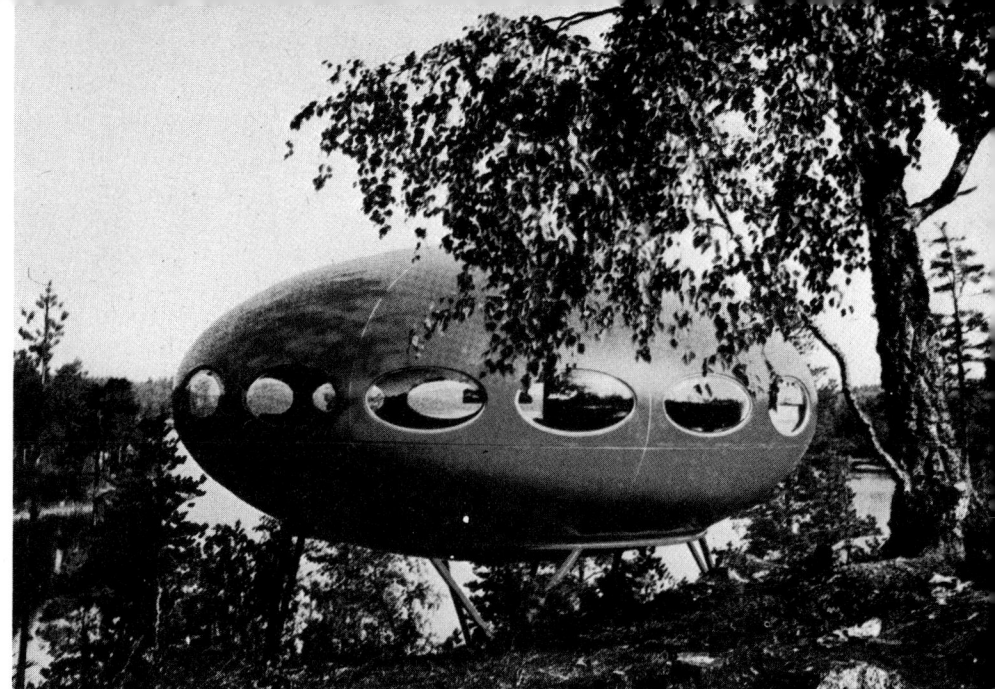

151, 152 'Futuro' house by Matti Suuronen. Finnish weekend house with drop-leaf door, carried on tubular steel cradle. Below, detailed plans.

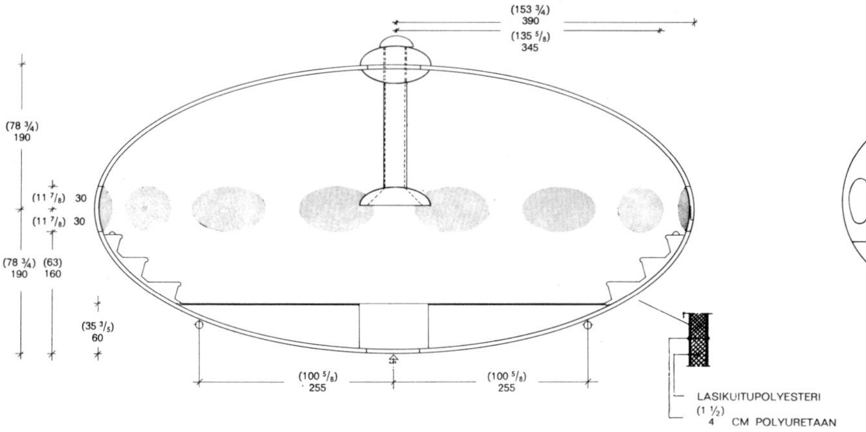

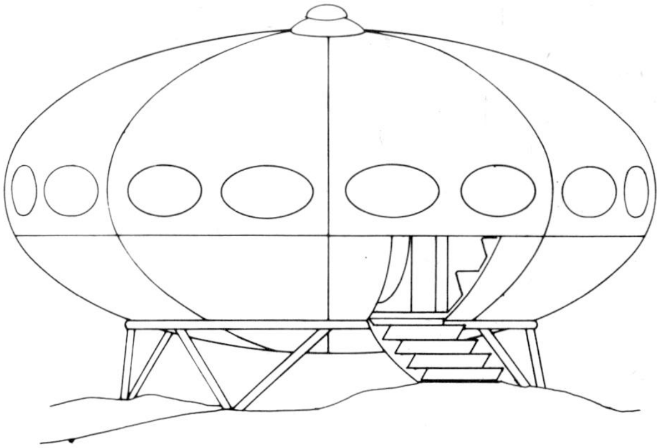

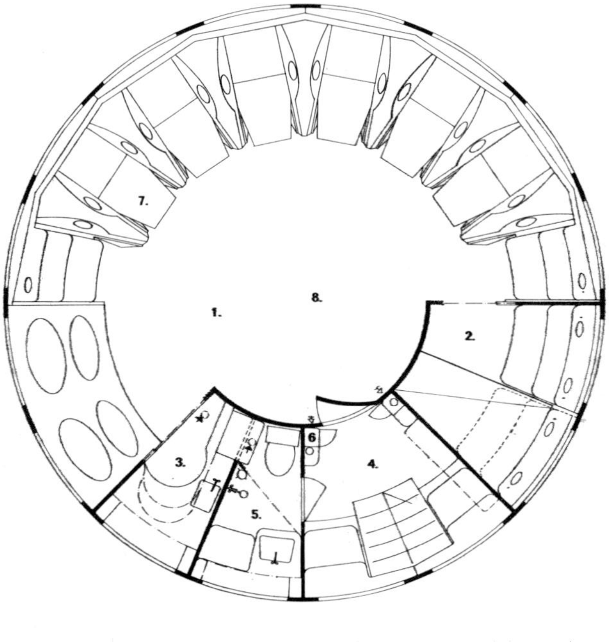

1 HUONE
2 MAKUUHUONE
3 KEITITÖ
4 ETEINEN
5 WC JA SUIHKU
6 SÄHKÖKAAPPI
7 ISTUIN
8 TAKKA

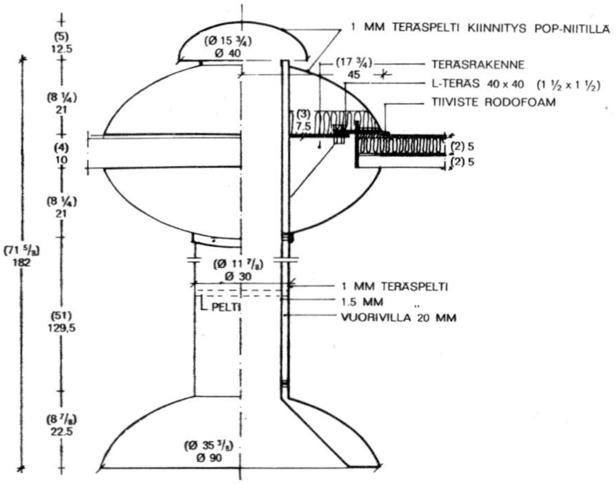

153, 154 Prototype junction unit for cellular housing system, exhibition at Chambéry, by Chanéac and (right), plan of 'Aixilia' floating town for le Bourget lake, by Chanéac.

155, 156 Below, left, 'Aixilia', showing houses folded and unfolded; below, right: Chanéac's project for stacking shell units, forming an apartment block.

 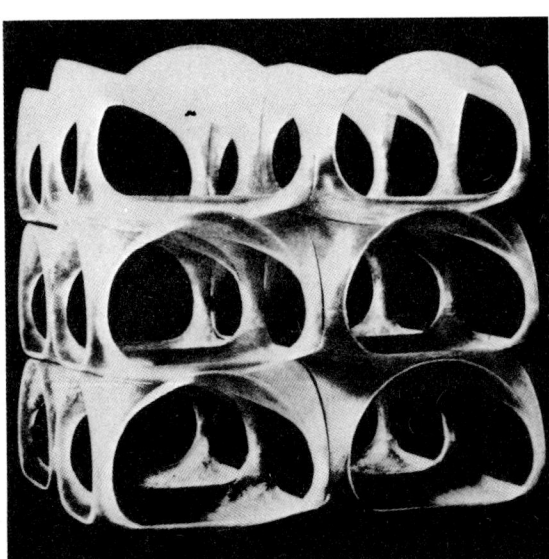

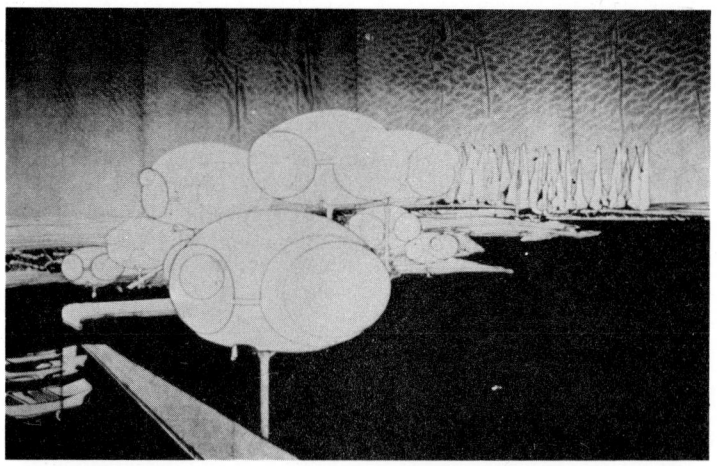 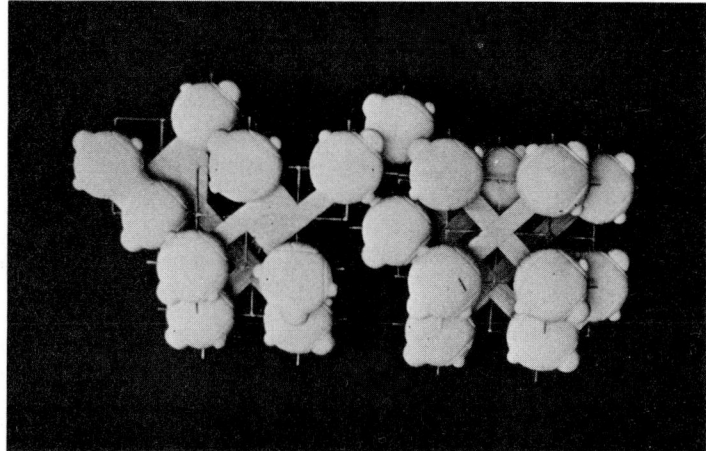

157, 158 'Cascaron Argentino', industrialized housing units for the Parana Delta in Argentina, by Jean Manéval. G.r.p. shells, polyurethane foam core. Perspective showing the units in the Parana Delta (left) and plan of model showing typical grouping of units.

well-meaning disaster operations lies surely not so much in the product (unless something basic like insulation or the need to sleep on the roof is involved) as in the way in which it is done. Take the inhabitants from an intimate, complex and, in planning and sociological terms, sophisticated group of little units and put them into a sterile, straight, flat and crude row of other little units and they will rebel. Just look at the high-level rehousing of people from the slums in developed countries, and the troubles which this generates.

I believe that a house can successfully be as simple in function as a car, which is basically a means of getting from A to B. However the way in which the house is used—the environment it creates and community which it helps to form—is of paramount importance.

Unfortunately the will to tackle this problem throughout the world seems as lacking now as it was one or even two decades ago. So many projects which were initially so promising become hopelessly bogged down in complexities, like the magnificently conceived HUD 'Operation Breakthrough' in the United States. Each project needs a clear-sighted leader capable of seeing through and beyond problems and irrelevancies to the goal beyond.

Many of us are still driven on by the complete certainty that the logical application of plastics materials and technology can, and one day will, produce an industry of building capable of curing the housing ills of the world, and feel the need to revise Roosevelt's definition of human rights to include 'Freedom from housing want'.

However I doubt whether the answer lies in less sophistication—in the tendency to think of providing the poor peoples of the world merely with a basic shelter—and think that the answer may lie in a new type of housing altogether.

I am a great believer in providing people with what they want, and cannot help but be affected by the activities of immigrants from the poorer parts

159 Component housing project, Isago, Yokohama, by N. Kurokawa. Low-rise high-density housing units. Standard concrete components with inserted plastics service components.

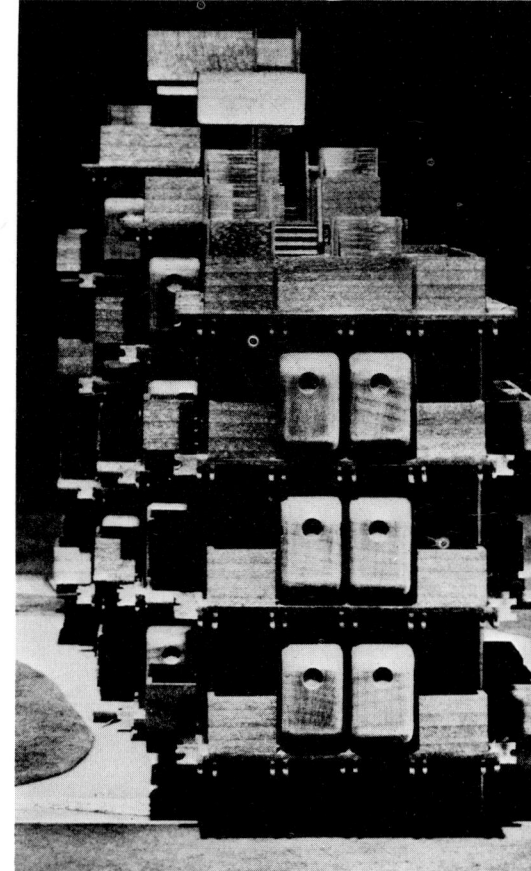

160, 161 Ski lodge units by Komatsu Plastic Industry, Japan, are delivered with two service units stacked inside. Four-berth capsule, with entrance lobby and bathroom unit. G.r.p. shell on timber frame with plywood lining, weight 2,100 lbs. It can be set directly on the snow or on four jacks. Above, the unit; below, cut-away detail.

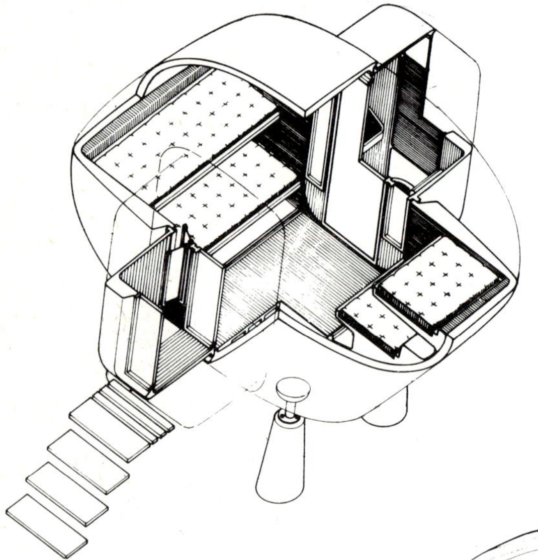

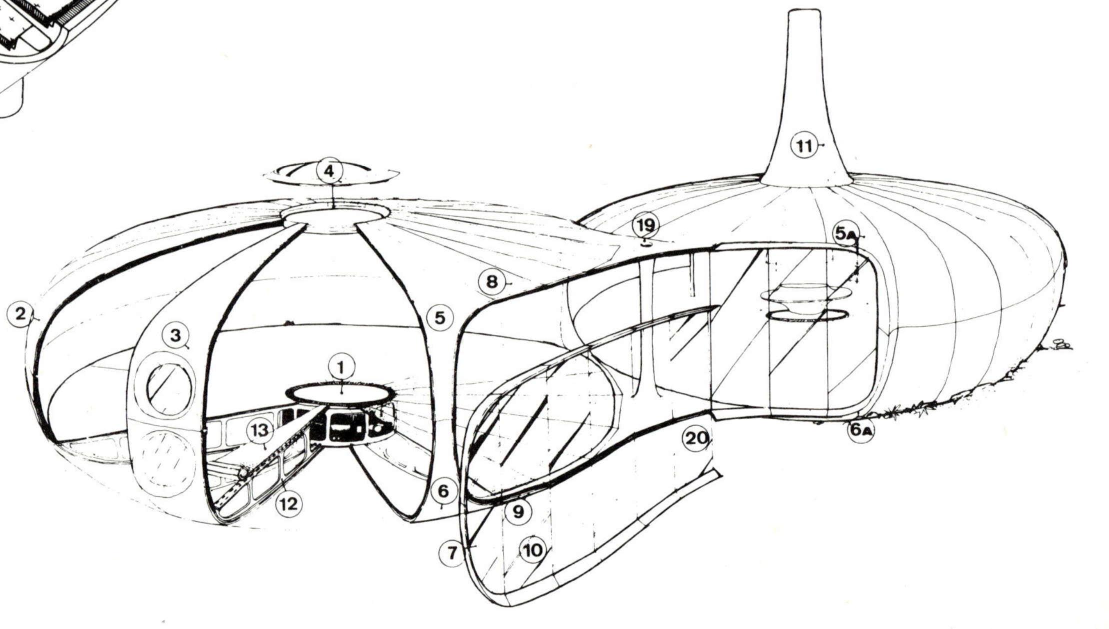

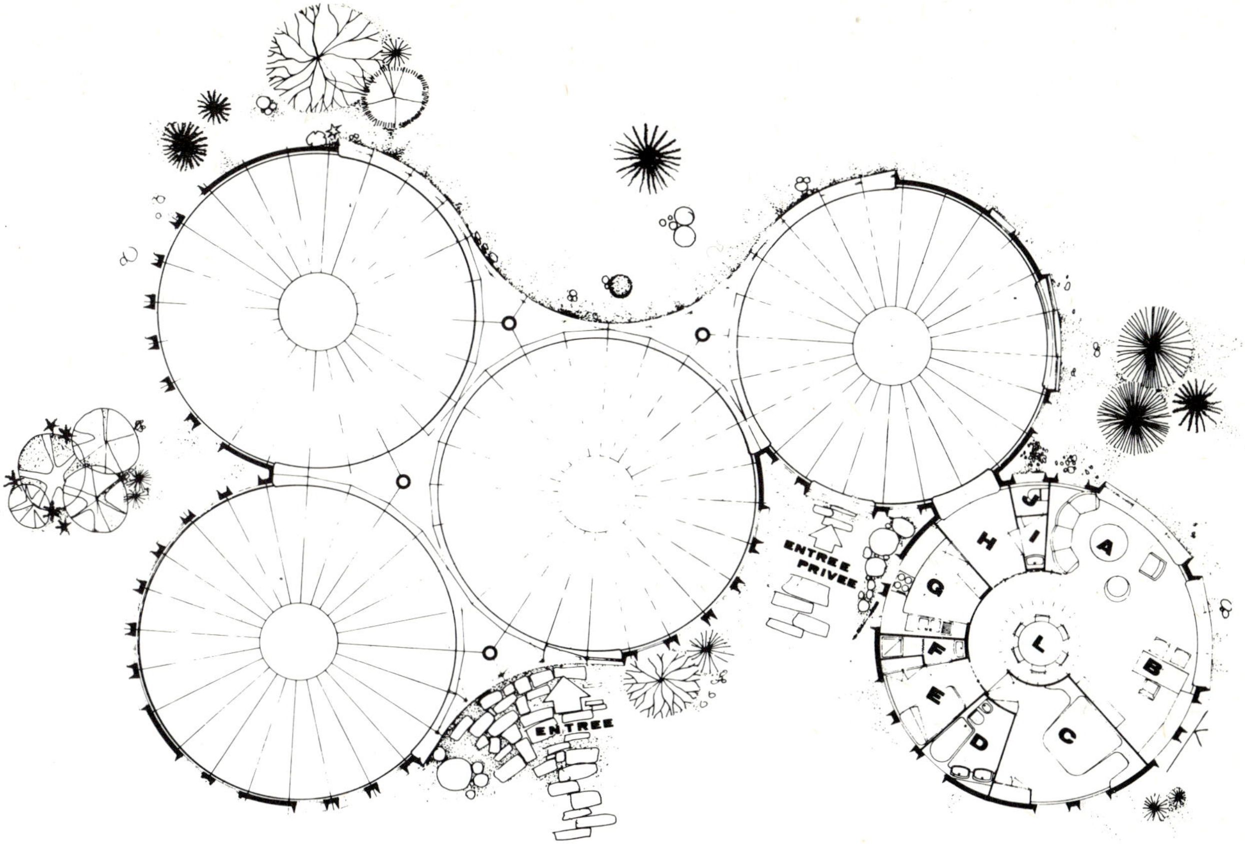

162–64 Spheroid housing project by Guy de Moreau. Facing page, cut-away sketch showing central service disc core with water, electricity, heating and telephone. Note timber framing in floor, and roll-up ribbed floor surface, for access. G.r.p. shells with foam core generally. This page, above, plan; below, prototype unit.

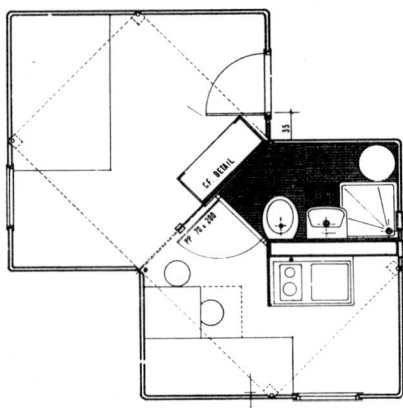

165–67 'Maison 12E' by Atelier 4. Flexible system in g.r.p. sandwich construction. Left, typical plan of double unit, showing diagonal steel square-tube frame, on which the corner-angle shells are hung; right, general view showing frame continuing through shells to ground and below, window and rooflight detail.

of Asia and the West Indies who have in recent years settled in great numbers in my home town. So often it seems to be the sophistications of civilization which give them the greatest delight—televisions, transistors, and cars for example. It is a mistake to assume that they should progress slowly and logically from a primitive state to the toys of the mid-twentieth century, when so many seem to jump in joyfully at the deep end.

Perhaps we might look on housing in this way. The house is a cave, and it is time it became something more. Perhaps if we cease to aim at the minimum and go for the maximum we might make more progress, especially when the minimum normally achieves merely a reduction in air-space. More space not less, and more sophistication—for we could hardly have less than we have at the moment. Houses today have only two technological delights—turn a tap and water gushes out; press a switch and a room is flooded with light.

Electrically-operated automobile windows affect me in this way, and I like the idea of power operation for windows, walls and roofs, of being able to change the volume of a structure and its atmosphere at will. And I hope to be able to realize something of this delight in a new house for myself which is on the drawing-board at the moment, and which illustrates some of these points.

Imagine a central living garden with lawns, trees, rocks, a waterfall and a pool, surrounded by enclosed rooms and covered with a translucent power-operated sliding roof, the garden being air-conditioned and with artificial sunlight so that the plants and trees grow all the year round and one can keep a modest sun tan. The surrounding rooms have complete sliding walls to the central living-garden so that one can throw them open to the central living space or close them off completely.

This particular project is to be partially buried in the ground of a sloping site with turfed soil ramped up the outside and over the roof, except for the facetted translucent sliding roof unit, an observation tower in one

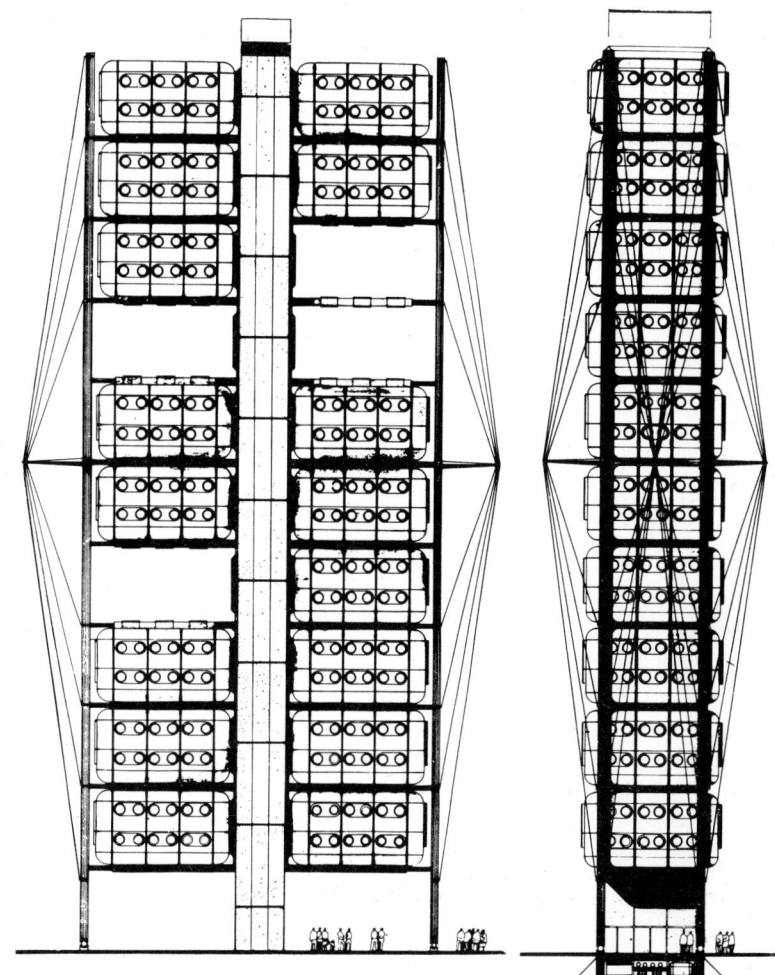

168, 169 Stackable room shells from the Spatial Housing project by Wolfgang Doring. The units are integrated into racks connected to the central core with wind-bracing cables.

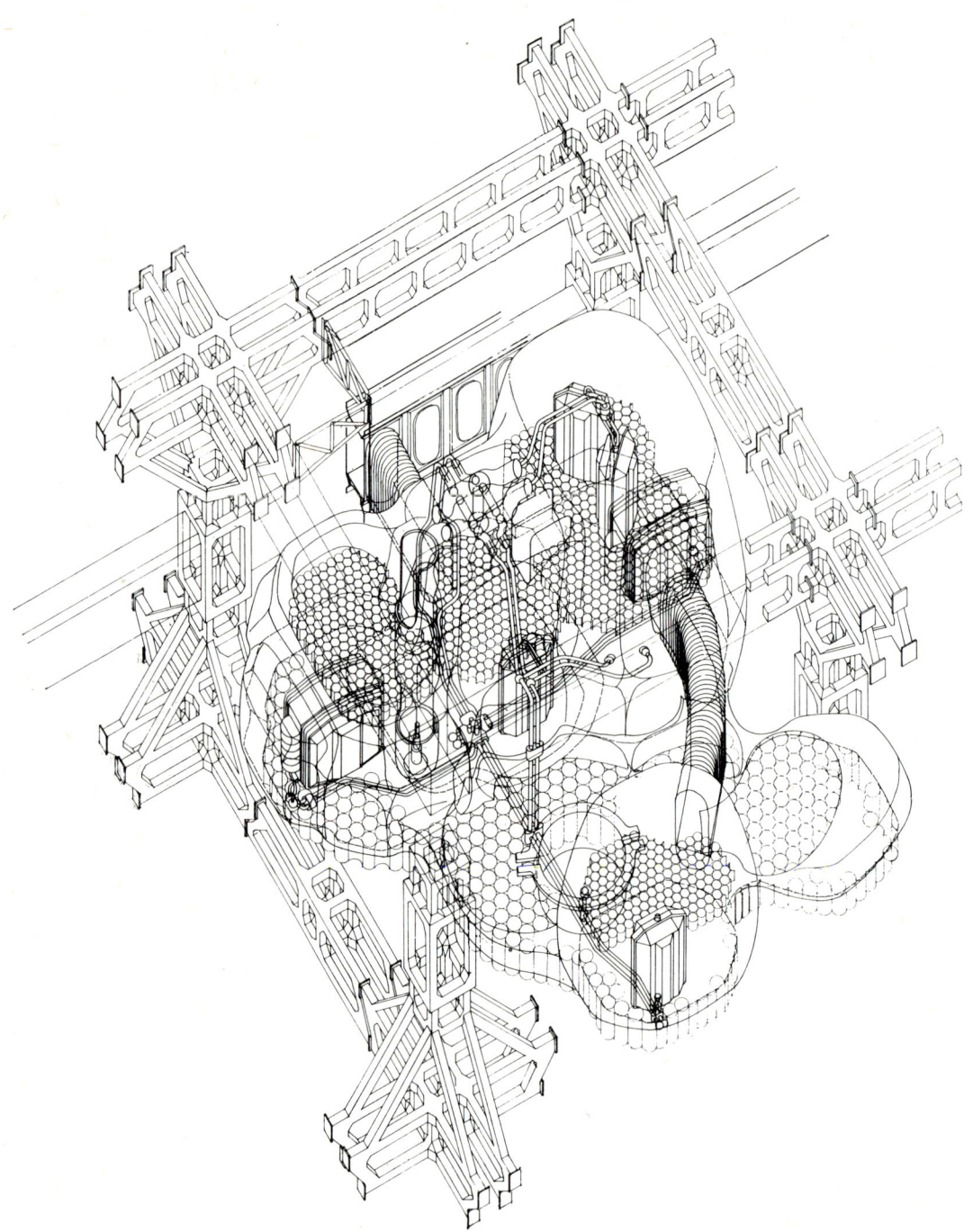

170 Proposal for the 'form of an industrialized urban habitat' by Domenig and Huth: individual volumes on several levels, terraces and suspended gardens, flexible divisions; designed for community ownership of land and superproperty, with subproperty held on lease.

171 (Facing page) transportable units by Angela Hareiter. Basic kitchen/bathroom to which living and sleeping rooms are added. The units can be clipped to high-rise structures with a central service core, hoisted by crane and mounted on rotary arms. The balcony unfolds and membrane living area extension is applied.

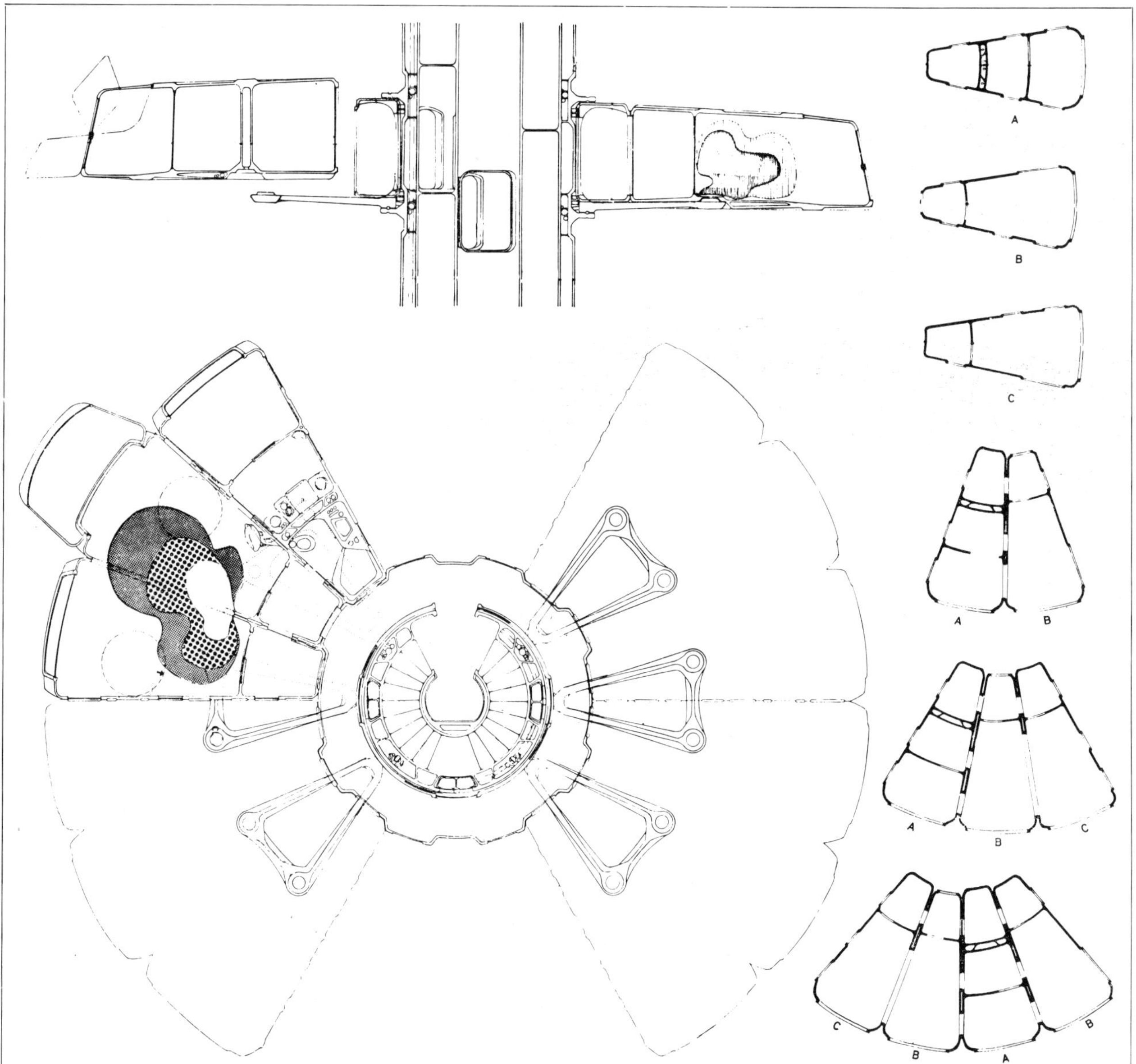

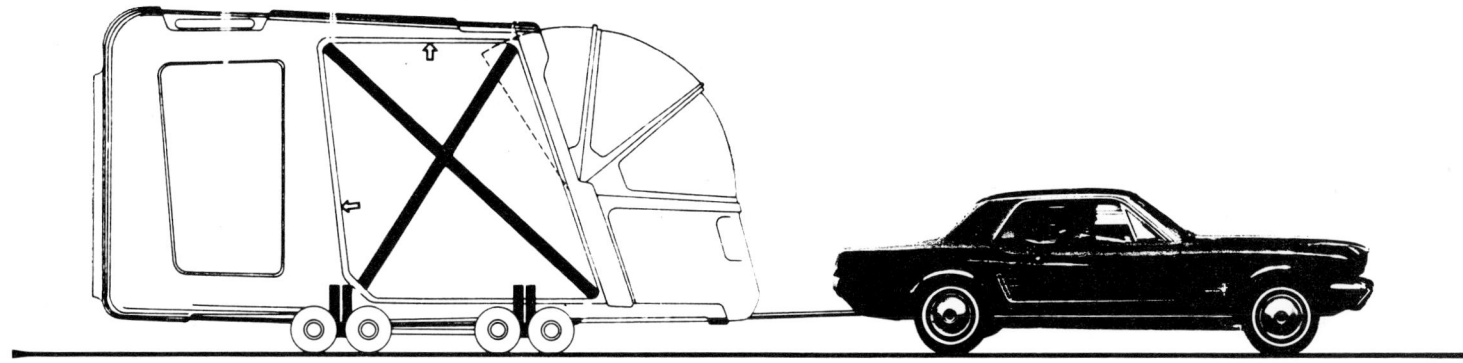
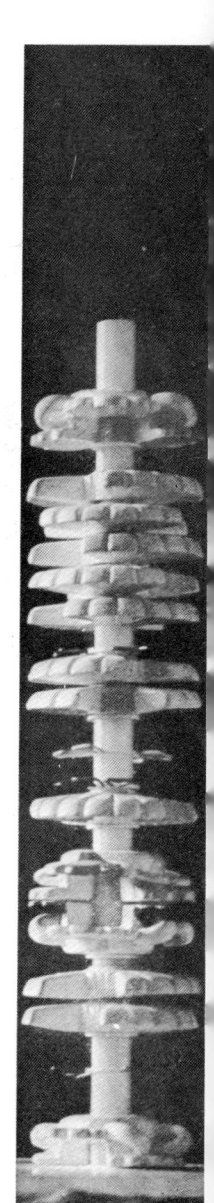

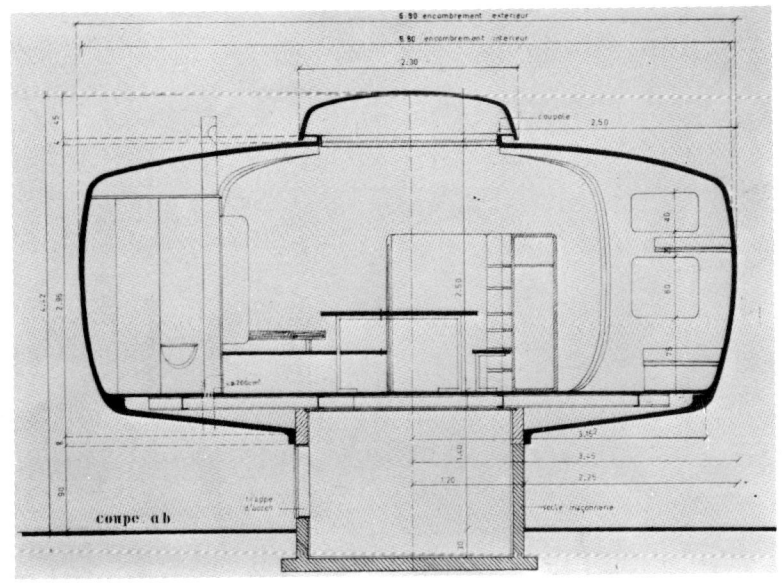
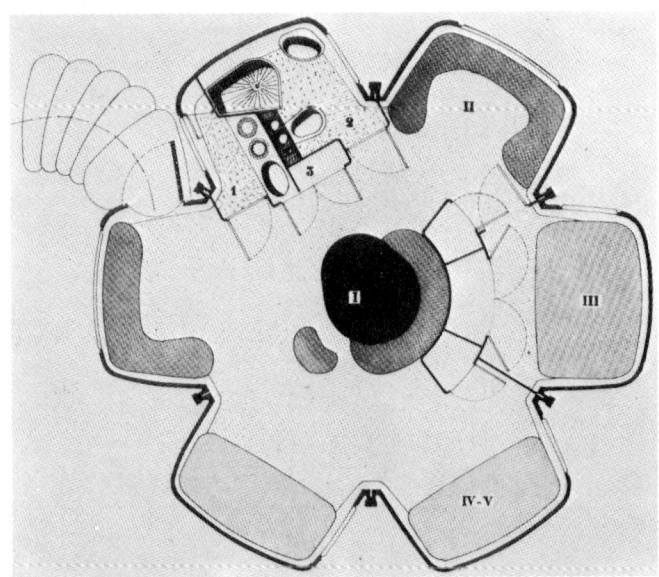
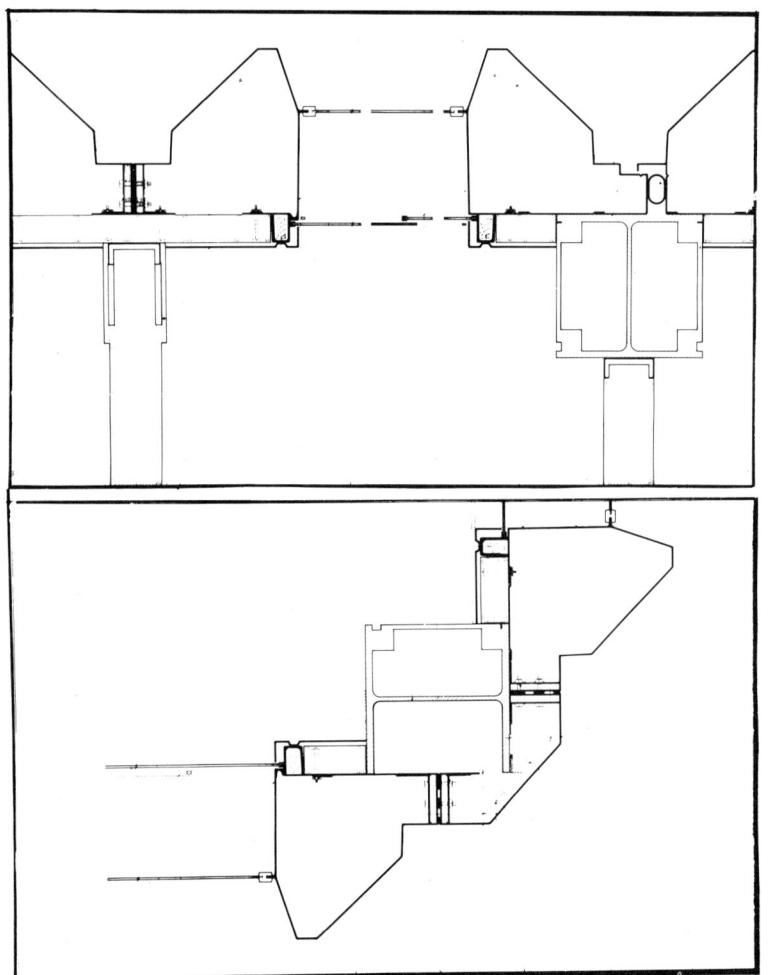

174, 175 Terminal 3 building, London (Heathrow) Airport, by Pascall and Watson. Left, plan through window, and through corner junction. Moulded g.r.p. shells, strawboard back-up panel, cavity filled with glass wool quilt. Removable inner face panel of g.r.p.; right, exterior.

172, 173, 176 'La bulle six coques' by Jean Manéval. G.r.p./polyurethane foam sandwich shells on a concrete base. Successfully launched and sold under license (like the Futuro house), in several countries. Facing, above, far left: section and right: plan; this page: exterior.

corner and a section of sliding wall to give a sudden impact view from the living garden. And the grassy ramparts would be turned around themselves to enclose an area of land outside, and to form a circuitous entrance.

It is very difficult for anyone to try to stand apart from the housing of our environment and to imagine what housing should be. Reyner Banham gets somewhere near a definition when he attacks the preoccupation with enclosure at the expense of services and equipment. 'The hearth makes the home' he says—'four walls make a prison.' And again '... holes in the wall do not ventilate in a flat calm when the need for ventilation is most urgent. Nor do windows admit light when you really need it—after dark.' And in conclusion '... a habitable building works by combining structure and powered equipment—be the structure inflated polythene and the equipment a multi-service standard-of-living pack (*A home is not a house*) (249, 250).

He gets near to it, but then I feel overstates his case by claiming that the service pack is more permanent than the enclosure it serves. Functioning equipment out-dates more and more rapidly—who wants a ten-year-old cooker or a five-year-old stereo outfit? And yet the enclosure, if it permits a degree of flexibility and perhaps mobility, could at least equal and possibly exceed this life-span.

Nevertheless it is impossible to overstress the need for more sophisticated functioning for housing. The majority of British houses are still not properly heated—and yet their owners would not dream of buying an unheated car. I would like to be able to create an atmosphere—a mood—by varying lighting, colours, sound, music, views, smells, feeling. Why do we not build such facilities into housing? Perhaps because we in building are frightened of technology—we think that mechanical things are expensive and go wrong.

And we are wrong on both counts. Compare a refrigerator with a joiner-made kitchen worktop unit with a drawer and a cupboard beneath. The unit will cost more than the refrigerator, which has automatic lighting and

component construction

177 G.r.p. cladding units, store in Bedford, by E. H. C. Inskip. Consultants Polyplan Ltd. Sixty-four units each 18 ft. × 4 ft. 6 ins. and weighing 550 lbs.

component
132 /construction

defrosting, magnetic door, tremendous insulation, a complex moulded lining, variable temperature control of individual compartments and goes stop-start-stop all its working life and is guaranteed for five years.

This is what we should be doing with housing. Yet we concentrate on trying to achieve the same old result at a cheaper rate and somehow fail in this even, spending £7 ($16·50) per sq yd on external walling when plastics sandwich panels are available to do the same job with many times the insulation, at a tenth of the cost.

Even projects for plastics housing, such as those illustrated, fail to offer any real advance. Some could give mobility, some could float on water or sit on land, but each is still the same basic cave with a face-lift.

So Banham is right, and we should design the servicing first and then enclose it—for real, or even with an air curtain as he suggests. David Greene is nearest to the core of the proposition with his Living Pod (see 225, 226). The servicing of this unit includes hydraulic jacks for on water or sloping site, power-operated sliding entrance, two wash capsules with automatic body-cleaning equipment, rotating silos for disposable and non-disposable clothing, vertical body hoist, climate machinery (with connections to sleeping mats and warm section of inflating floor), mobile food dispenser with self-cook modifications, mobile teaching media and teach and work machine. The actual enclosure is then of very secondary importance.

Perhaps the realization of this advance is simply a marketing exercise with parallels in the development of the hypermarket. (One-stop shopping—sell everything under one roof and you can take over the trade of the thousand-and-one specialized shops of the city centre.)

Most houses contain a considerable amount of sophisticated tackle—several types of heat (mobile fans, odd electric fires, hair dryers and electric blankets); also food mixers, a refrigerator and deep freeze, electric clocks, toasters, radios, record players, stereo, television, tape recorders, telephones, vacuum cleaners, power tools and power gardening equipment, additional lighting units, shavers, cookers, washing and drying machines for clothes and utensils—quite an impressive list when you think about it. And all bought separately and carried back into the cave. To quote Banham again: 'Certainly we would survive in weatherproof shells without services, but it would be only surviving'.

So housing contains a tremendous range of servicing equipment—which the owner has to add for himself, because the architect somehow assumes that this is not a necessary part of the house.

The servicing equipment only scratches the surface, and we should add furniture—beds, wardrobes, dressing tables, chests, tables, chairs of all kinds, couches, benches, stools, divans, desks—and the in-betweens such as pianos. All furniture is actually brought into the house by the owner—except for bathroom equipment and a few bare pieces in the kitchen. Why do we draw the line in this arbitrary way—why not design fully fitted houses into which one can step and simply live, complete, in much the same way as one can sit in a normal fully-fitted car and drive away?

178, 179 Large g.r.p. façade panels by João Honorio, Rio de Janeiro. Twenty-five four-storey buildings have been faced with these panels, at Novo Iraja. There are six units to each façade. Below: the units (9 ft. × 32 ft.) in transit.

What scope all this could have as a marketing exercise—how cheap built-in furniture and equipment could be, if all these expensive retailers and their showrooms (which are a necessary service for the loose equipment currently in use), could be eliminated. And if we could have built-in, permanent finishes for the interior—there are so many more interesting ways of developing the personality than by changing the wallpaper or buying a new carpet.

Undoubtedly the sum total of these servicings and fittings is the core of housing, and the actual enclosure comes a very poor third, after the external environmental and community design. Perhaps this is one reason for the real lack of progress in housing—we concentrate on the enclosure, and largely ignore these far more important factors.

PANEL CONSTRUCTION

As many plastics housing projects lack any real conceptual advance, few of them get built, because the mere sculpting of the enclosure into different shapes is insufficient to justify the cost of production runs. However, the moulding of simple panels for cladding framed buildings is making much more progress, following the impetus given by the Indulex panels used on several Greater London Council high-rise towers. This is the 'Spatial Enclosures' end of component construction however—a very limited concept usually restricted to turning the weather, resisting the elements, providing insulation, and a window. Few, if any, go as far as the Schein panel of 1956 which incorporated furniture and heating. Therefore low capital cost in tooling up, and small runs are a definite possibility.

Consequently simple cladding panels are second only in importance to spatial enclosures in the current development of plastics structures, and in actual tonnage of material used, come way out first.

It is possible to note a movement first of all away from the profiled and sculptural panels of some of the earlier projects, such as the sectional house by Cesare Pea, to a flat, plain and absolutely smooth panel which was indistinguishable from half a dozen other materials, and more recently a swing back again towards, and more recently, beyond, the earlier proposals.

The Indulex panels were the first real advance—lightly sculptured and hoisted into place in preassembled units three storeys high, and consisting of six panels.

Since the above application, and encouraged by its acceptance under building and fire regulations, large numbers of rather more flamboyant panels have been produced and used, and there would seem to be a distinct possibility at long last of the simple cladding panel coming to rival pipe production as the major outlet for plastics in building.

In addition to cladding panels, a range of simple systems of construction has been developed in which a limited number of panels can be assembled together in a variety of ways to give a variable size of structure. Notable amongst these might be the Relay Room system for British Railways referred to earlier, the Clamp system by James Dartforth, and the elegant bus shelter project by students of the Hochschule für Gestaltung, Ulm, Germany.

180 New faculty building at Lyon-Bron by M. Detland, with Prouvé-Petroff, using 'Matra 2' cladding panels. Self-extinguishing g.r.p. skins, expanded phenolic core.

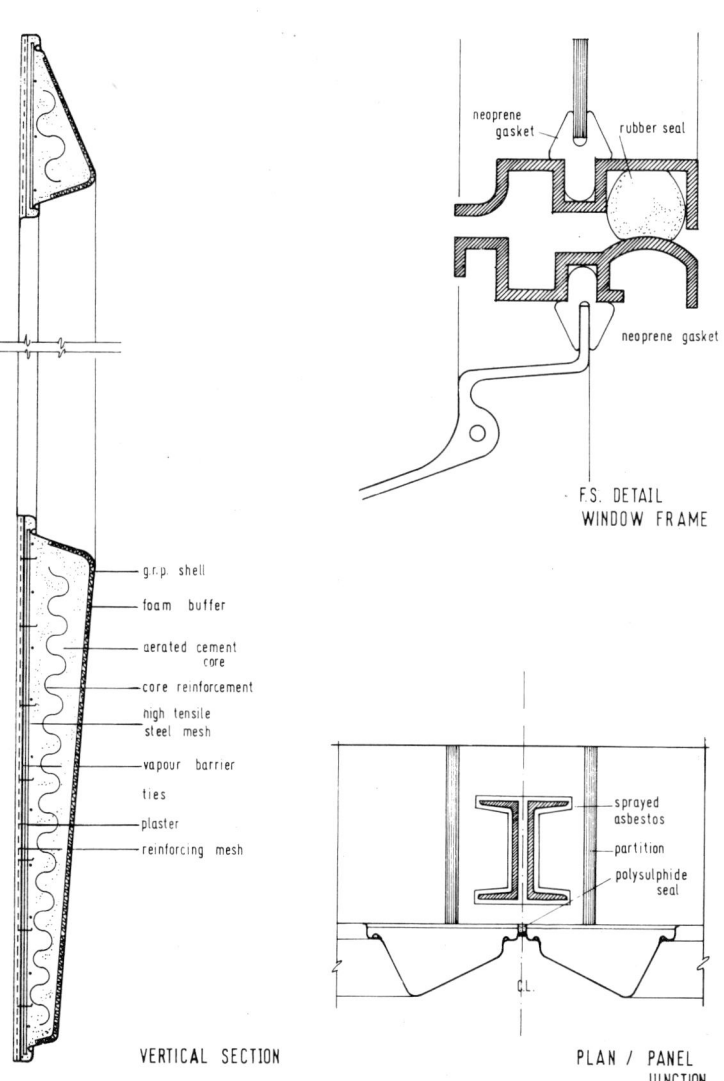

181, 182 SFI cladding panels by the Department of Architecture, Greater London Council. Manufactured by Indulex Engineering Co. Ltd. G.r.p. shells with an aerated concrete core. Left, constructional details; right, six panels are assembled in a light steel frame prior to erection.

183–85 'Maisons par éléments' by A. Christen. G.r.p. skins with foam core. Left, external corner detail, showing housings for fixing bolts; centre, interior detail; right, general view, showing window and ventilators.

186 Shell service station by the Compagnie de l'Esthétique Industrielle, Paris. G.r.p. kiosks, corner detail and general view.

187, 188 Left: B.P. service station at Baldock. Arthur Quarmby with Polyplan Ltd. Steel goalpost carries double-cantilever g.r.p. roof. G.r.p./polyurethane foam profiled wall panels, profiled acrylic windows, preformed sanitary core. Right, minimum, unfolding container service station project for B.P.

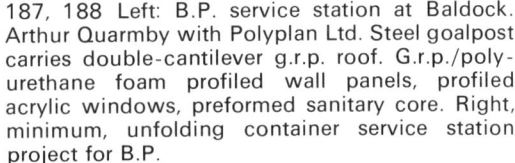

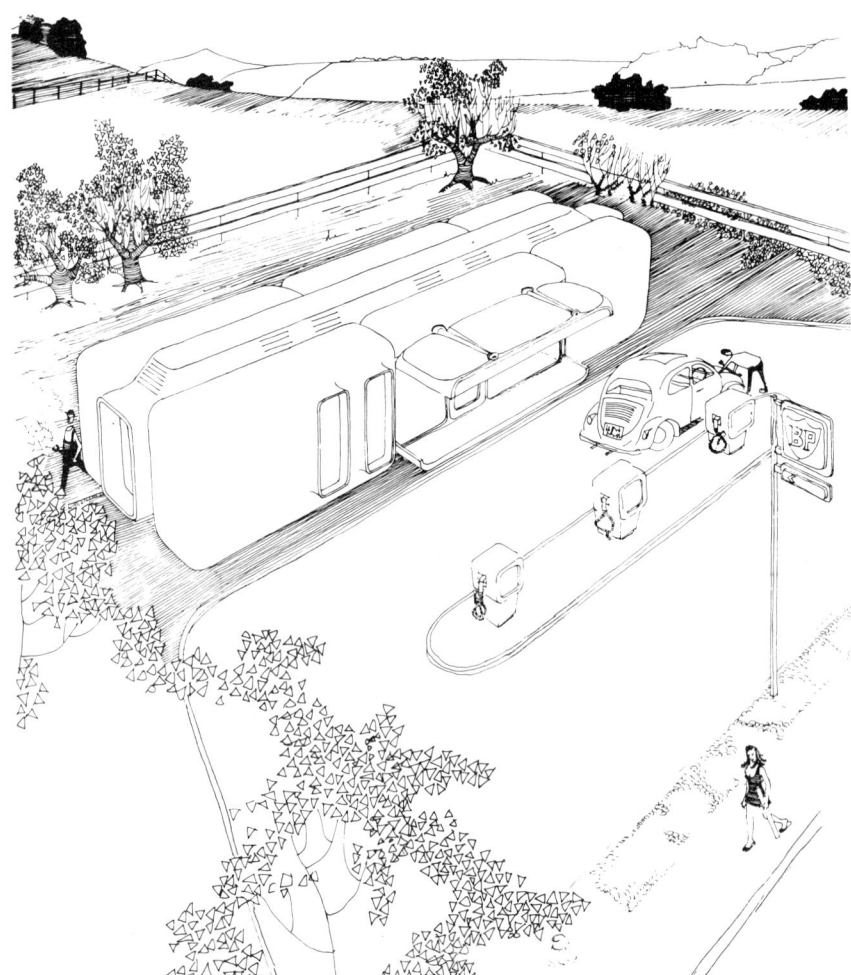

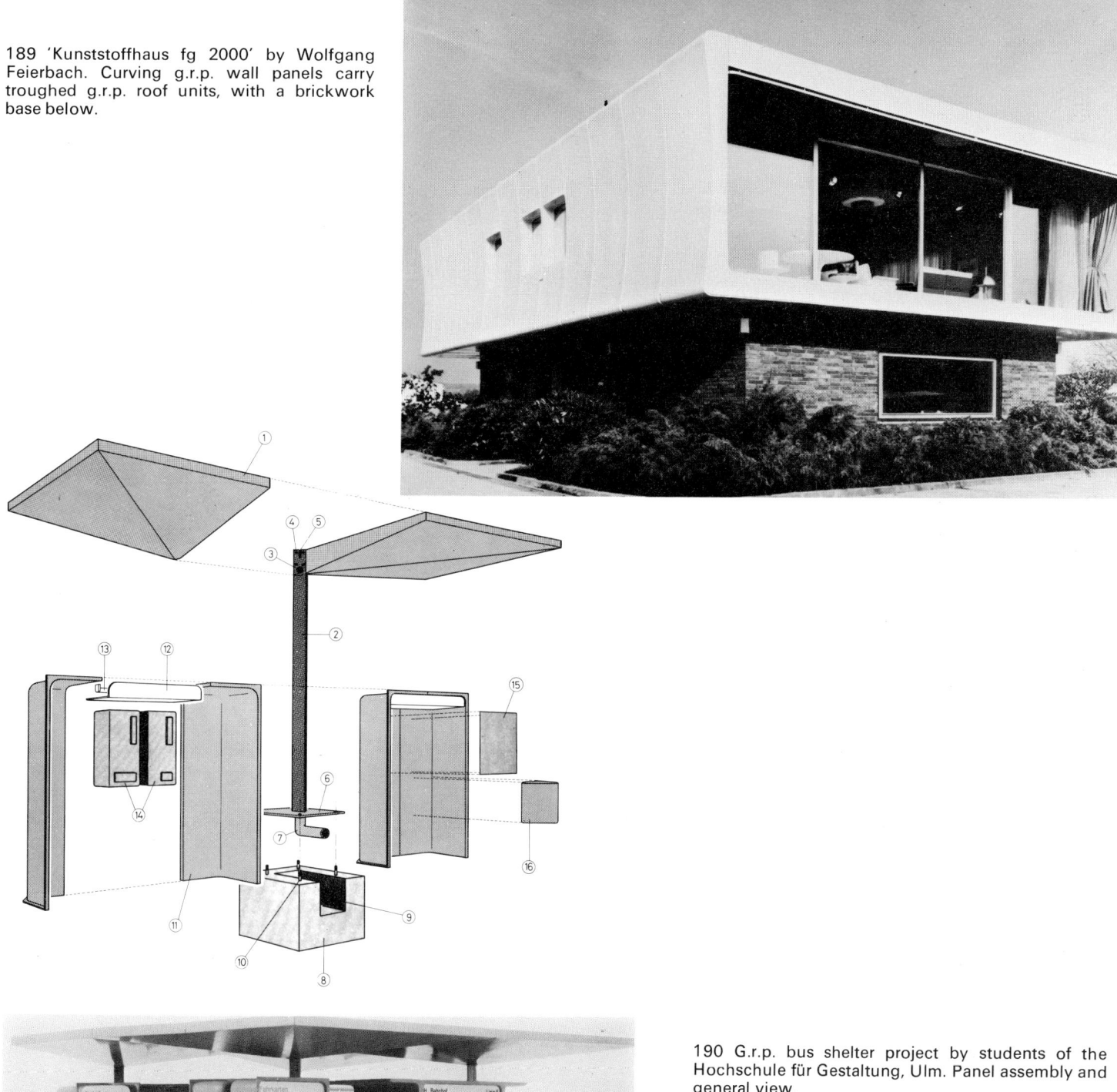

189 'Kunststoffhaus fg 2000' by Wolfgang Feierbach. Curving g.r.p. wall panels carry troughed g.r.p. roof units, with a brickwork base below.

190 G.r.p. bus shelter project by students of the Hochschule für Gestaltung, Ulm. Panel assembly and general view.

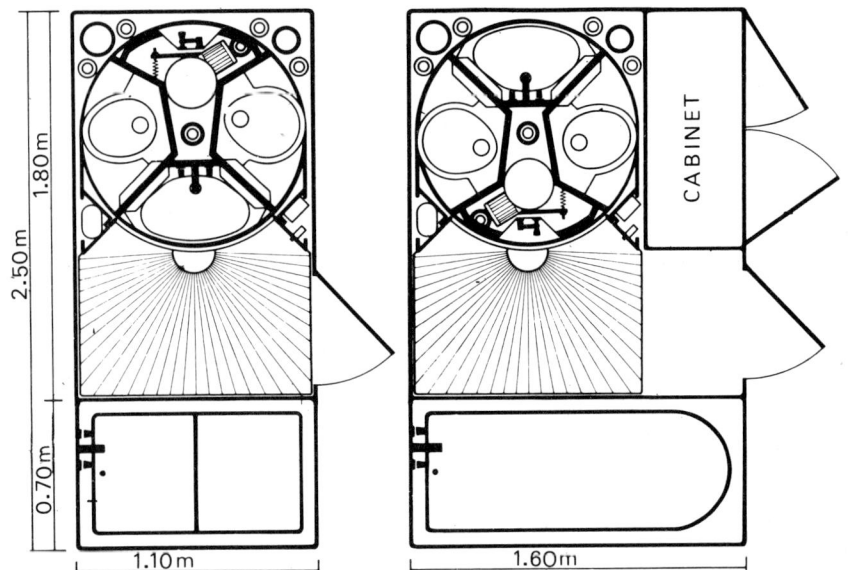

192, 193 (Facing page) packaged bathroom by Arthur Quarmby. Packs into box 2' 6"×2' 6"× 1' 10". Contains water heater and spring-loaded flush from mains water feed. Left: units and container; right, the units assembled in one of the several permutations.

191 Revolving bathroom by R. Bucher. (a) with hip bath; (b) with full-sized bath. The unit contains four sections—w.c., bidet, washbasin and shower, and may be turned by hand or by motor.

One project in this vein which dates back to around 1962 is the *Maison par Elements* scheme by the Swiss architect, A. Christen. Unfortunately but little known, this project is an object lesson to all designers in plastics in its simplicity and complete elegance. Little is attempted, but what is done is done superbly. The slim and crisp detailing of the window, the soft, delicate moulding of the panels and the articulation of the fixing points all work together to produce what may not be the most important or dramatic, but which is to me the most elegant little structure yet built in plastics.

BATHROOM UNITS AND FUNCTIONING CORES

Although little work has been carried out on reconceiving the servicing of housing, bathroom units and heart units (containing bathroom, kitchen and heating) have received a great deal of attention in recent years.

Starting in Scandinavia, the heart unit idea made rapid and extensive progress without three principles being fully grasped: (1) a heart unit no matter how flexible must inevitably impose some restrictions on the structure or planning of the dwelling in which it is to be contained; (2) the principle of putting the units of a bathroom and the kitchen into a box which is then put inside another box may often be illogical; and (3) unless the unit offers some advantage to the customer in performance or appearance, it can only be sold on cost terms—it must be cheaper than the traditional, site-constructed element.

For these reasons the majority of heart units developed during the past ten years have failed to survive—too rigid, too expensive, and with no functional innovation.

There are exceptions in the few cases where a reasonably-sized production run could be guaranteed—notably the Farrell/Grimshaw spiral tower, and the Moeller acrylic bathroom which was used in the competitors' accommodation for the 1972 Olympic games at Munich.

This latter unit is the first to use a plastics W.C. in full production, and fabricated in acrylic. Prototypes have been constructed before in g.r.p. and

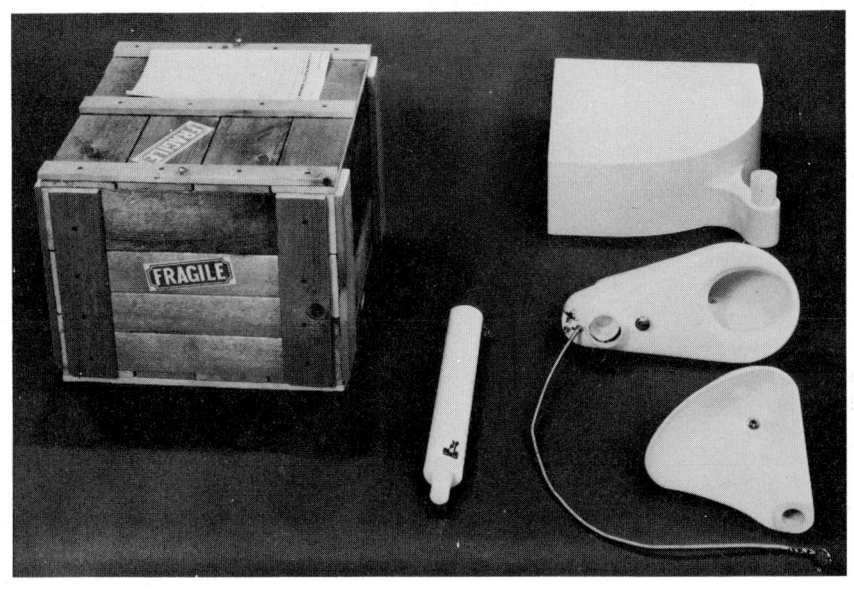
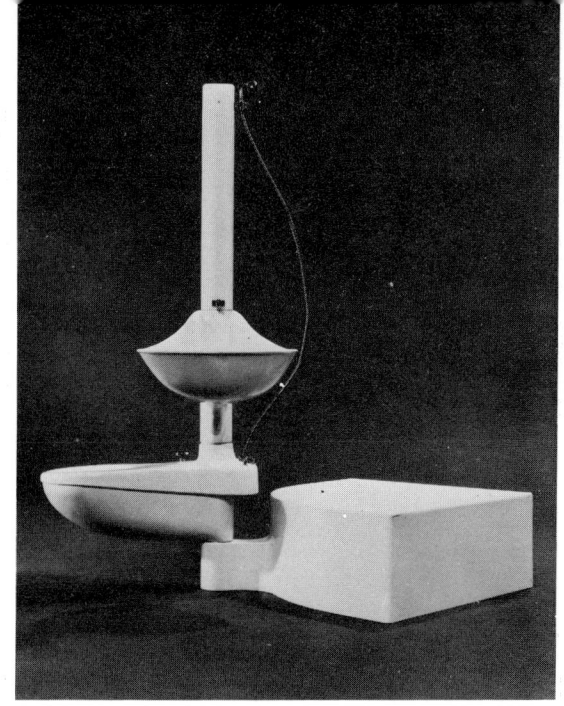

194 G.r.p. bathing cabinet by Mario Scheichenbauer. Double unit, in four sections. P.v.c. sealant strip down end joints.

195 Moeller Sanitar bathroom unit by H. G. Müller Kunststoffwer, for the Munich Olympic village. Acrylic shells, with external stiffening coating of g.r.p.

196, 197 'Bloc sanitaire monobloc' by Mario Scheichenbauer. G.r.p. construction, containing built-in water heater, w.c., washbasin and shower. The longer unit consists of w.c., washbasin and hip bath.

198 Unita bathroom block by Alberto Rosselli, for Soc. Montecatini.

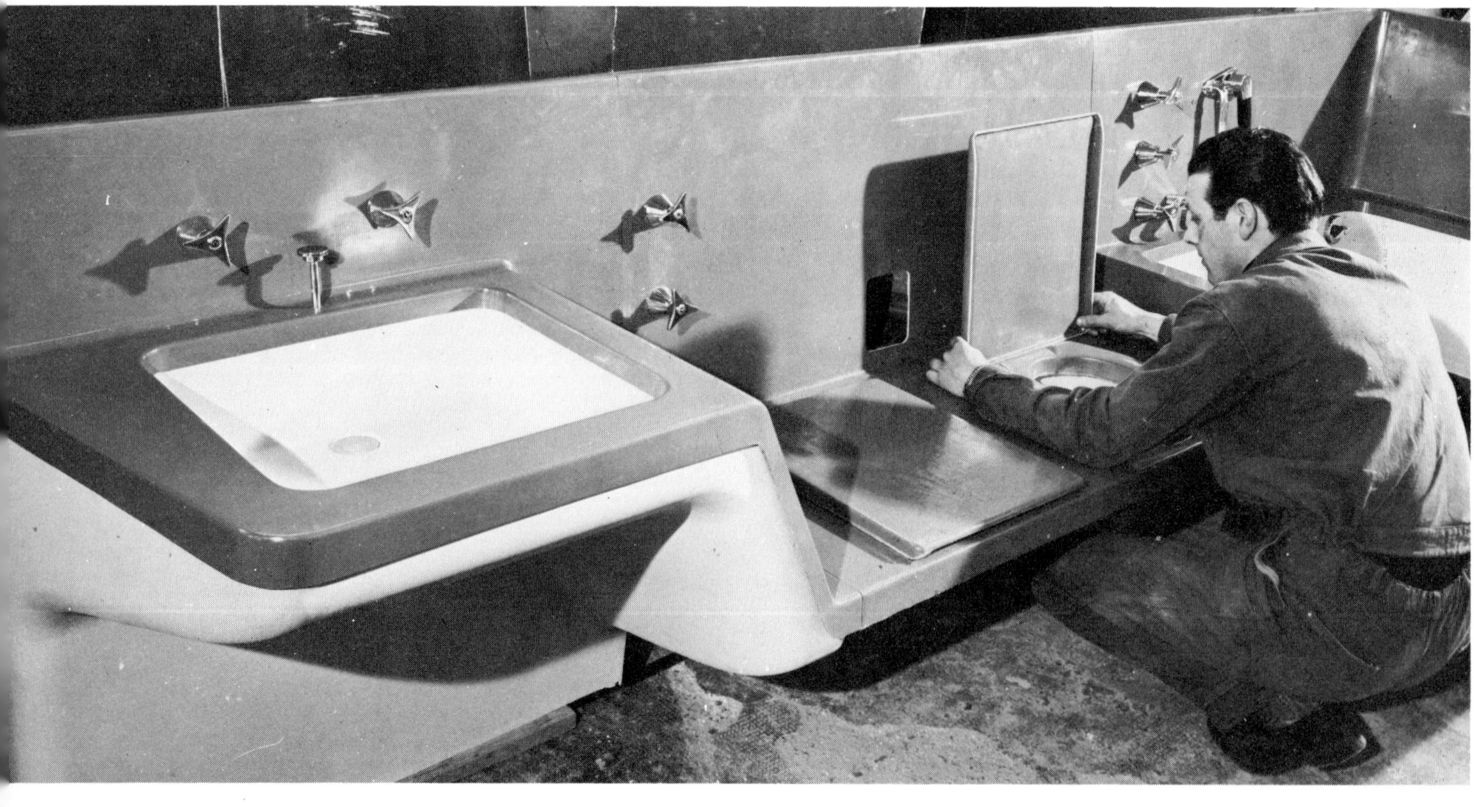

in p.v.c. (in Holland and Italy respectively), but the convoluted form of the normal W.C. trap has until now discouraged manufacturers from putting them into production.

As architects of plastics housing projects have failed to reconsider the present and potential function of the house, so designers of kitchen and especially bathroom units have failed to produce any real innovation with their projects—which too often consist of the same old units in a box with rounded corners.

Even the Moeller bathroom still has a built-in recess for the roll of toilet paper, the whole concept of which is so incredibly crude and unhygienic—hardly better than the monastic wisp of hay or the goose head of the later Middle Ages. The amazing thing is that we have put up with it for so long, and public outcry has not demanded something better. A combined W.C. and bidet has been developed in Switzerland, a sophisticated and fully automatic unit. Why do we not use it?

Moreover the whole basic principle of water-borne sewage is becoming ridiculously extravagant in an age of exploding demand on our water resources. It is calculated that each person flushes 4,000 gallons of water down the W.C. each year, in a ratio of 60 parts of water to 1 part of excrement.

In an attempt to tackle this problem, a British architect has developed and fitted in her house a compact recycling system which purifies and puts back into the system waste water from all domestic fittings including the W.C., and only needs topping up with collected rainwater. Many similar experiments are being carried out around the world. Can we now doubt that eventually the dwelling will be as self-contained as the transistor radio, and that the umbilical cords which tie buildings to the ground—water, gas, electricity, drainage, will one day be cut?

Of course, the real technical innovation in bathroom design would come as a result of redesigning the functioning of the human body—perhaps a perfectly-balanced diet so that all we produced were small, hygienic pellets like the hamster, or we might even apply the shrink-wrapping technique now used for food, at a later stage in the process?

Lacking such possibilities at the moment we must perhaps concentrate on accepting the bathroom into the house—and in some countries the W.C. is still only half way in—and redesigning it as a place not only of contemplation but of relaxation and recreation. Perhaps we might eliminate some of the clinical Spartan feeling for a start.

Take the bath—smooth, hard, cold and shiny because until recently only smooth, hard, cold and shiny materials could do the job. We now have flexible foams and decorative, waterproof skins which allow the bath to be built like a couch—warm soft and inviting, and available for relaxation and enjoyment rather than simply for getting clean.

Water is fun to play in—but is it essential for cleaning purposes? Should we make use of Buckminster Fuller's atomiser gun and could we go one further and consider other techniques such as ultrasonics? Could one clean teeth by ultrasonics? And hair?

199 Bathroom tower for students' hostel, by the Farrell/Grimshaw Partnership. Steel structure slung from mast, containing thirty inset g.r.p. bathroom pods around the spiral.

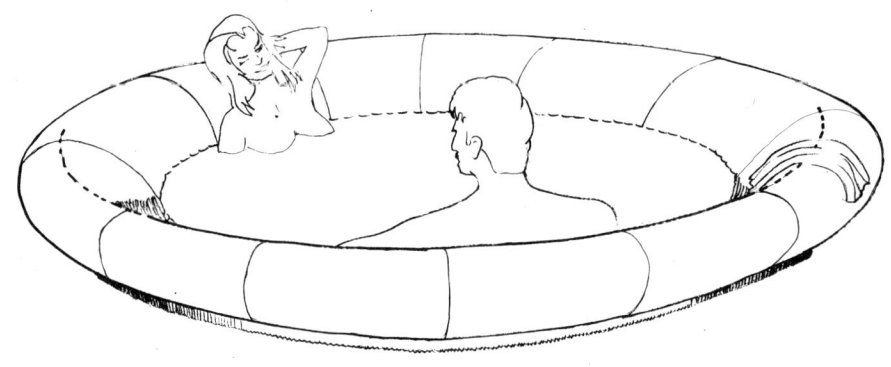

200, 201 Soft bath design, Arthur Quarmby. Leather-look p.v.c. on 1" flexible foam on segmental rigid foam or g.r.p. shell former.

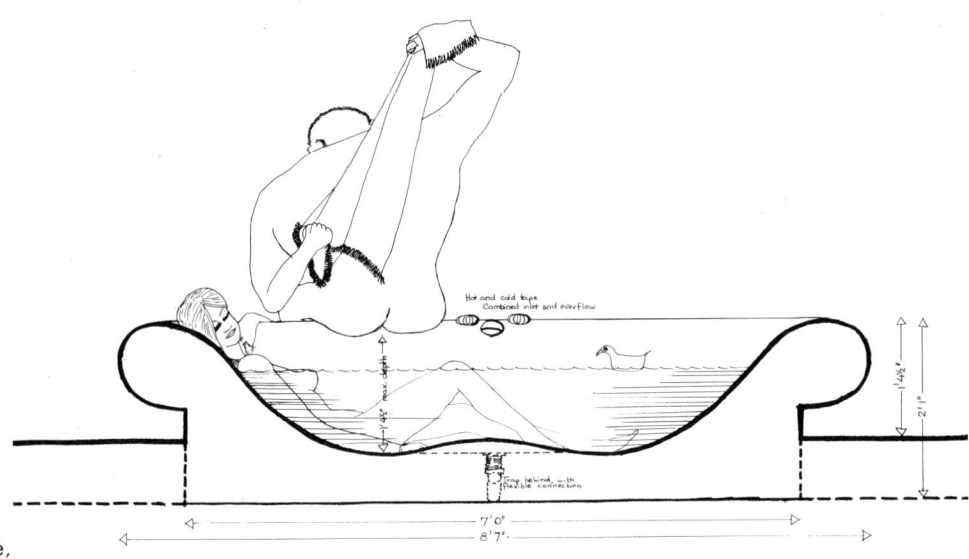

202 'Les Jours Mailleurs' house, Jean Prouvé, during assembly. Service core carrying spine beam. The house was erected in 24 hours on a base prepared in three days.

We need to use more imagination as far as the design of living conditions as a whole are concerned, and this applies to the bathroom even more than elsewhere. It could and should be both functionally efficient and a pleasure to use, and ought to be provided as a matter of course with every unit of sleeping accommodation.

This chapter on component construction should have been full of sophisticated functioning elements making complete use of the speed and complexities possible with plastics materials and techniques, and illustrating countless innovations in living techniques which were contributing significantly to the way of life of the peoples of the world.

Unfortunately it is not, for work to date has accepted too much of the traditional way of life and of the elements of housing. We condemn the plastics industry for its tendency to substitute plastics for traditional materials—but is this not what we are doing ourselves, in a very slightly different way?

CHAPTER 8 sculptural applications

Plastics materials were seized upon by architects as a means of achieving the type of curved, bulbous forms which were impracticable with traditional materials. Schein pronounced that 'egg shapes are best', and this was a simple way of explaining the fact that plastics materials were expensive and should be used in the most economical way, and that materials with a tendency to creep must avoid bending stresses.

This is probably the best sculptural idea which has been produced so far, and it came at a time of reaction against the right angle and the post and lintel, a reaction which is still developing. The extreme bulbosity of some of the earlier projects and structures has been modified in recent years, and a delight in the crispness of detail and accuracy of production is beginning to emerge.

However plastics materials in themselves have other sculptural characteristics which have yet to be fully exploited, and this applies particularly to the two factors of colour and texture.

It is probably fair to say that most architects are unhappy when faced with the necessity of using colour. Nurtured on the natural (or semi-natural) materials of stone, brick, timber and concrete, we are at our best when using these in conjunction with black and white, with only the occasional splash of synthetic colour for punctuation.

Perhaps for many of us this has been the easy way out. As students we used masses of colour in earlier years with little success, and finally made the discovery that a scheme based upon the careful use of natural materials cannot go wrong. And this is not just from a colour point of view—it is rather that many natural materials have a special aura of their own containing the magical ingredients of warmth, familiarity, childhood and comfort.

However this subconscious approval can be fooled—melamine-faced plastics panels can have a colour photograph of timber laminated into them in such a way that they become indistinguishable from real timber with a polyurethane lacquer. P.v.c. wallpaper can simulate hessian—plastic panels can effectively imitate genuine stonework.

203 Typical decorative, wood-effect panel in self-skinning polyurethane on flexible neoprene mould.

These factors have tended to inhibit the exploitation of the colour and texture potential of plastics. Why work on this when natural materials can be simulated so effectively, and when the subliminal aura of these materials can be tapped as an added bonus? And we are not at the end of this simulation yet—not by a long way. Recent developments in high-impact polystyrene, water-filled polyester and self-skinning polyurethane have provided the means of reproducing carved timber panels or furniture, Grecian porticos or adzed beams at an incredibly low cost, and one would hesitate to predict an end to this movement.

Not that I am entirely against it—synthetic it may be, and the purist may shudder when on closer examination he finds that he has been taken in by a fake—but for the majority of people it works. It produces that magical aura which we have, to our cost, ignored in architecture. We have designed a cool, elegant and chilling environment since the early days of the modern movement and, as so often happens, have blinded ourselves to something which non-architects always knew, the fact that it is often emotionally unsatisfying.

In consequence we now have stick-on Georgian trimmings decorating the fronts of the same old terrace or semi-detached houses, also the current enthusiasm for the delightful fake village of Portmeirion, and a rash of new traditional villages around the coastline of the Mediterranean and in the Canaries.

These all work, because they tap the magic of traditional materials and traditional techniques, and are in marvellous contrast to the common sterility of modern housing and town centre developments.

They do something else too: all of them make use of decoration. We have had fifty undecorated years, since the end of the Art Nouveau movement, and have forgotten the subject so completely that one now almost hesitates to claim that decoration is a completely viable element of architecture, and one which must inevitably return.

What better time for a return than now, and what better reason than the potential of plastics?

The death of decoration followed the demise of the craftsman in building. Traditional decoration is so labour-intensive that its cost is quite prohibitive. In contrast a plastics element or component planned for bulk production can be enriched—and there is an evocative word—at a cost which is utterly negligible. Engrave the mould and it is done, for a thousand off or a hundred thousand off.

The question is, are we inevitably tied to the effect of traditional materials, techniques and decorations, or can we create the aura which they possess afresh, in a novel way which is not dependent upon the subconscious or conscious memory? Is the magic based on wood and stone, egg-and-dart and Grecian fret, or is it rather certain colours and textures, certain patterns of light and shade, which could be analysed and used to create the same or even better results?

Ironically plastics are perhaps more responsible than anything else for the current flight into the cosiness of tradition. Plastics materials are entirely

204–206 The work of William Mitchell, in plastics and in concrete formed on plastics moulds, demonstrating the textural potential which is available for use on structural components.

207 'Ensculptic III' spray polyurethane house by W. E. Wedin. Nylon cables slung from a central mast carry a tensioned fabric skin. 3" sprayed polyurethane foam with a finishing coat of $\frac{1}{4}$" sprayed g.r.p.

cold, hard, smooth and shiny to most people simply because designers have used them in this way, and have totally failed to exploit their more desirable characteristics of warmth, texture and richness.

Totally failed—and yet there are exceptions, there are designers and sculptors who have seen into the heart of plastics, and have shown the way in which we might travel.

Chief among these is William Mitchell, who specializes in large and highly decorative murals, cladding panels and ceilings. He at least is entirely aware of the over-clinical effect and sterility of much current design, and contends that plastics could be used to bring back the sheer enthusiasm of some of the most successful late Victorian and Edwardian architecture.

His work, both in concrete and in plastics, is as rich as the Maya Toltec *Palace of the Governor* at Uxmal—and some of it merits comparison with the Aztec *Stone of the Sun*—and yet it is rarely derivative in form or element. Perhaps one might venture two criticisms—that too often he limits his sculpting to the decoration of a large flat panel, rather than using the form of the panel to add its own contribution to the whole, and that he frequently feels the need to evoke the warmth of the past by using a simulated bronze or gold finish, rather than by evolving an equal richness afresh. However, his work will, I feel sure, be seen in years to come as having had a profound influence not only upon the course of plastics in building, but also on that of architecture generally.

One quite different approach to this matter was demonstrated in an electricity substation at Fresnes in France as early as 1960. This small structure is composed of a number of g.r.p. panels laid up on rubber moulds which were deliberately deformed prior to lamination to give an erratic, beaten metal effect to the final components.

The structure was designed by Genier, Kowalski and Muel, who also developed a large number of cladding panels based on the same technique.

146/ sculptural applications

208 Monumental sculptured wall at Viry-Chatillon, by P. Kowalski. Reinforced concrete cast on deformed plastic moulds, leading to similar treatment of g.r.p. in the artist's later work.

209 'Sprayform' house 2, at Weston, Connecticut, by John M. Johansen. Construction planned for spring 1959 but never carried out.

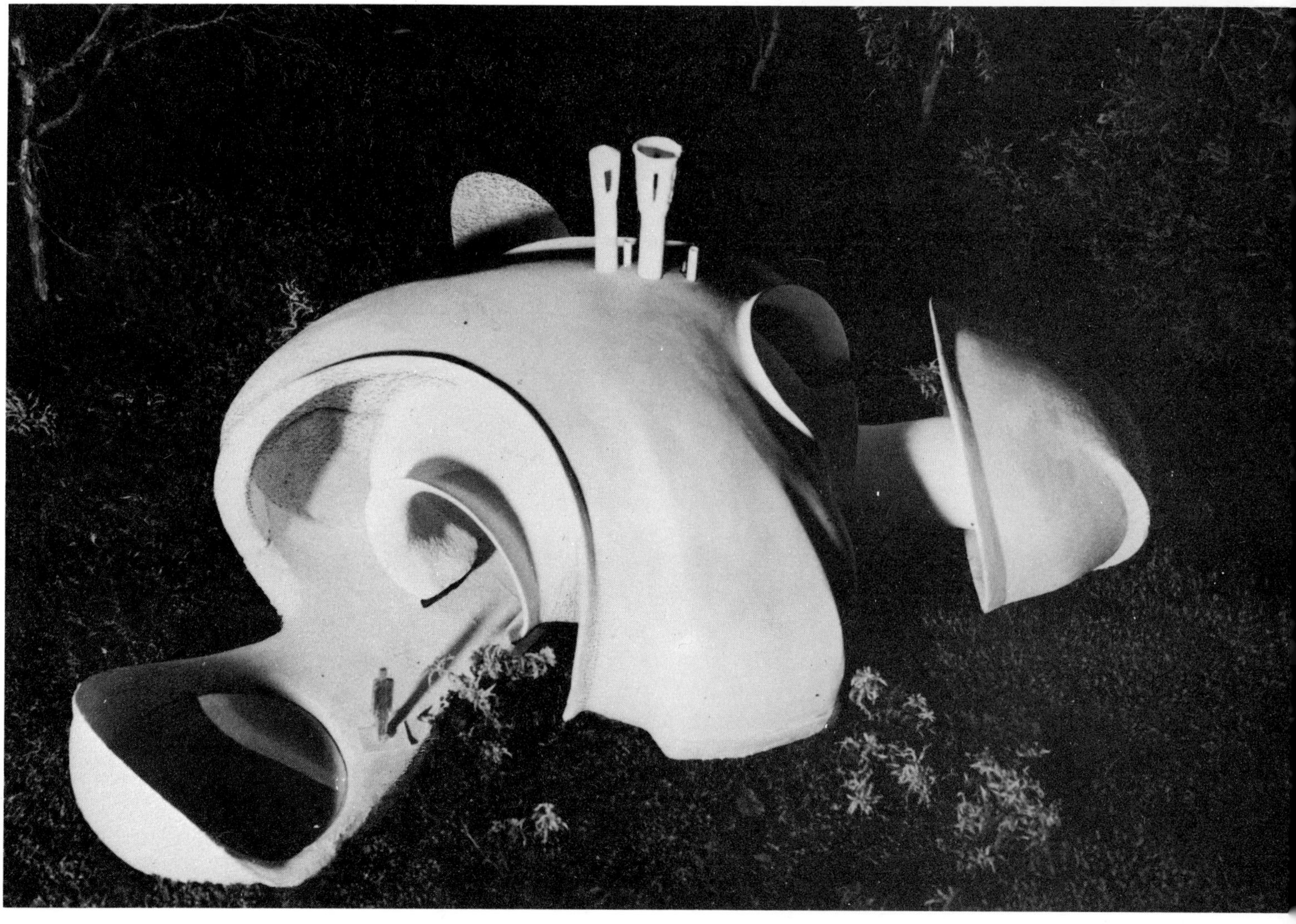

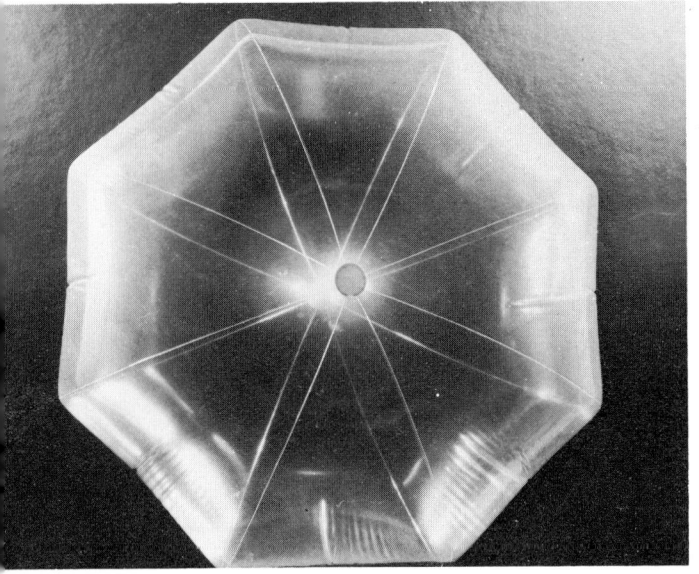

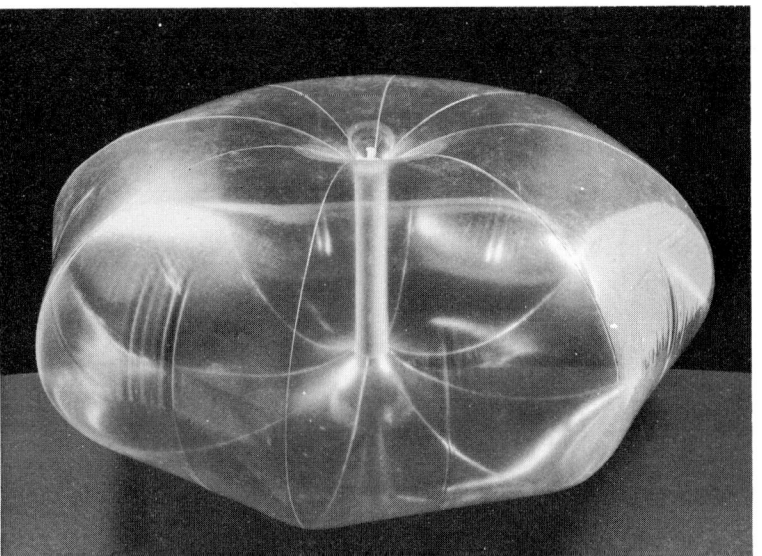

210 First pneumatic pouffe. Transparent, high-frequency welded p.v.c. with pigmented central tension tube in the same material. Arthur Quarmby.

211 Plaster model of housing components (*cellules polyvalentes*) by Chanéac.

However, none of these has as yet had any great influence upon other architects—largely on account of the long-standing fear of decoration which is normally defended as a desire to express the form of the structure with the utmost clarity, and without distractions.

John Johannsen is probably still the most potent visual influence on the free form of a large number of plastics structures and projects. The impact of his U.S. Pavilion at Zagreb, his project for a Lutheran church at Norwich, Connecticut and above all his house project for Weston, Connecticut—all spray concrete and all designed in the mid fifties—can still be felt in the work of Chanéac, Pascal and Claude Hausermann, Manéval and many others.

Almost all designers of plastics structures have experienced the delight of sculpting a structure in two or three dimensions—in manipulating double-curvature forms and sweeping shells over, around and through each other. Of attempting to think clearly about the form of a structure and whether the right angle has any special validity in the design of living space.

The conclusion one reaches is normally no—people are not rectangular in plan or elevation, neither beds, baths nor chairs need to be rectangular—we use round and not square plates and pans, and so cookers and cupboards can be curved.

One is therefore encouraged to produce projects to illustrate this fact, to demonstrate that the right angle is not ideal either in plan or in structure—but in most cases such projects are considered to be too lacking in general appeal to be put into general production, and to sculpt them by hand on site is prohibitively expensive. Nevertheless some have been built, and others will be.

However one stumbling block lies in the path of a totally sculptural construction, and that is the force of gravity.

Gravity dictates that when moving about people stand upright—they walk about at right angles to the earth. This means not only that the inside wall of a curving shell may be beyond reach on account of the curve from

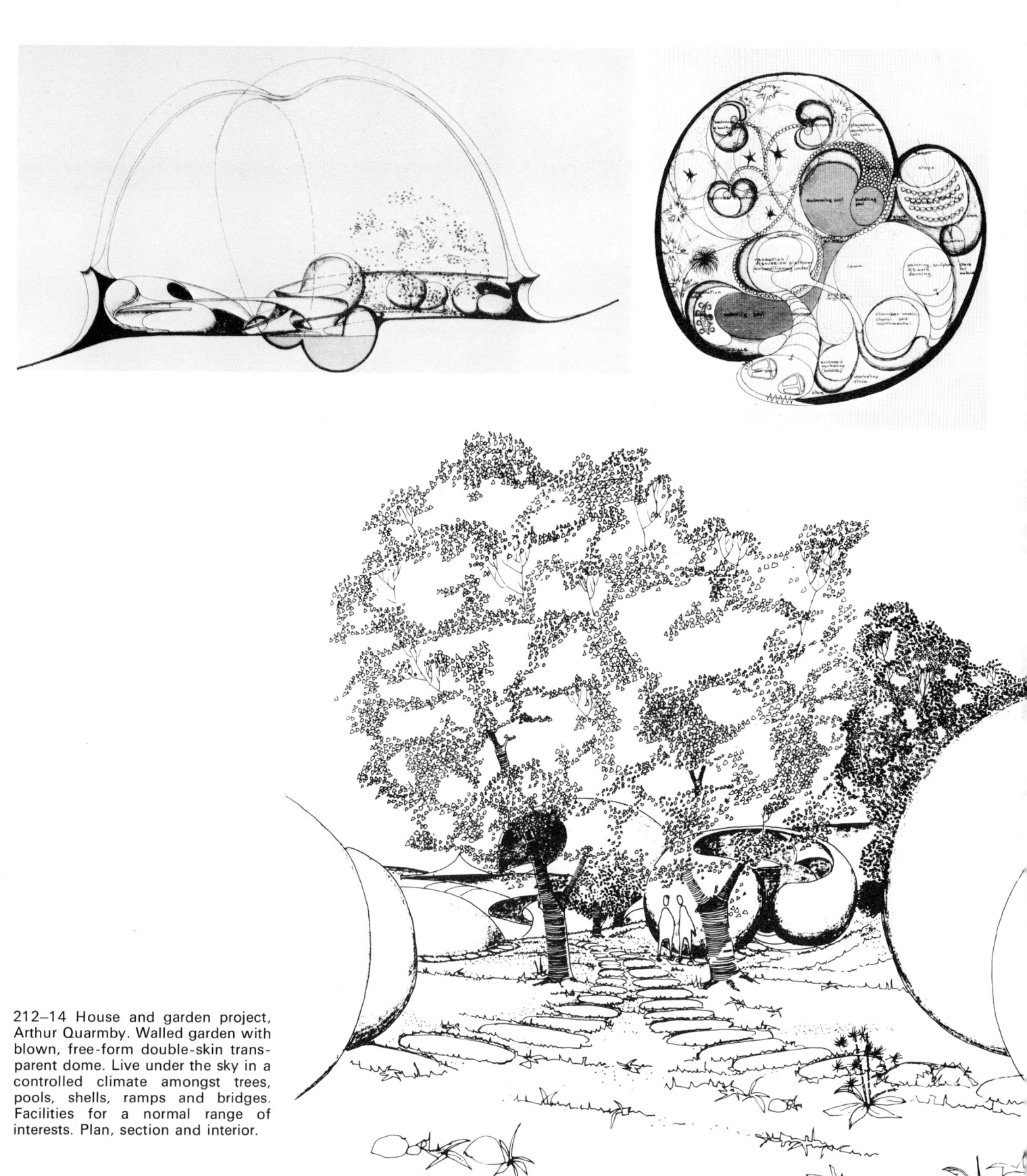

212–14 House and garden project, Arthur Quarmby. Walled garden with blown, free-form double-skin transparent dome. Live under the sky in a controlled climate amongst trees, pools, shells, ramps and bridges. Facilities for a normal range of interests. Plan, section and interior.

215–17 'Yellow Heart', by the Haus-Rücker-Co. of Vienna. Pneumatic structure for two on a metal supporting frame. Entrance lock and main space filled with transparent, pulsating p.v.c. bubbles. Inmates wear stereo headpieces giving out jumbled sounds, and changeable coloured glasses. Below, section and plan.

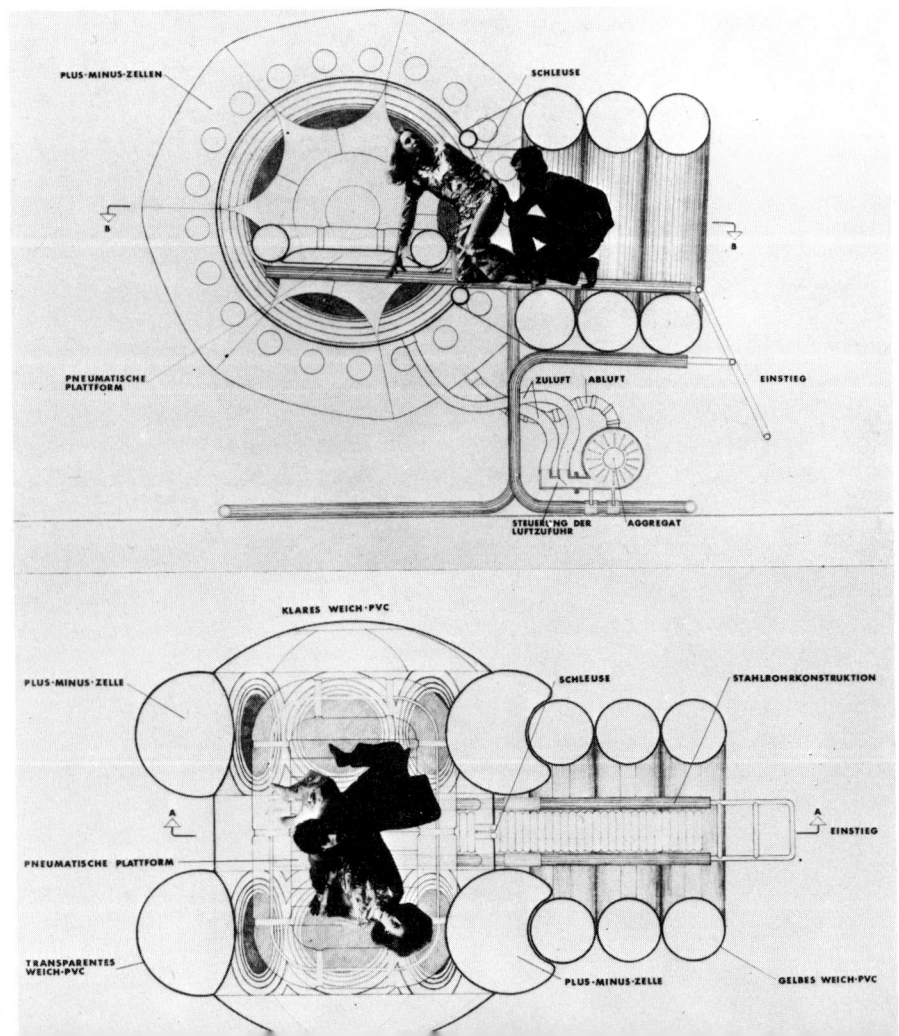

218, 219 Facing, furniture carpet by Gernot Nalbach. Each unit contains 16 cells which can be elevated or lowered by a pressure-and-vacuum cell, controlled from a switch box. Below, two units, one with cells retracted.

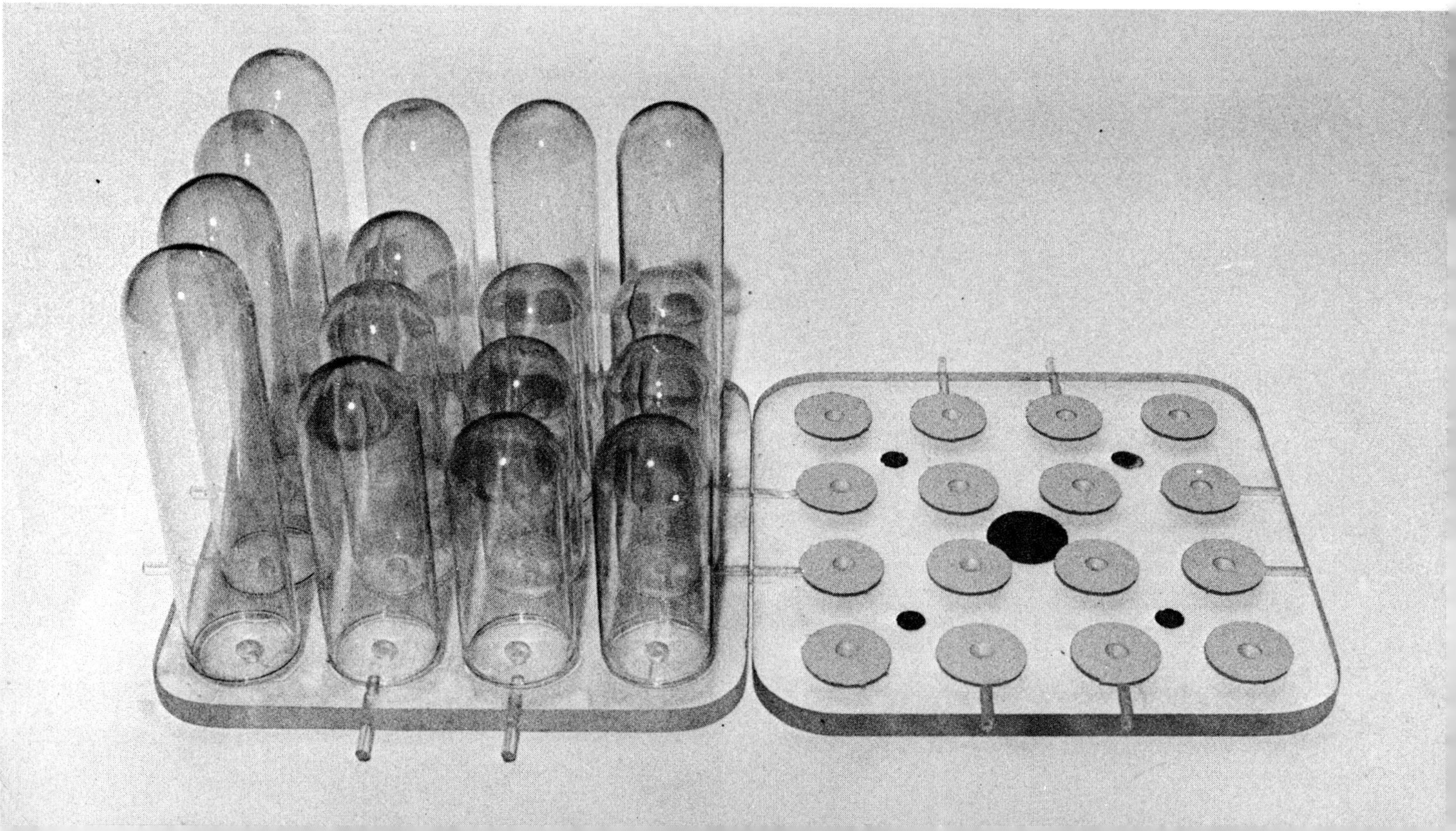

220 Utopian pneumatic town, 1966, model by Gernot Nalbach.

221 Roman leather airbed. Sixteenth-century woodcut based on Roman literary sources.

floor to wall (if one may use such terms in this concept), but also that a horizontal surface is needed for walking upon.

It is needed for walking upon, but just how essential is it? Do we inevitably stumble when encountering a slope or an otherwise flat floor, or is this simply the result of our upbringing? We stumble over the miscounted last step of a staircase, over an unexpected slope in a floor, over a paving stone projecting slightly above its fellows. And yet oddly enough we do not stumble over rough ground on a moor or amongst rocks.

Could it be simply that we are conditioned to expect flat walking surfaces in architecture, with changes in level only occurring by clearly-marked staircases or ramps? If so should we perhaps move away from this, and extend our sculpting to the floor and the ground?

Perhaps a lead might come from certain furniture designers who have been working on responding floors—floors which can change their shape as required, and can not only mould themselves into varying forms of depression and mount, but which can also be varied from softness to hardness—which leads one to the pulsating yellow heart environment of the Haus-Rucker-Co of Vienna, the water bed from Aquarius of New York, the furniture carpet by Gernot Nalbach and the Enviro Machine of Wolfgang Doring.

Furniture designers have in some respects been far more enterprising in their use of plastics than have architects. Perhaps their task is easier because furniture can be fun, whereas buildings and the environment are all too serious? This may rather be a simple matter of cost, but is perhaps also something to do with the fact that eccentric furniture may be enjoyed in private, whereas eccentric architecture tends to announce itself to the world at large.

Whether this is the reason or not, the fact remains that the basic function of furniture has been questioned far more effectively in recent years than has the basic function of housing.

152/ sculptural applications

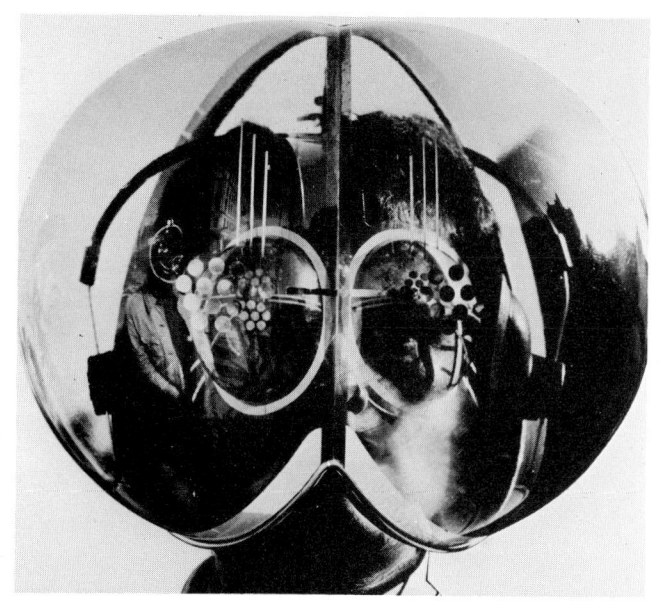

222–24 Top left: 'Flyhead', a transparent p.v.c. helmet and visor with special optic and acoustic qualities. An 'environment transformer'. Below left: 'Mind-Expander' chair for two, with a collapsible balloon over the two heads, generating an audio-visual adventure. Below, right: 'Balloon-for-Two'—a place for concentration in the street, all by the Haus-Rücker-Co. of Vienna.

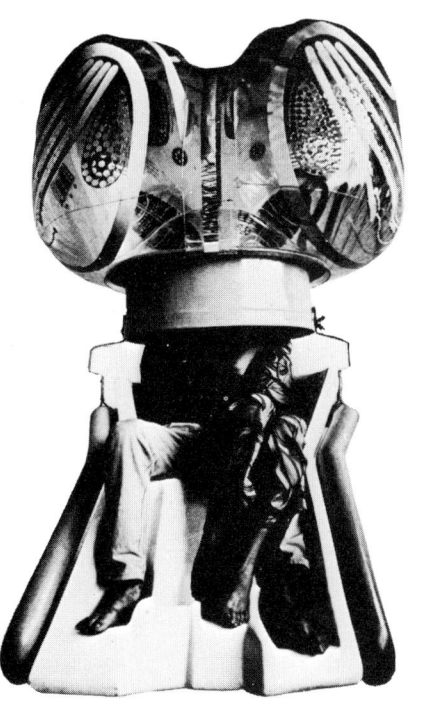

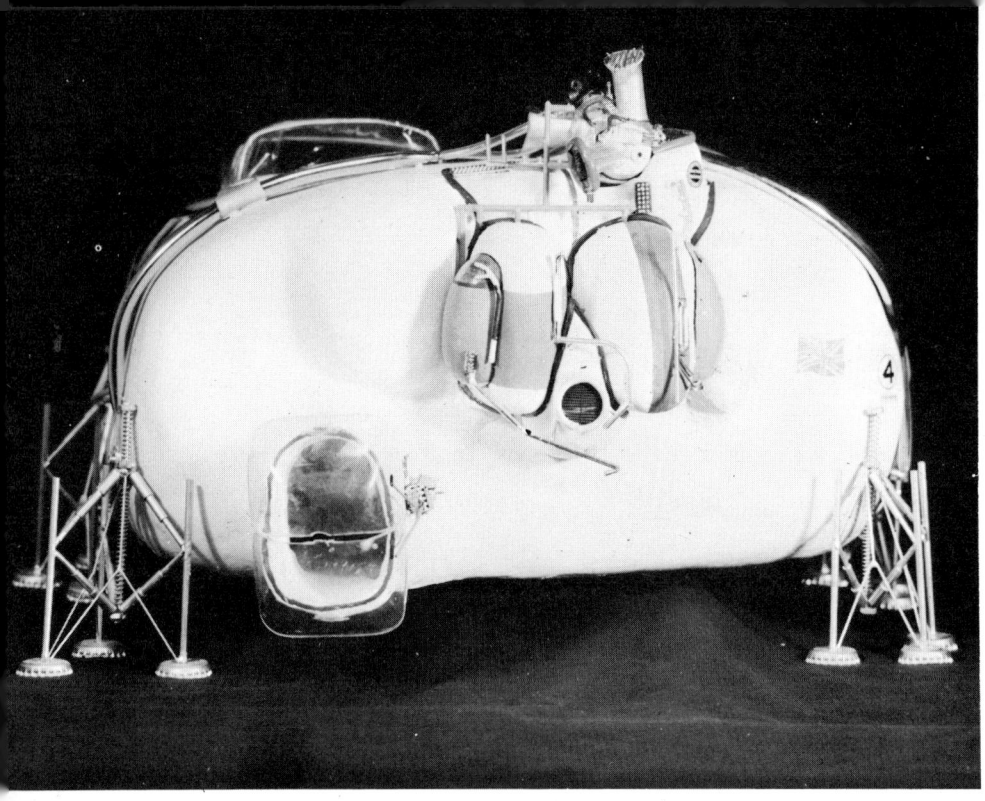

225, 226 Living pod by David Greene. Cleans and clothes, feeds, sleeps and teaches the inhabitant(s). Exterior and cut-away interior.

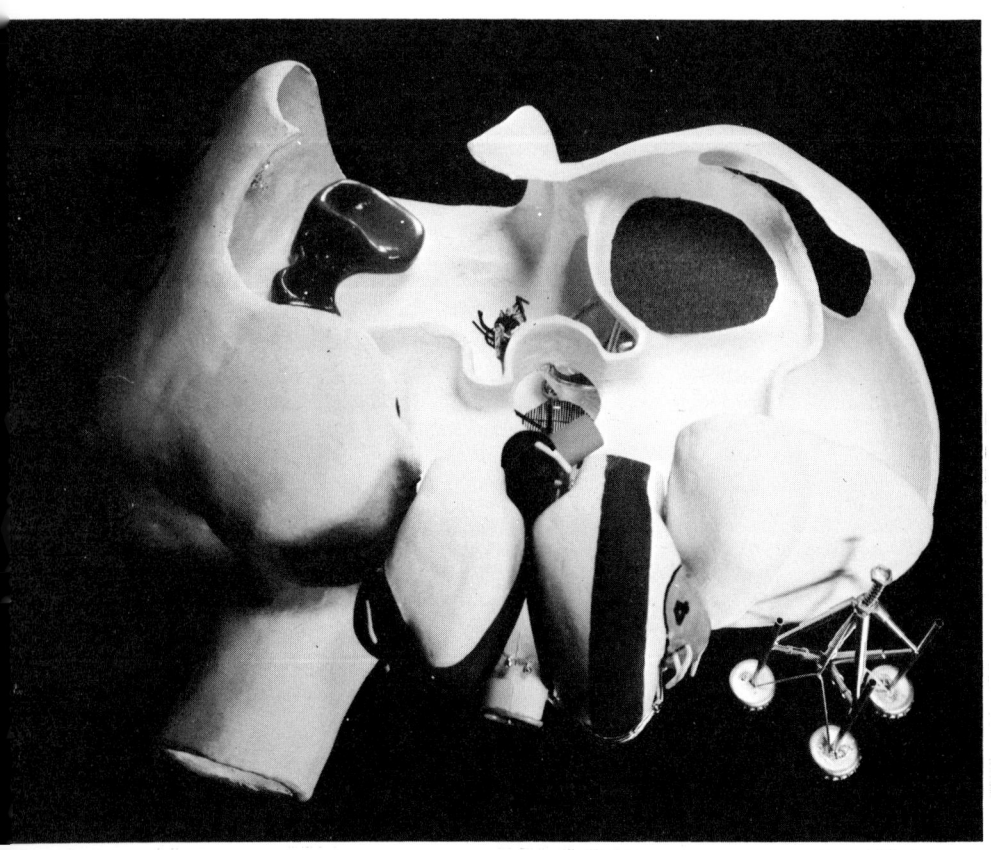

227, 228 'Dyodon' habitable pneumatic by J. P. Jungmann, Beaux-Arts School, Paris, under D. G. Emmerich. Elevation, section and perspective.

229 'Biotecture 70.6'. Experimental model for edible architecture, by Rudolf Doernach.

230 One million feet of wrapped coast at Little Bay, Australia, by Christo.

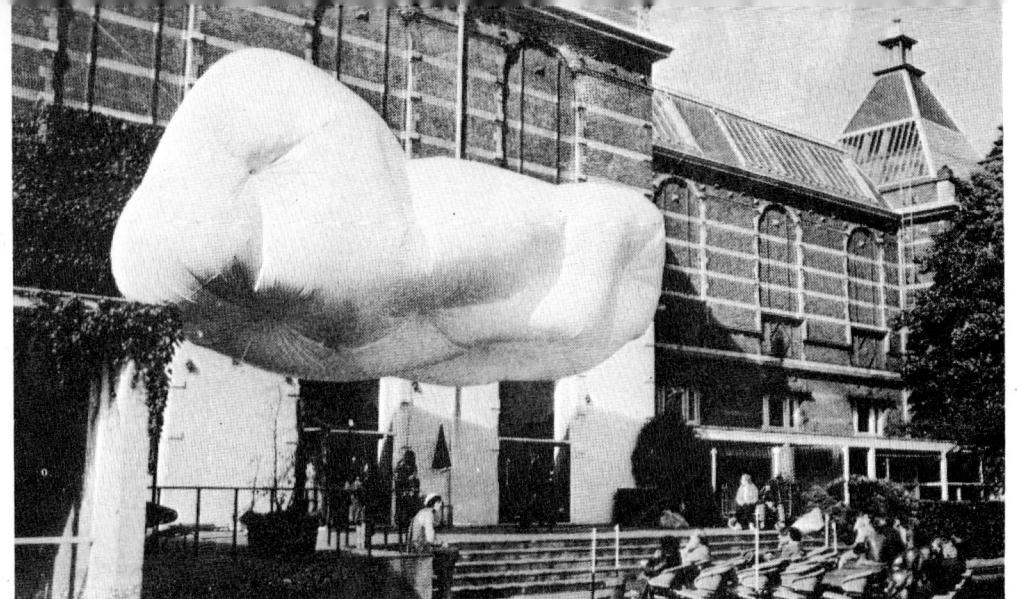

232 (Facing page) 'Projekt Canaris' by Herbert Distel. Giant g.r.p. egg, floated across the Atlantic.

231 'Cloud'. Eventstructure Research Group, Amsterdam.

One could quote Werner Panton's sculptured interiors, the inflated cushions of Kohlmaien and von Sartory which can clip together to make anything from furniture to domes, and of course Michael Webb's Cushicle (see 247, 248).

These and many other projects examine the way in which we live at the moment, and by their design suggest a new approach which is more relaxing, more stimulating or just plain different.

The danger in basic questioning is, of course, the fact that any problem, no matter how simple, if taken back and back to its roots and beyond inevitably spreads out and envelops a myriad of other problems and eventually leaves the designer sprawled out with all the problems of the world in his lap and the conclusion that it is all really too overwhelming.

This was a recognized disease in architecture when I was a student, and the only cure seemed to be either to cease questioning, or to restrict the enquiry to a limited area—to be aware of all the mass of problems looming around beyond the perimeter of the investigation, but to prevent them obtruding on the problem in hand. I have always found it necessary to work in this way, which is why my concern has been restricted to innovation in the elements of architecture rather than on a broader scale, in the environment. One might consider that a harmonious whole might best be created from the small scale upwards, rather than from the grand scale down.

And this is why the grand approach in so much planning doctrine is so horrifying; planning which incidentally seems to manifest itself to a more marked degree in France than in any other country: such tremendous, all-embracing projects based upon such a small and often insignificant theme. People are far too complex to be manipulated in this way. Perhaps such grandiose schemes are the twentieth-century equivalent of the architectural 'follies' of past centuries—but far more dangerous in that they may be taken seriously and applied to the community. Many of us have lost the ability to enjoy follies and fall into the trap of taking ourselves too seriously.

It is therefore refreshing to find that follies are still being constructed for fun—follies such as Distel's Projekt Canaris—a giant plastic egg which was floated across the Atlantic and lost for months, only to be found shattered and plundered in Trinidad. Or the Cloud by the Evenstructure Research Group of Amsterdam. An inflated form 12 m long in white p.v.c. which was intended to be floated through the streets of the city accompanied by the amplified sounds of wind, rain and thunder.

Projects such as these have to me a beautiful and wholly enjoyable simplicity about them.

233, 234 Dome over Manhattan, by R. Buckminster Fuller. Geodesic dome project two miles in diameter: total weight 80,000 tons. Aerial view and (facing page) perspective.

CHAPTER 9 prospective work

Much of the work already considered may be classified as prospective or forward-looking in that in concept or construction, it is in advance of currently-accepted standards. For example, some plastics housing projects incorporate sociological proposals which would as yet be unacceptable for general application, and, less frequently, some designs include physical or structural elements which are either beyond the capabilities of present-day industry, or are only available at such a high cost that their use is, for the moment, prohibitive.

However a certain number of important general tendencies may be separated and considered in more detail. Chief among these is the growing world-wide interest in climate control by the use of very large enclosures, or by other less constructional means.

Except in a few favoured areas, the climate of the world is hostile to man, and consequently simple protection from the elements has been the largest single factor in the evolution of architecture; a certain volume is enclosed and a more favourable climate is created inside. This is almost invariably carried out on a small scale, and our towns and cities therefore consist of thousands of little micro-climates all doing the same job and all huddled together, yet each completely separated from the others.

For many years now we have had the ability to create a more logical town or city with an overall benign climate, in which normal buildings would not be required. Perhaps we are simply afraid to try the experiment—afraid of a different way of life where normal standards of inside and outside do not apply, and where other standards of property, dress and behaviour might undergo radical change.

One of the earliest enclosure projects was Buckminster Fuller's design for a 3,200 m² dome to cover a substantial section of Manhattan Island, and at around the same time incomplete news kept arriving from the Soviet Union of vast pneumatic domes for agricultural purposes in the Arctic regions, and also projects for enclosed polar towns.

235, 236 Arctic city project by Frei Otto and Ewald Bubner, with Ove Arup and Partners, Kenzo Tange and Urtec. A temperate climate is forecast for the interior without heating, on account of reduced heat loss from the earth. Interior and (below) exterior. On an island at the extreme right is the atomic power station with, to the left, the air circulation tower. The covered harbour and the airport are on the left.

237, 238 Above, interplanteary city project, under a cable net restrained pneumatic form. Frei Otto. Below, project for a transparent suspension roof (with opaque edges) to cover the parks at Expo '64, also by Frei Otto.

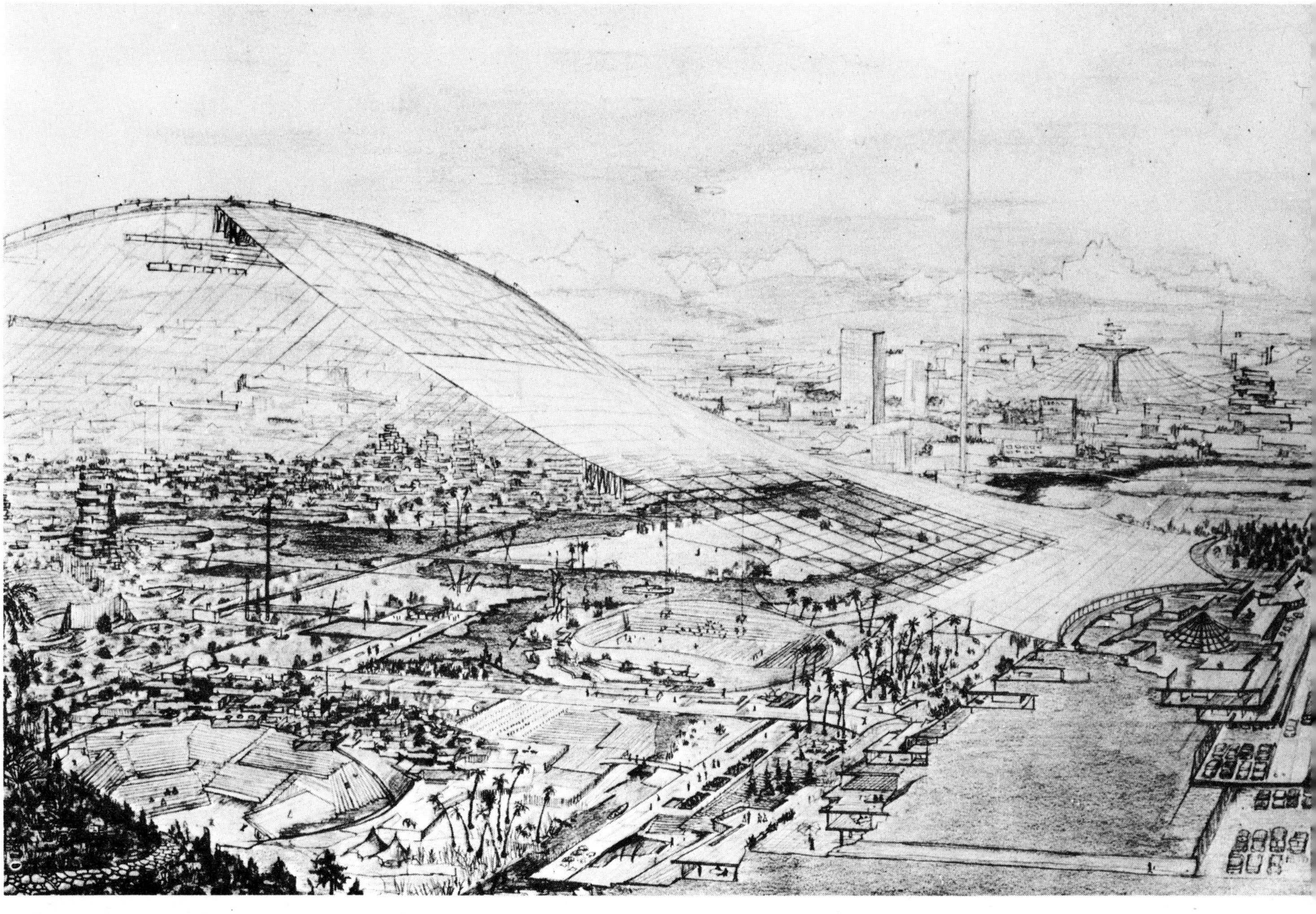

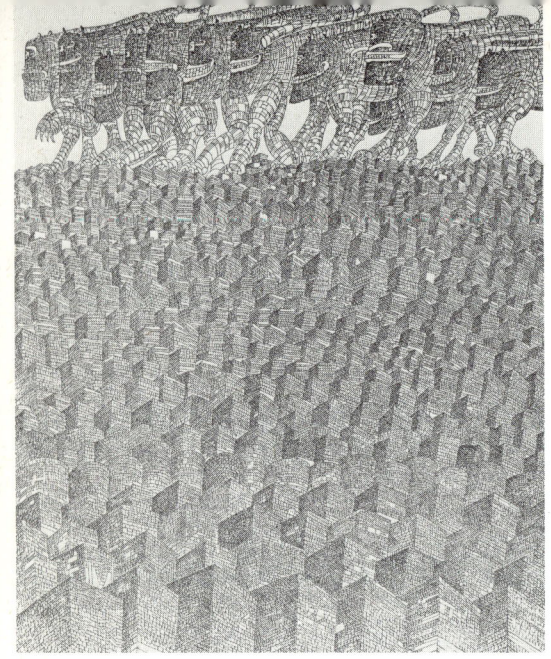

240, 241 (Facing page) Hunstanton Leisure Centre project, by Gillinson, Barnett and Partners. Geodesic triodetic solarium, multi-purpose hall and dolphinarium. Above, model; below, interior sketch of solarium. Pool, beach, wave machine, palmtrees, waterfall, restaurant and bars, sunbathing.

239 Cartoon, 'System Building', by Alberto Longoni.

More recently an increasing number of designs for enclosed Arctic cities have been produced in many countries in the Western world, stimulated not so much by the escalating need to house the growing populations of the world, but rather to service the exploitation of the natural resources recently discovered in those regions.

However the real implications of the total enclosure of a new city have yet to be fully grasped. Virtually all projects aim at the control of the climate and then assume the current construction of a conventional town or city within the enclosure. And one can just see it happening—brick walls, reinforced concrete, opening windows, individual heating—all out of habit. Just like now, only more so.

Perhaps we shall have progressed beyond this early stage by the time the increase in the world's population compels us to live in more harsh areas than we do at the moment, and perhaps then we shall be able to test Robert Ardrey's *Territorial Imperative* and discover whether under circumstances of total enclosure we shall still feel compelled to fence ourselves in—or to fence the other fellow out. And so far as this is concerned, I have found a significant difference in the races. An English family approaching a beach with only one other group on it will position themselves as far away as possible. A German or French family will tend to come and sit on top of you.

Under circumstances of total enclosure—one tends to think of the really large-scale application of low-pressure pneumatic structures, but always with the realization that it may well be feasible to achieve the same end with less physical means, by air curtains or by reconstructing the natural climate.

An idyllic, South-Sea island existence for us all, contemplating our navels under palm trees? Why not—or at least let us try to use climate control as an opportunity to examine our way of life, to create more fun for all, to re-examine the relationships within our Society and of man with his surroundings.

164/ prospective work

242, 243 Above, Biotecture project by Rudolf Doernach, who has been pursuing his own unique ecological path for many years. And sometimes his dedication surprises his guests. Below, Hydropolis I prototype, Rudolf Doernach: 'Reinforced foam bone being colonized by micro organisms—eroded by wind, sun and women—breeding Maritime Society'.

244, 245 Biotecture house, Rudolf Doernach. 'Architecture must become an externalized, technical, artificial super-system. Biotecture. . . . Live Biotecture is the greatest challenge to industrial man'. Below, Hydroponic Biotecture. An expression of Doernach's Maritime Society theory, including 'Man to be generalist, machines specialist'.

246 Summerland recreation centre, Japan, by Kinji Fukuda and Minoru Murakawi.

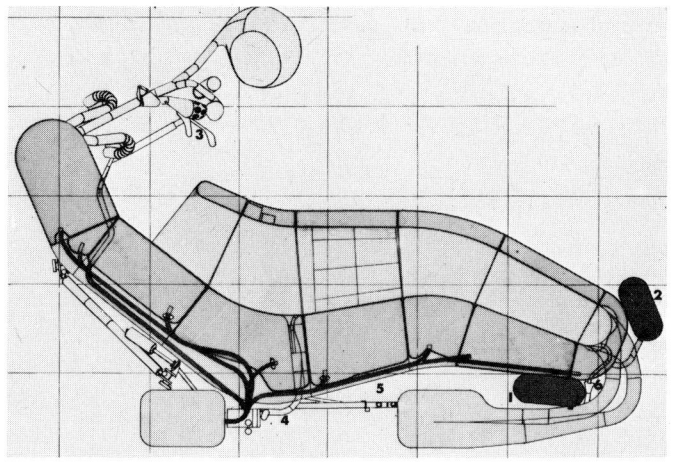 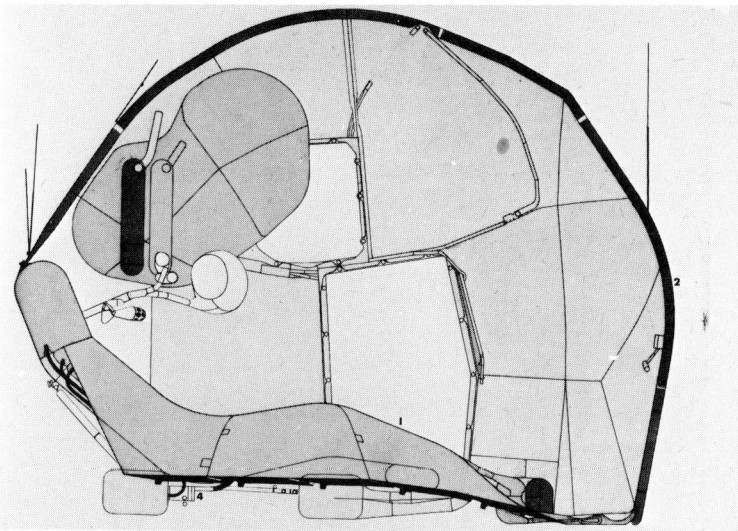

Some modest research is already being carried out in for example the inflatable enclosure projects at Princeton and Antioch Columbia universities, both in the United States, and in the enclosure of holiday resorts.

So many of us have simple tastes in our holiday requirements—sun, sea, sand and solitude figuring high on our lists, and some of us in Britain have felt for years that our traditional holiday resorts such as Blackpool could be economically re-created by the enclosure and climate control of a large area of sea and land, with dramatic tropical landscaping and artificial sunlight. This line of thinking has generated the Derby Castle Solarium, Isle of Man and the Summerland playground near Tokyo, but these two examples are far too small for the possibilities to be fully realized, and in addition suffer from the absence of any safe form of artificial sunlight.

This is a serious problem, which will have to be overcome if climate control is to develop as it should. A means of providing simulated sunshine which will be warm, bright, and will produce a moderate and even tan.

Silly really that we should feel the need of such simulation, that we are not yet ready to accept the far more dramatic effects that could be provided by a free approach to artificial lighting, and that we should go to such trouble to change the colour of our skins and our hair.

Nevertheless artificial sunlight will be probably required in the enclosure of towns and holiday resorts for the foreseeable future, and despite claims to the contrary it is simply not available at the moment. Sophisticated sunray lamps of course, or even unscreened fluorescent tubes. Unfortunately both of these tend to reproduce some of the nastier constituents of natural sunlight, leading over a period of time to skin cancer and other equally unpleasant complaints.

We need to be able to generate the desirable characteristics of moderate sunlight. This would not appear to be beyond the wit of man, but indicates those capable of developing a suitable output unit have not yet been made aware of the growing and unsatisfied world demand for such a product.

247, 248 Above, left: 'Cushicle' by Michael Webb. Suit and cushicle combined as couch. Right, couch transformed with a second suit into a home, with images projected onto the sheath. 'The ultimate in Drive-in living'.

prospective work

Perhaps such artificial sunlight may also be required in projects for submarine cities, unless recent experiments to convert the human apparatus to breathe water proves to be successful, and certain sections of the human race in consequence become able to beat the other marine mammals—porpoises, seals and whales—at their own game.

A growing interest is being shown in the sea, not only as additional living spaces both on the surface and beneath it, but also as a source of raw materials and foodstuffs. Rudolph Doernach has examined maritime possibilities in considerable depth in his three projects of Hydropolis, Biotecture and Maritime Society.

In Biotecture he puts forward proposals for 'soft and hard, contractable and re-usable organic matter as the universal building material, invented and programmed by the environmental scientist, the comprehensive architect'.

On the other hand his Maritime Society is a complete attack on the present materialist world, based upon the Edible City concept, and proposing the colonization of the Mediterranean as a first stage by a new post-Christian post-industry society.

Then Hydropolis, followed by Dropolis—a strange blend of lighthearted drawings and all-too-serious writing. Doernach is one of the chief early pioneers of plastics architecture, having developed shell structures, domes, slot-in low-cost housing systems, Land-Air-Sun 'Habitainers' and many other structures, but since the early days his work has become far more world-wide and more complex. His obsession with future food supplies is perhaps a result of his continuing work on plastics, and may be an organic spin-off from the research into synthetic foodstuffs being carried out by a number of plastics companies.

One of the most promising of these investigations is the growth of protein on oil waste at a B.P. operational plant in the south of France. The bacteria/fungus-like growth produces an entirely neutral material, something like soya flour, which is then flavoured and shaped into acceptable and palatable form. The protein can be extruded into a stringy substance and then be converted by a variety of means, including knitting, into a fibrous material like meat. The company say that a good steak substitute is already available.

There are also prospects for growing protein on plastics waste—at a later stage in the oil-conversion process—and a wide range of by-products of the plastics processing industry have parallel potential. (And shall we be able to avoid the name 'Polyfiller'?)

The future of raw materials supplies for the oil-based plastics industry appears to be rather gloomy at the moment, with forecasts suggesting a mere fifteen years' life for world resources at the current consumption growth, and taking into account the present rate of discovery of new oilfields.

Fortunately, however, other carbon-based raw materials can conveniently be used (including timber, coal, milk etc.) and current research is opening the way for rocks, sand and salt to be employed; and syntheses of water and air are undergoing examination as a further possibility.

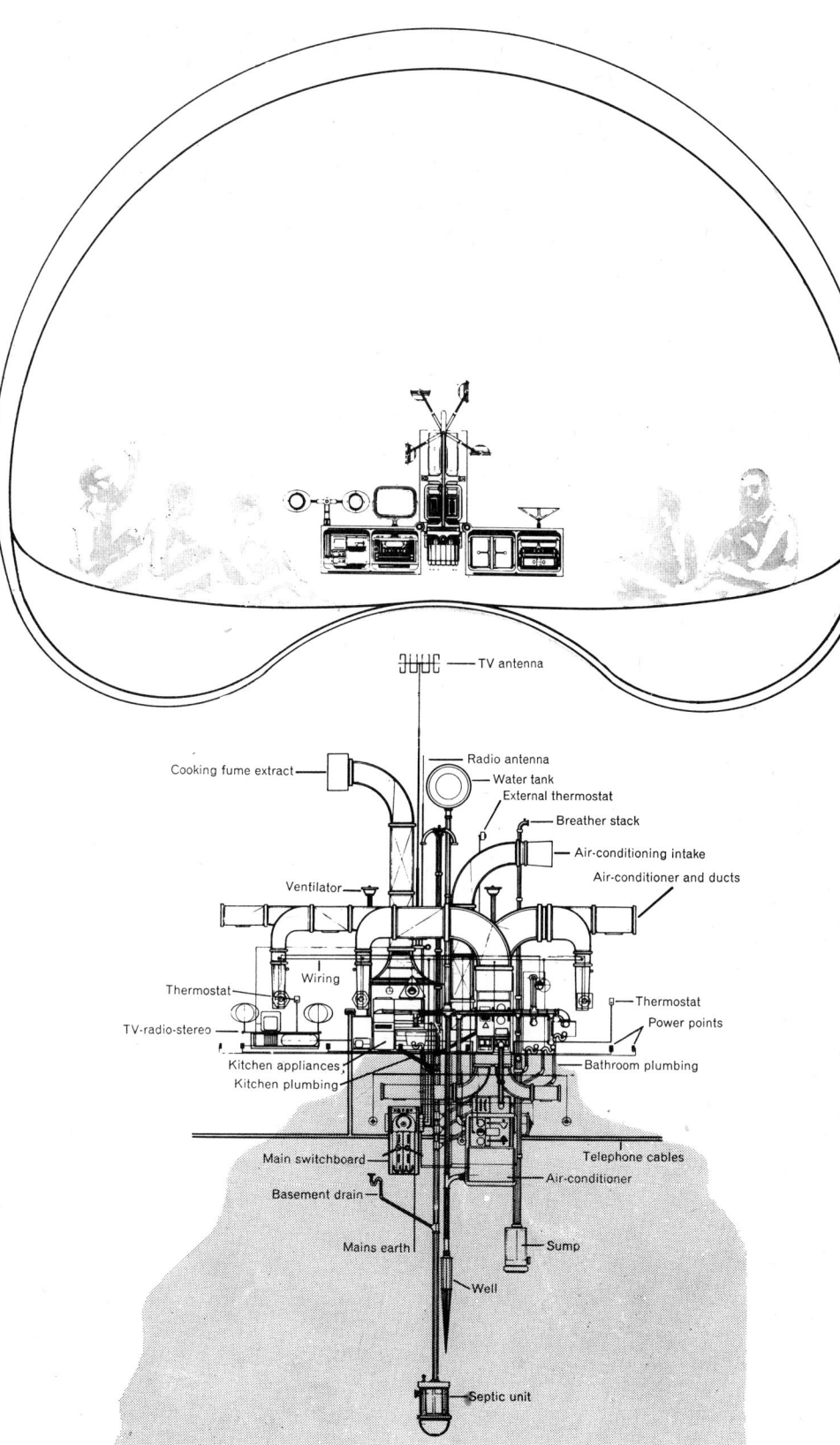

249, 250 'A home is not a house' project by Reyner Banham. Complex service module and simple pneumatic enclosure. Below, detail of module. 'With very little exaggeration, this baroque ensemble of domestic gadgetry epitomises the intestinal complexity of gracious living—in other words, this is the junk that keeps the pad swinging. The house itself has been omitted from the drawing, but if mechanical services continue to accumulate at this rate, it may in fact be possible to do away with houses'.

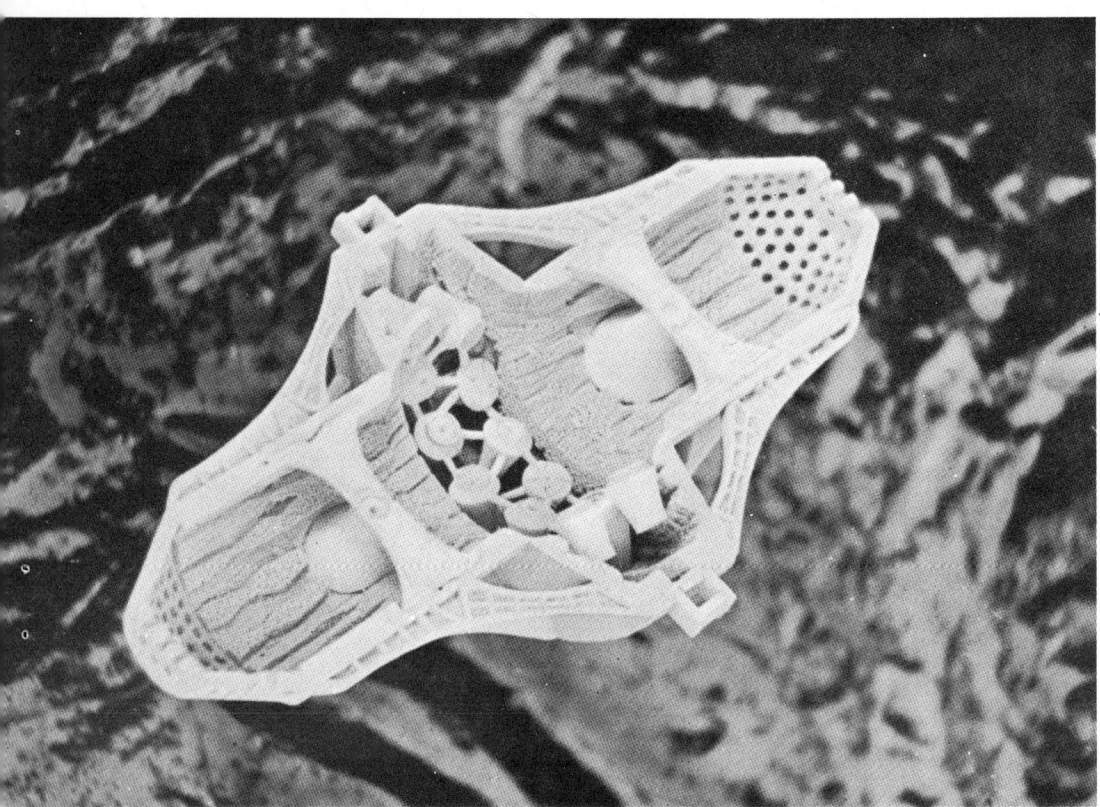
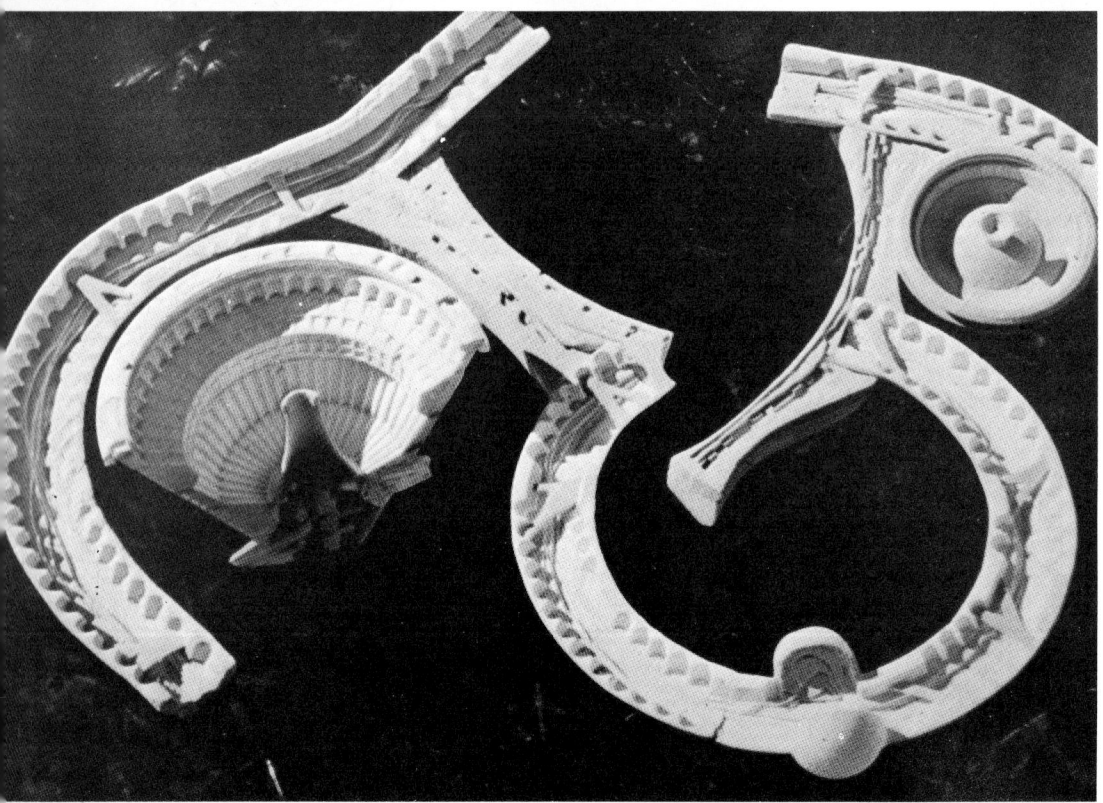

251, 252 Above, 'Asteromo', a double-skin inflated asteroid, for a population of 70,000, by Paolo Soleri. Below, 'Novanoah A', a floating city designed by Paolo Soleri.

253 (Facing) Drive-in housing by Michael Webb. The house is a unit within a megastructure. Mobile containers travel horizontally or vertically along the megastructure and provide all internal circulation. Interchange with car in parking racks on perimeter: (A) mobile unit; (B) fixed floor space; (C) bed; (D) dressing; (E) bathroom; (G) garden; (J) study; (K) kitchen.

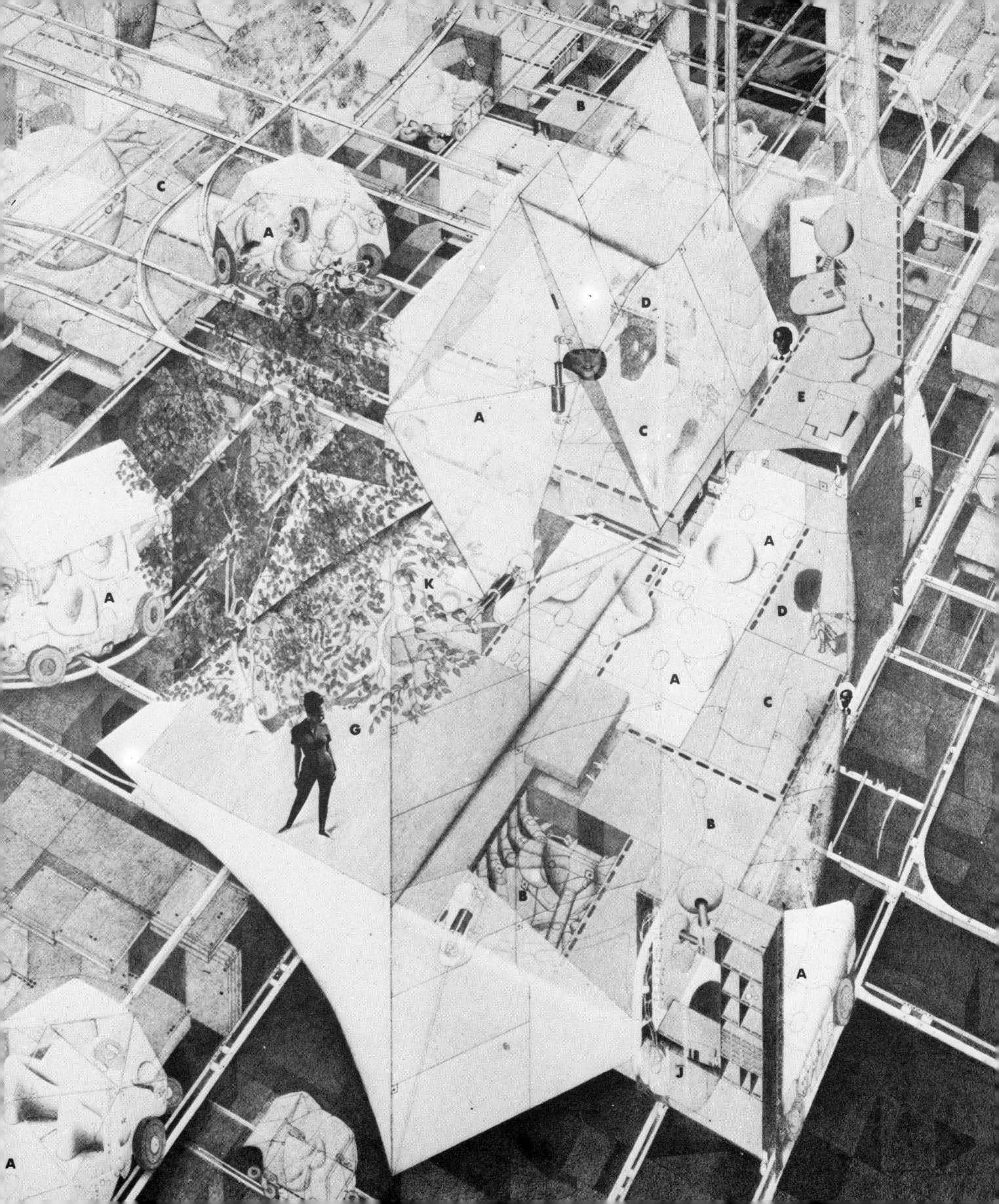

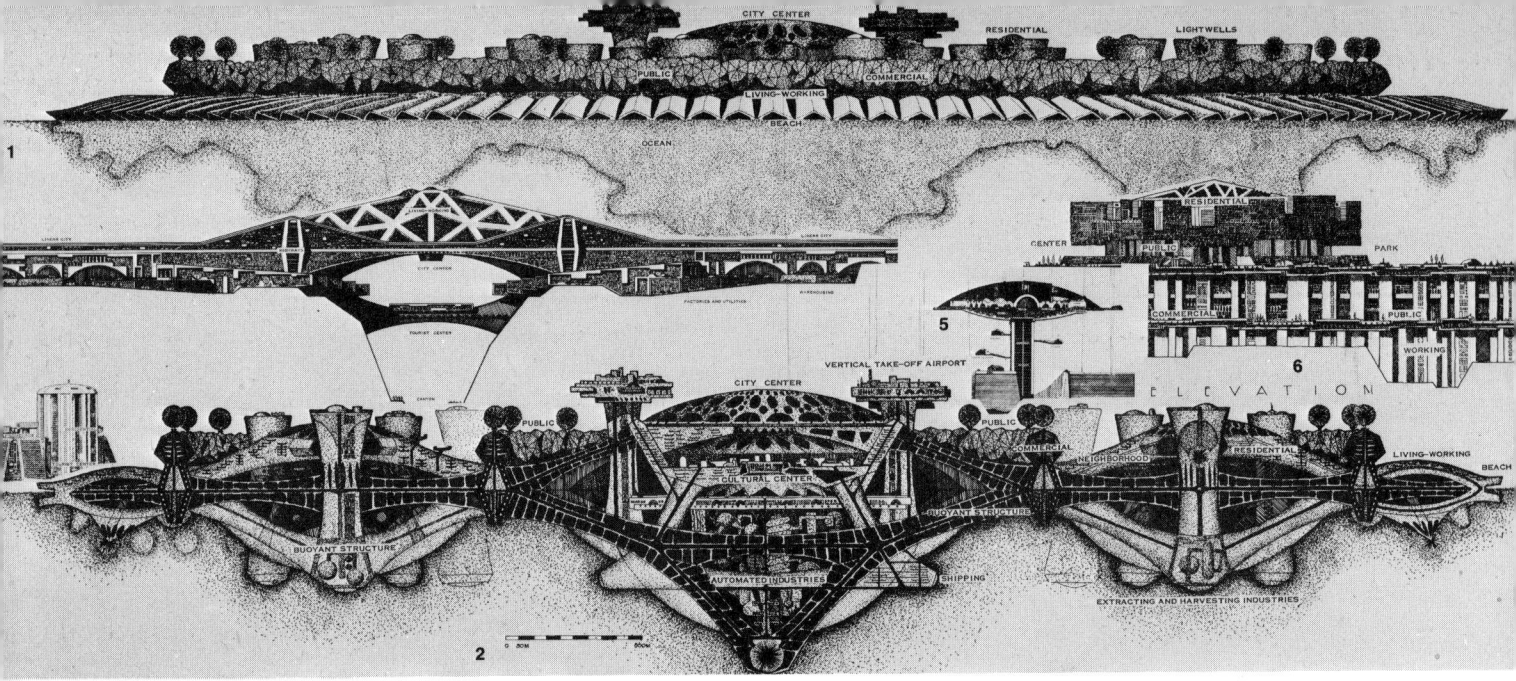

254 'Novanoah B', floating city, elevation and section.

So the work of constructing new molecular building blocks from the basic atoms from which the world is made can be expected not only to continue, but to grow apace. Even with present carbon-based materials, it is forecast that by A.D. 2000 the volume of plastics in use will outstrip that of metals by a factor of four.

One may therefore feel optimistic about the future of the plastics industry and its developing ability to provide materials tailored to any performance, but perhaps less so about our ability to use these resources effectively.

As has been pointed out, the new materials provided by the plastics industry have outstripped the ability of architects to make use of them. In by far the majority of cases, the same old wine has been used in these new bottles, largely because we design out of habit, and construct what we think people should need or what we decide they ought to have.

I fear that this is an increasing danger, and one which is linked to a reduction in communication and the growing tendency for all of us to act as spectators rather than participants—as critics rather than creators.

And there is such a world of difference. The human brain is all too adept at closing off compartments within itself and consequently blinding its user to reality. We can read about horror in the world around us, but the reality is so shattering that the mind glosses over it, even from childhood. We have to train children to think of others—to project themselves into another's experience—by means of 'do as you would be done by'. And yet what child—which of us—projects in this way during a murderous scene in a Western film? Or at news from a civil war or a concentration camp or of starvation? And so down the line to architecture. Unless we can understand one another, how can we possibly design for others save at the most rudimentary, box-like level?

Understanding stems from communication, communication depends upon self-expression, and all three are grossly neglected in present day education. We can all smile at the plight of the expert whose work is so specialized

255, 256 Floating house by Masayuki Kurokawa. Designed for water sports, it consists of three cabins, two for living and one for mechanical equipment. These are linked by two gangways; the upper for a sundeck, the lower to link the two cabins. Steelwork beneath acts as stabilizer when afloat. Below, an exploded diagram.

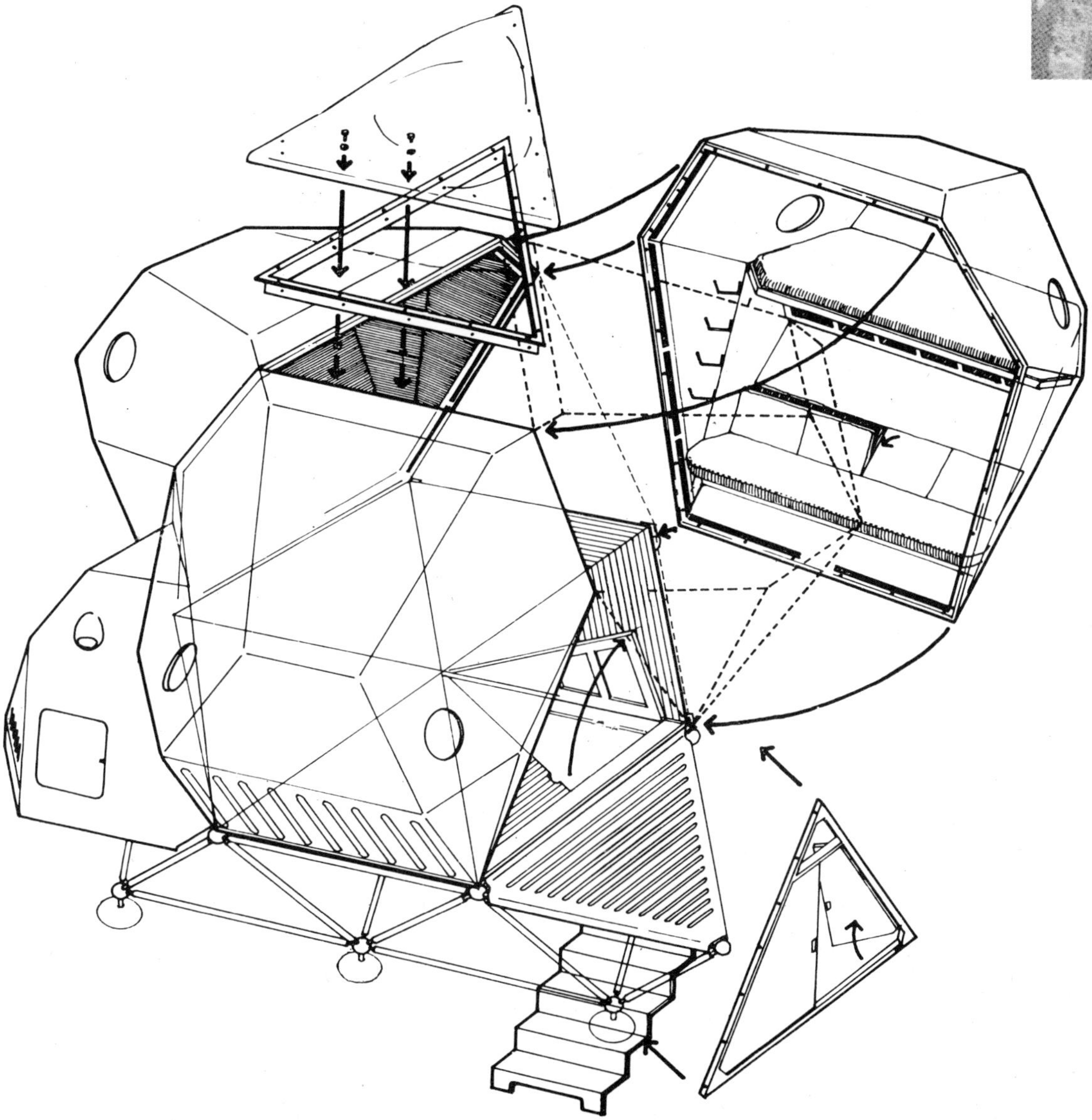

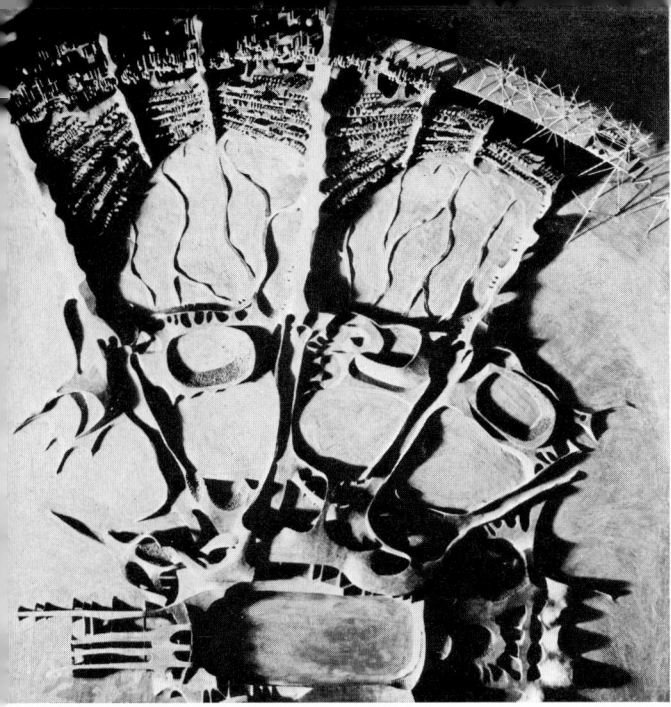

257, 258 Aerial view, new town for the Seine valley by the Group Miasto (Lefevre, Bezou, Karcewski and Zandfoss).

that he can only talk to two or three people in the world, and yet which of us is much better off?

Teaching was originally a dialogue between pupil and tutor, each learning from the other and each sparking off new ideas and understanding in the other. Teaching nowadays is increasingly carried out by machines (which follow on where books led), and in consequence we confuse the power of thought with mere memory. We neglect intellectual ability for a simple storage capacity which can be bettered by any computer. One could quote in evidence the 'Brains Trust' and the 'Brain of Britain', which have been popular radio contests in recent years, yet which test memory alone and never imagination or intelligence. This is perhaps why we are so bad at defining the way in which we would like to live—even for ourselves. The mind throws up memories and the result is visual or functional eclecticism.

So much prospective work admits and panders to this breakdown in communication. For example, in a description of his Induction House, Hiroshi Hara states that 'we no longer have the time and opportunity to build up the associations and relationships vital to humanity. These must therefore be induced by electronic devices. The Induction House is thus made up of a collection of self-controlled learning cells in which one can enlarge both one's experience and acquaintanceship by electronic means.'

Experience of an acquaintanceship with—the machine? Is this really the future for humanity—sitting dazed the livelong life through before a hypnotic screen? Such a proposition has in fact been the subject of a number of science fiction stories, and has since been taken up with world-wide enthusiasm by designers including such diverse names as Montes and Tschumi, Azuma, Cedric Price, Colani, Hans-Walter Muller, Aida and the Archigram Group. The difference being that the sci-fi writers passed beyond the initial stage and often examined the situation of the individual when he finally rejects his drugged stage and tries once more to come to terms with people and the world.

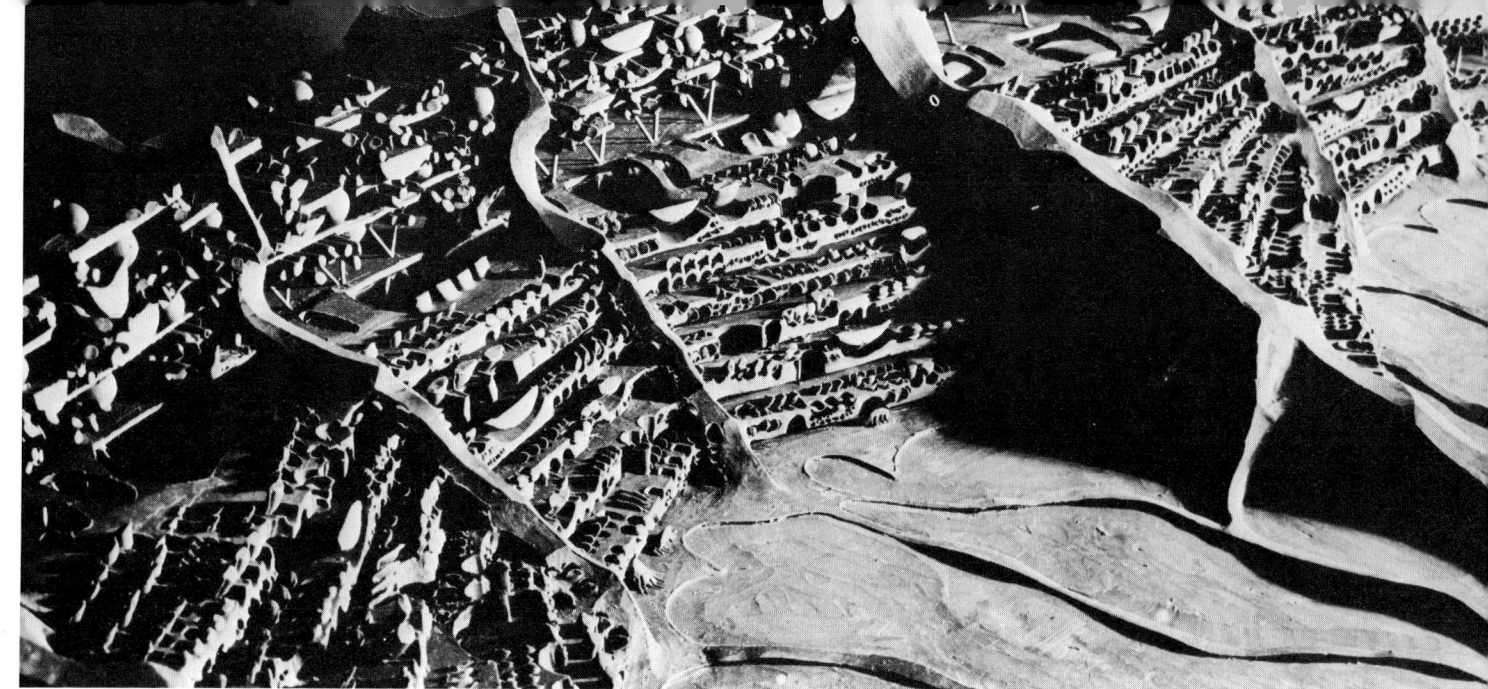

Perhaps therefore the more simple prospective projects where innovation is limited to image-making are, in fact, more desirable by being simply less dangerous. The plastic city of the Miasto group, Chanéac's crater cities, Soleri's Mesa city and Hausermann's egg forms, Ekuan's truncated octahedra, the projects of the N.E.R. group, Rossi and Mazzoleni's tower city and much of the work of the Archigram group fall into this category.

However some Archigram work—Instant City, for example—also contains those elements of stimulation, lateral thought and constant revolution which form the basis of another developing school of thought, and one which may well prove to be the generator of a whole new era in architecture. A school of thought which makes use of the shock tactics of 'black is white', of the long-forgotten intensity of the excitement of discovery, of the delight of ideas and the stimulation of communication—these form a part of so many proposals which unfortunately make an inadequate impact because their clarity is obscured by visuals. These are ideas which cannot be set down in the form of designs, and indeed are so much more important than any space which may be sculptured around them.

This, of course, is the root problem of prospective work. Architecture is the servant of people, and art form or no, it fails in its task if it ceases to serve. The ultimate service which architecture may eventually be called upon to render could be its own self-elimination. As leisure increases, when we finally get to grips with and solve the problems of food supplies, when we accept self-control of the population of the world, when we make use of our ability to create comfortable living conditions, and when we move beyond the confines of a materialist society, then perhaps we shall find that Architecture has evaporated into a total irrelevance, and that we are launched upon a new world of *poésie faite par tous*.

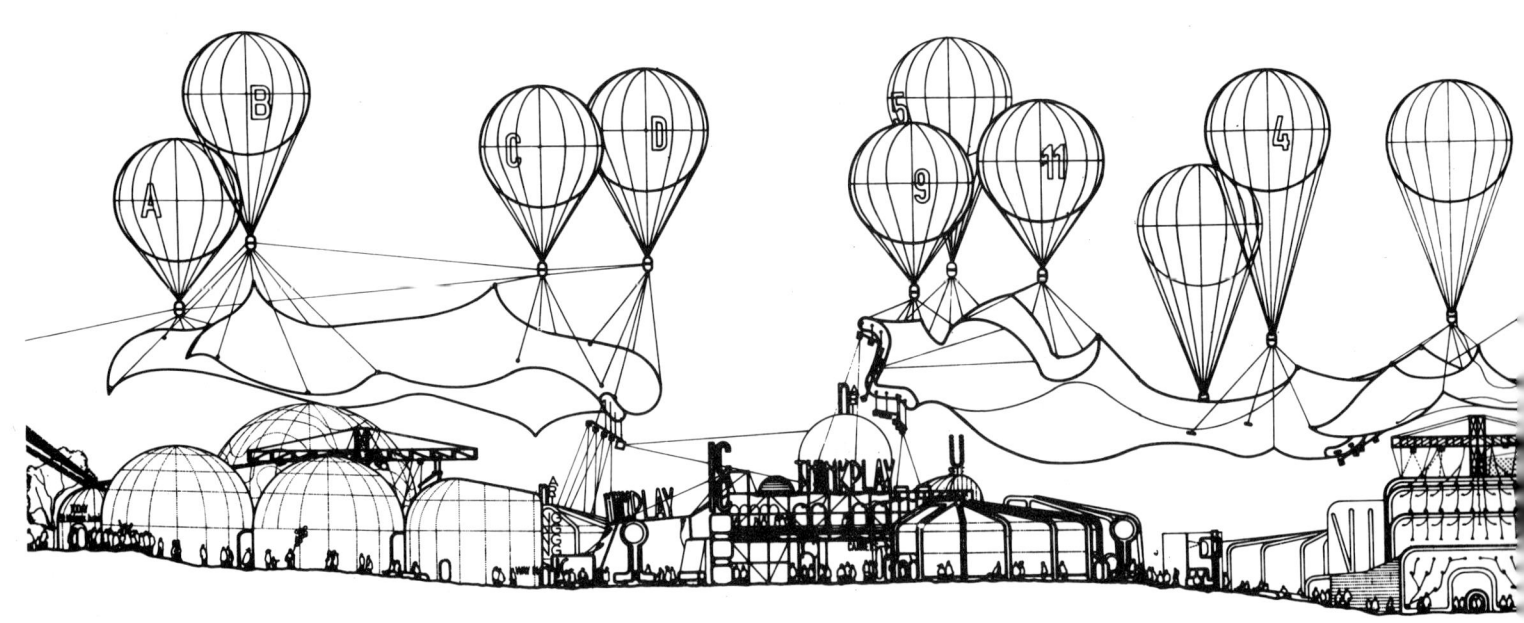

259, 260 Above: 'Instant City', by the Archigram Group (Cook, Crompton, Herron), sets out to provide environmental shock, intellectual and emotional excitement. Below: 'Control-and-choice' living, also by the Archigram Group, aims at an exploitation of 'the means by which enclosure, sustenance and any other kind of response can be made available but not allowed to take over'.

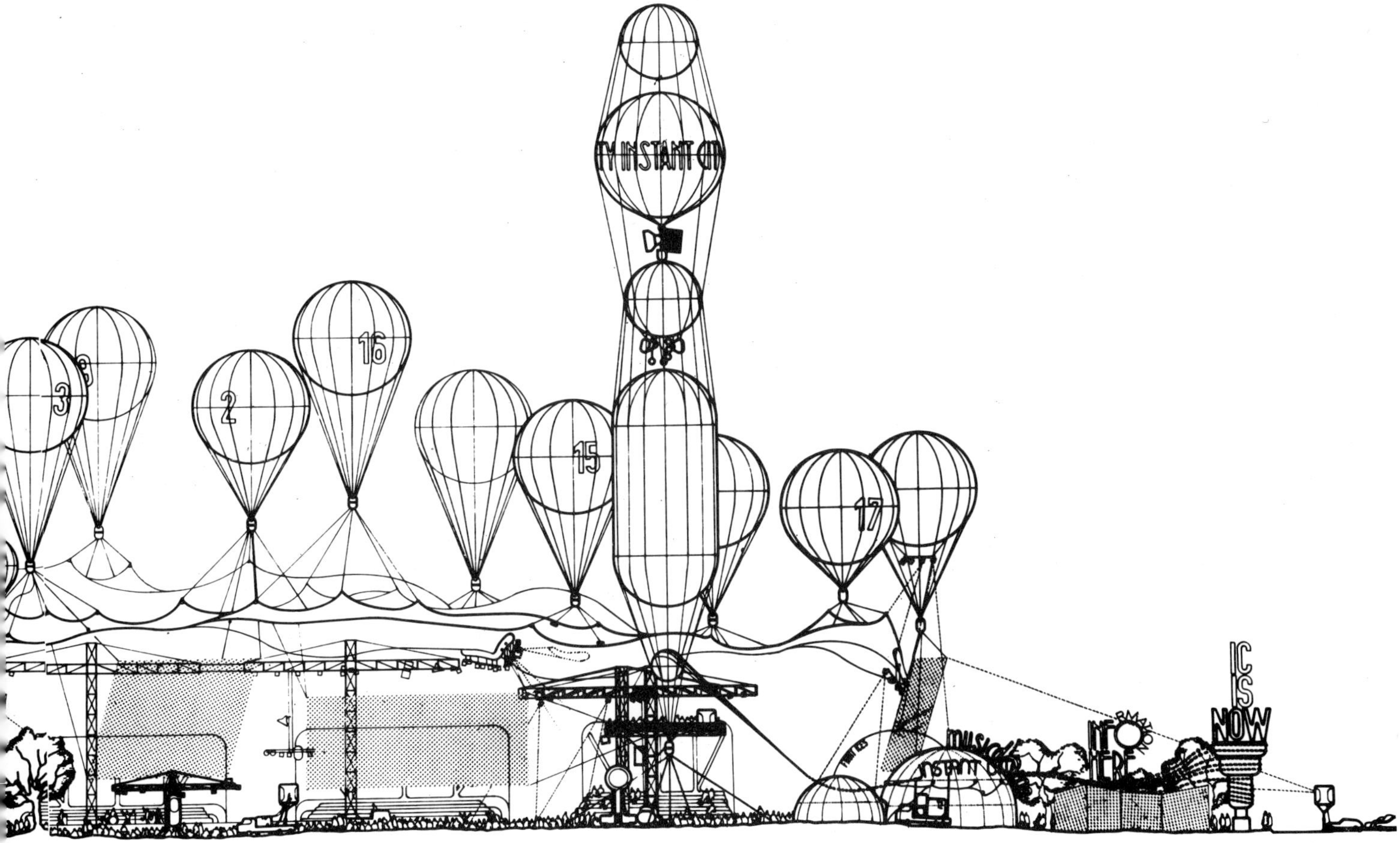

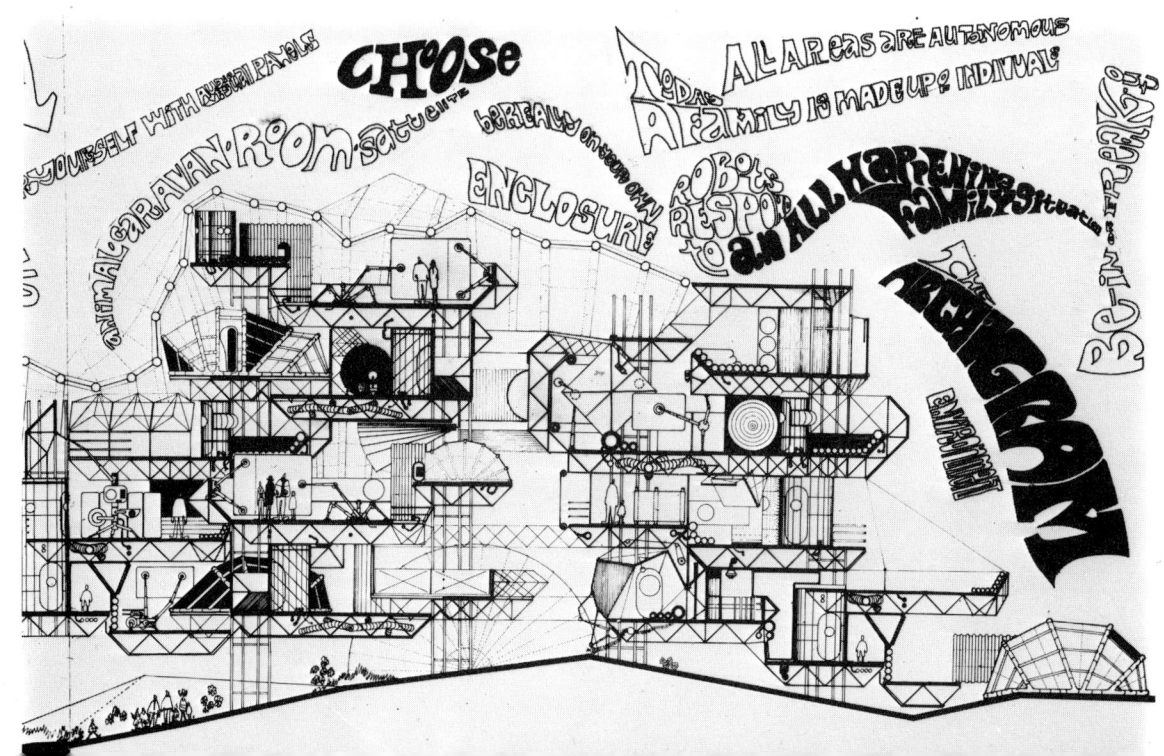

261, 262 Above, 'Walking City', Archigram Group. 'A mobile city intended to congregate at any point of the earth, grouping and un-grouping, changing existing concepts of static societies'. Below, 'Plug-in City', Archigram Group. Is one right in suspecting that the thinking behind this and the other Archigram projects has already had more effect than the physical concepts will ever have?

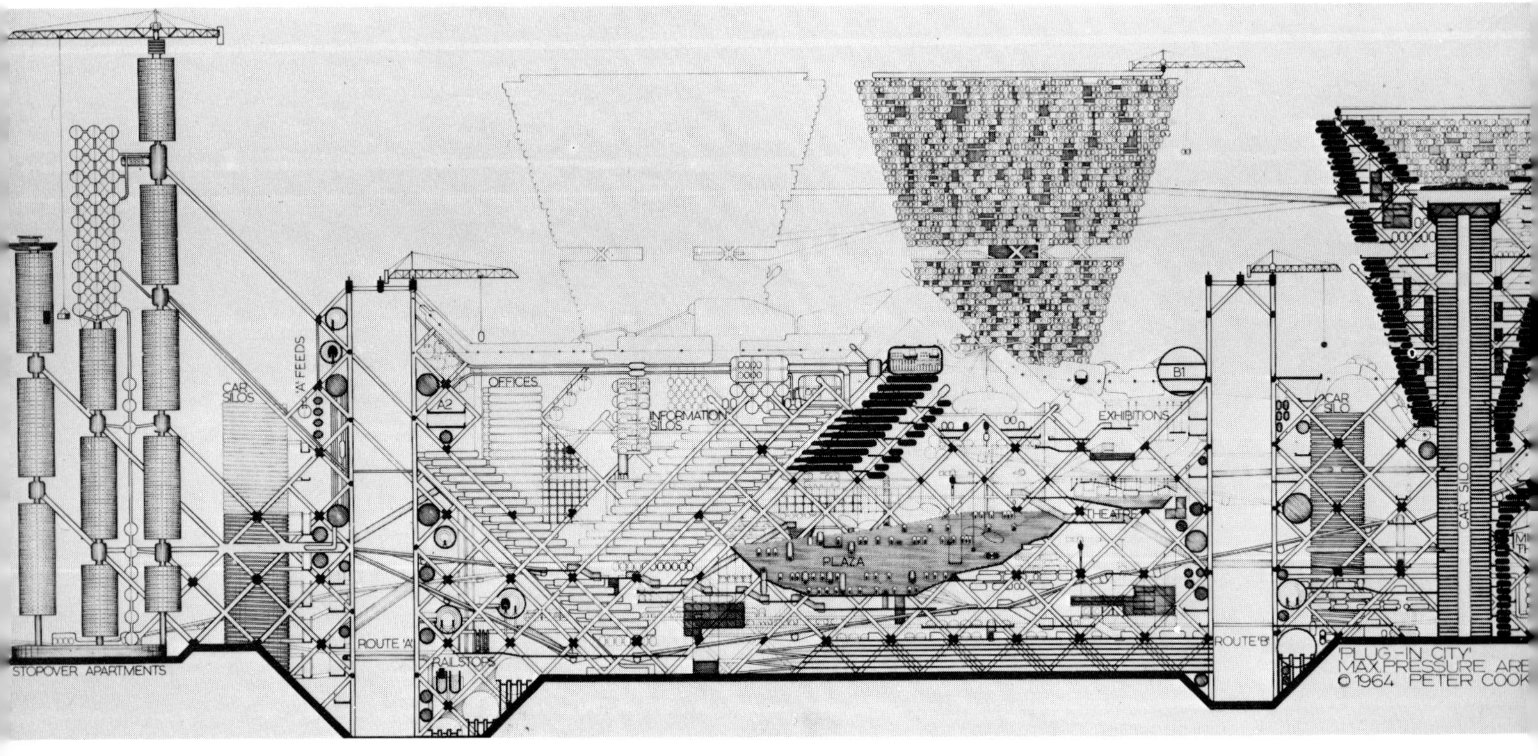

263 'New Town—vertical' project by Aldo Rossi and Donatella Mazzoleni. Fully flexible vertical circulation which is limited horizontally.

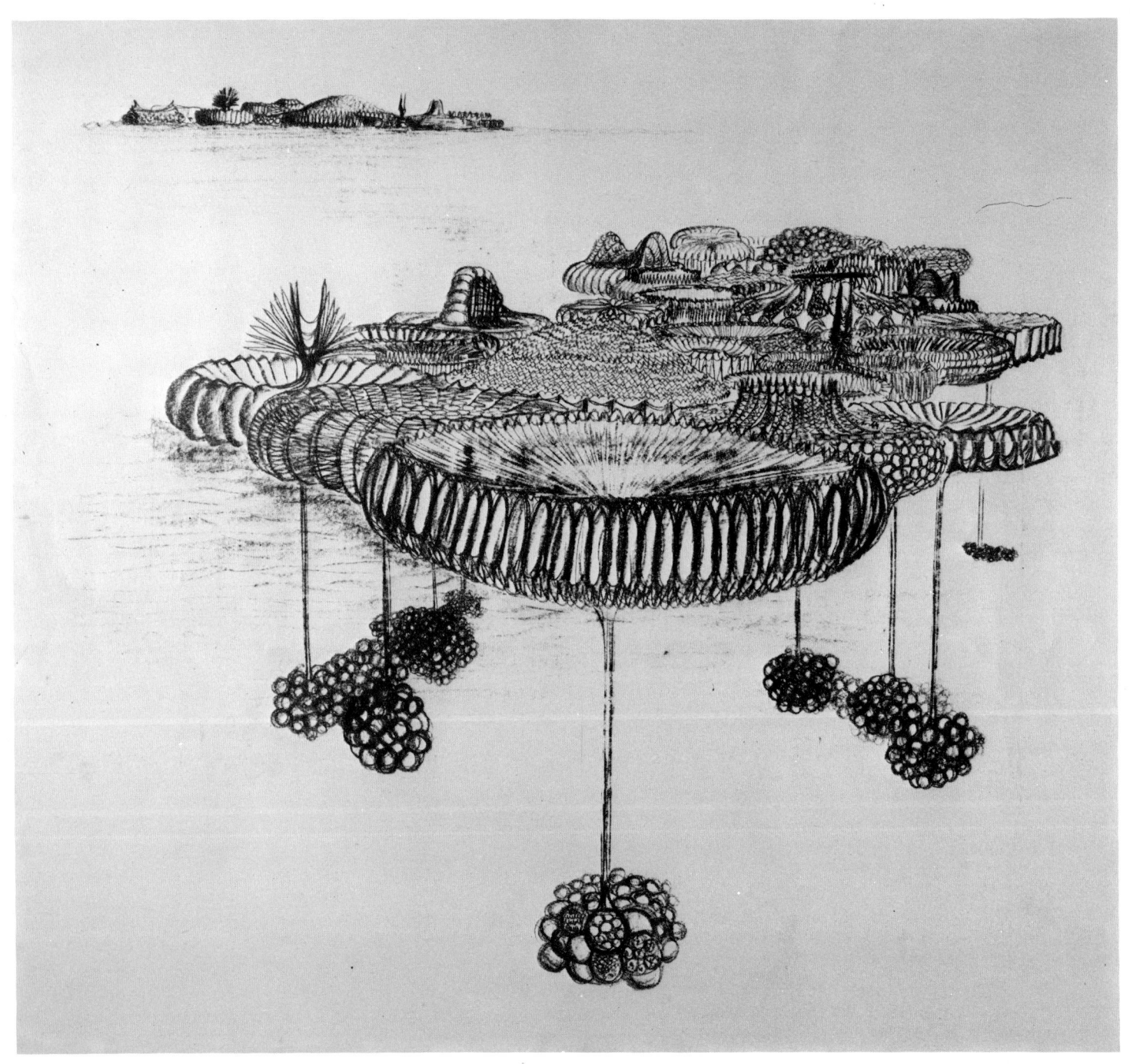

264 Plastics floating city by William Katavolos.

CHAPTER 10   in conclusion

The future of plastics in architecture is utterly dependent upon the future of architecture. This may seem self-evident, but the world-wide industry of building is finally nearing the watershed in its development which, but for an odd quirk of history, it would have negotiated half a century or more ago.

The industrial revolution of the nineteenth century affected the building industry but little. Pointers to the future such as the Crystal Palace had little effect, and the architectural profession wandered up the blind alley of eclecticism and cut itself off from the real business of building.

As a result technological advances and mass-production techniques were not brought into building, which has largely continued in its old craft-based ways, and has attempted to cope with the problem of exploding demand with tools which seem to be ever more and more out-dated as the century progresses. Buildings have remained crude, and have become increasingly expensive.

Jan Bobrowski has pointed out that at the time of the First World War, when both houses and cars were built by hand, one could buy two modest houses for the price of one cheap car. And when one considers the relative complexities of the two products, that is about the right price difference. However although cars have long since been mass-produced for a standardized market, houses are still largely made by hand. As a result one can now buy twelve cheap cars for the price of one modest house. And yet the car of today is vastly superior to its counterpart of fifty years ago in terms of comfort, performance and economy. In what way is the house of the seventies different from the house of the twenties? The only real difference lies in the price, which may have gone up by as much as 2,000%.

A comparison between the automobile and building industries is dangerous because the two products are not yet of the same nature. Nor is housing by any means the whole of building. Nevertheless I believe that this comparison illustrates the result of the basic inability of the building industry to make use of the tools of the twentieth century.

And housing is an extreme case of a relatively standardizable product which is built in such an incompetent way that its price tends to get out of reach of the lower paid sections of the community, and so the supply of sufficient housing at reasonable cost has in many countries become the subject of political action.

But how ridiculous this is! Could one imagine a vast international demand for cheap automobiles remaining unsatisfied, or becoming a matter of political debate in the countries concerned?

Perhaps we need to regard buildings entirely as consumer durables rather than as extensions of the personality or minor household gods (as is often the case with housing).

It is worthwhile comparing the costs of consumer durables with those of building products. We tend to accept building costs as being in the same category as acts of God—awful but inevitable. Awful they certainly are—£10·00 ($24·00) per square foot for an individual house, when land can be bought freehold for as little as 10p (10c) per sq ft. Or a garage: the British build garages to keep their cars in (a very doubtful investment this, and one which is used equally as a store for toys and garden implements), but if the garage is solidly built—say of brick—it can cost as much as the car which it is supposed to protect.

Buildings undoubtedly offer terrible value for money, and we grope about with so-called systems of industrialized building trying to find the solution which is self-evident, and right in front of us. (Not uncommonly of course—the man who works closely with a problem is often the last to see the simple solution because his vision is cluttered with habit and tradition.)

The solution is this. We have a vast international demand for buildings of all kinds—and I mean really vast. (In Britain 8% of the gross national product is spent on building, and in the United States the figure is almost 10%.) In order to satisfy this demand effectively (or in some parts of the world to satisfy it at all), we need to draw upon the existing resources of general manufacturing industry.

This must seem quite obvious to all architects working with the plastics industry, which makes use of some of the most sophisticated mass-production technology in the world. The contrast between designing a unit for mass-production by injection moulding, and then perhaps the next day designing a factory or office building in normal building terms is quite ludicrous. And when one realizes that the increasing sophistication of the plastics industry is producing materials and fabrication technologies which, if properly deployed, could revolutionize our concept of building, then the frustration of not being able to make use of these facilities is quite unbearable.

Plastics is only one of several industries to have developed such advanced technology, and to have realized what immense potential lies in the international building market—perhaps the only remaining tremendous market where real manufacturing and marketing techniques have yet to be employed, and a market moreover capable of considerable expansion.

Unfortunately these industries have not yet been sufficiently dynamic, and have simply tagged on to the coat tails of the building industry by concentrating upon substitution techniques and the production of relatively small components within the traditional framework of construction. They have yet to realize that we in building desperately need their technical and financial resources, and that if only they plan ahead in a clearsighted fashion, then large sections of that marvellous building market could fall right into their laps.

The key to this development, and the reason why it has not yet happened in any country in the world, lies in the organization of the building market. Although so vast, it is entirely fragmented into individual units of non-standard, uncertain demand in such a way as to prevent the easy application of manufacturing technology. So in order to benefit from modern production methods, which could so easily give better buildings for less money and a consequently improving product, we need somehow to induce the building market to cohere.

This could happen in any one of three ways. The slowest is the gradual evolution of the building industry—and yet not an evolution but a metamorphosis—from a construction to a manufacturing industry. Such a change-over cannot be easy, as is exemplified by the recent fumbling and erratic development (and subsequent demise) of systems of construction in Britain—all traditional in concept, all low-output based, all very vulnerable to slight changes in the monetary situation, far too many of them, and all handicapped by being owned for the most part by large building companies who are very nervous of involving the manufacturing industry giants in their production runs, for if manufacturing industry has not yet realized how vulnerable the building market is to them, this has certainly been appreciated by the construction industry, which is setting out (and how short-sightedly) to guard its traditional dominance very jealously. I do not think that we can afford to wait for this to happen.

A quicker way would be for the largest customer or customers for buildings to rationalize their purchasing by organizing bulk orders. This already happens in Britain, where we have a handful of customer-organized systems for the construction of schools (SCOLA, CLASP etc.). These are as yet on far too small a scale, and bedevilled by local county politics, but a start in the right direction, were it not for the fact that the customer actually designs his product and invites the building industry to tender for it. This is a really basic error, because for the full benefit of the exercise to be obtained, we should have not a design but a performance specification, in order to allow new techniques and processes to be introduced.

The development of this customer-organized market would probably be as slow and erratic as the present development of the building industry, were it not for the fact that there exists in many countries of the world one really large—even dominant—customer, in the form of the government. It is not generally realized that in Britain, government (national and local—and the latter largely directed by the former) purchases each year roughly 55% of the total output of the building industry. This is, in fact, a controlling interest, which is at present quite haphazardly deployed. However studies are being carried out in certain political circles to find out how the bulk-purchasing power of the government could be used to revitalize certain industries—and building is very high on the list.

This is a very delicate operation—for two reasons. Firstly because such a revitalization by the organization of bulk orders would inevitably produce a very different building industry very quickly indeed. Consider the order book of the British government—some £3,000 ($7,200) million of it. What would happen if out of that book half a dozen annually-renewable bulk orders of around £200 ($480) million were put together, in the form of performance specifications rather than designs?

First of all, the individual construction companies could not cope. Although in Britain we have some of the biggest and most efficient and up-to-date constructors in the world, who work on a very large international scale, they are nevertheless very small indeed when compared to the giants of manufacturing industry. They have neither the financial nor the technological resources to undertake this type of mass-production operation.

News of the organization of governmental bulk orders would induce the very rapid formation of a few manufacturing and construction conglomerates on a scale not before seen, each anxious to obtain one or more of the orders, and equipped with a range of design and manufacturing capabilities which would enable immediate and tremendous advances to be made in building.

This would be a marvellously worthwhile operation from the point of view of the government, for it would not only result in a building industry which would undoubtedly lead the world and have considerable export potential, but would also (and this is the real purpose) bring about the development of more advanced building types, which would give the country far more and far better buildings for its money. Moreover, the government would by its action put the new conglomerates in a position to organize the rest of the building market around its advanced product range, set up on the basis of the bulk orders.

The danger is this. Once government exercises this degree of control it will be reluctant to let go, and what started out simply as a rationalization of the buying operation (in bulk, with all its attendant benefits, rather than in penny lots) might well lead to governmental control of the building industry.

The third and final alternative is the most attractive of all but, I fear, the least likely. This is that a really large and dynamic corporation will take a lead over its fellows and over the rest of the world by producing an interchangeable and flexible range of functioning elements and spatial enclosure techniques which could be as far ahead of present buildings as the space capsule is ahead of the horse and trap, and offering value for money to exceed the way in which the Model T initially outstripped its competitors; and that this corporation will organize the market by making it cohere around the image which it has produced.

This would be a very expensive undertaking and is generally considered, when it is considered at all, to be far too risky. Risky, because if one thing is certain, it is that such a product range, to be viable, would be very different from present-day constructions as it would be based upon manufacturing rather than craft techniques. A bulk market for such a product does not exist—but of course how could it? How could it exist when even those of us who are considering its development have only the faintest idea of what it could look like or how it would function?

Nevertheless the basis of the market is there in the international desire to have more sophisticated buildings at a cheaper cost. Would it really be so difficult or so hazardous to go for it? Not if we had more outfits like the Japanese railway company which had the imagination to guarantee its market by building a big new town at the end of its line leading into Tokyo.

One way or another, we shall have a complete change in the pattern of building, a change from construction by thousands of small building companies with little organization and no feed-back, to a handful of conglomerates handling a high proportion of all building in their country. This is surely quite inevitable.

Let us consider for a moment the form of this building industry unit of the future. The ideal would be a corporation which was integrated vertically from raw materials right through to direct sales to the customer.

Ideal for two reasons—firstly because in many industries the real giants are at the raw materials end of the chain and it is at this end that financial resources are available, not only to mount the operation which we have in mind, but also to carry the cost of the tremendous research which is so necessary in building, but is so lacking at the moment.

Secondly to include direct sales to the customer, so that the corporation may not only protect itself against fluctuations in demand by being able to vary the intensity of its sales campaign, but may also absorb a feed-back of sales reaction and experience in use, directly into itself. In this way the product can change and up-date itself more rapidly to meet public demand.

Immediately after the raw materials beginnings of the corporation, we should include basic materials and production research, and the group concerned with preparing the briefs for the products—the sociologist/psychologist/designer study team. This group would be working in very general terms, and would largely be concerned with forecasting demand fifteen to twenty years ahead. These materials/production/design teams would continue down the chain of the corporation, becoming progressively more detailed yet retaining the essential feed-back to all earlier groups, especially to the two groups first described. This would lead down to the bulk production of final raw materials and fabrication of the current range.

The building industry of a country might well be composed of three or four such corporations, each producing a selection of units interchangeable within the product range of the company concerned for housing (thus giving several hundred possible permutations from a relatively restricted range), or concentrating on spatial enclosure techniques flexible in three dimensions, with functioning element packs which may be incorporated in a completely free manner in order to convert the general space to specialized use.

This latter approach would enable a very wide range of building types to be catered for—perhaps almost all building types, for if one thing is becoming very clear to those of us working in building it is the fact that we can only design for uncertainty. The days when an architect could design a permanent building for a definite, firm brief are gone. If we are to cater for a function really effectively with a building then we must design specifically for change in order to stultify the development of that function, even with a structure which has a relatively short lifespan.

Which leads to the future of the architectural profession. In the manufacturing building industry of the future, the two chief design skills which will be required will be concerned firstly with the design of the components, and secondly with the creation of the environment with these units. In addition, there will obviously continue to be a demand for the traditional architectural service within the framework of the traditional building industry, but as the volume of building created from the large-scale use of components increases, so the traditional industry will contract and slowly decrease to relatively small proportions.

Several years ago, Reyner Banham wrote that the architectural profession must accept specialization, and that the initial division should be into architect-technologists and architect-planners. This fits well into the framework of the manufacturing building industry which has already been outlined above—but very little action has yet been taken on his suggestion.

Architects are generally not equipped by their training to prepare designs for jigs, moulds and tools. Traditional architectural designs make no sense at all to a production engineer. We need to be re-trained for this work, which is grossly overdue for inclusion in the curricula of most schools of architecture—in Europe at least.

Unfortunately, however, as the manufacturing building industry develops, so opportunities for this type of work will tend to decrease. Fewer and fewer component designers will be needed, but their work will have the greatest ever impact upon the environment. And if we are not careful, those component design teams will not include architects, but may well be dominated by production engineers and graduates from art colleges where the importance of the industrial process is, strangely, more widely appreciated. Although, on the other hand, perhaps this is not so strange, as the artist—certainly the industrial artist—sees manufacturing technology and particularly mass-production as a means of extending his scope, whereas the architect tends to see these things as a threat to his predominant position in the building field and even to his livelihood. Ostrich-like, we bury our heads in the hope that it will all go away.

To turn now to the second major field in which design skills will be required: the creation of a good environment from the components and elements of the manufacturing corporations.

This may well be the biggest task of all, as the quality of the future built environment will probably depend not so much on what we do but on how we do it. For example, one would imagine that the repetition of a great many identical or even similar units would inevitably result in sterility. But this is not necessarily so, for the imaginative repetition of identical units in the terraces and crescents of the Georgian era produced some of the finest townscapes ever realized in Britain.

I am reminded of an extract from a travel book quoted in a lecture on the theory of architecture when I was a student. The author described taking shelter in a hut on an island in the Aegean, and his delight in a small statuette which he found there. His pleasure was shattered when he turned round and saw shelves and shelves full of identical replicas. I did not understand this at the time and still do not, as shelves and shelves full of absolutely identical machine-made products, whether they be radios, torches, tools or toys have always held their own special delight for me, a delight which I know is shared by most children and some adults.

Not that I believe in any way that the future environment will consist of the repetition of identical units. Production technology already has the ability to pass far beyond this and to give considerably more choice than we can afford with our present one-off craft construction, and the future harnessing of computer control to mould and tool design and fabrication and to the cycling of production runs will greatly increase this flexibility.

Environmental design is at a very low ebb at the moment. When I contrast the accidental environment of the past with the supposedly-designed environment of the present, it often seems to me that we should have been better off without architects and without planning regulations, as delight can only be realized either naturally and accidentally or by the application of a very high level of design skill right down to the nuts and bolts of the environment. At the moment we get neither, just as with the individual buildings we get neither the delight of the handmade, unique work of art nor yet the equal delight of the accuracy, precision and somehow the inevitability of the machine-made artefact.

The architect has a real contribution to make in three sections of the future building industry. First of all—with proper training—in the field of component design, as he is the only artist who is entirely accustomed to achieving his ends entirely practically, mechanically and remotely. Secondly —with proper training—as an environmental designer; and this is probably the only function which will enable a few architects to retain their independence. And thirdly, with good traditional training, as a thinker; an ideas man. Good traditional training has this merit, it teaches the student not to accept but to question everything, even the most basic assumptions, in a way which if properly employed in industry can be as useful as a management consultancy. (The only field in which the architect cannot think clearly and in which he is unable even to imagine the basic childlike questions of the real innovator is his own—the traditional craft-based building industry.)

Unfortunately our future employers, leaders of present-day general manufacturing industry who will be drawn into a dominant position in the new industry of building, are unaware that architects have any contribution to make within that industry. We shall have to prove this to ourselves and then to them, and to create opportunities for ourselves within industry if we are to survive, for our future is most decidedly in jeopardy. The prospect of the demise of the blacksmith and farrier trades must have seemed much less likely at the turn of the century than the fading-away of the architectural profession does now.

The building industry, the architectural profession, and finally: the plastics industry. How does one define it, let alone predict its future? Perhaps a definition might be the industry which is unlike all others, in that it is capable of producing completely new materials, materials which do not exist in nature, for a specific purpose or problem. And that this definition is one which should become more and more applicable as time passes, so that we are no longer restricted to the use of a limited range of basic atomic building blocks but develop the ability to create new materials from all available atoms.

Up until now, the industries of the world have run on naturally-occurring, cheap materials—iron, clay, timber—and the products of industry have been designed in accordance with the natures of these materials. Many modifications have been made in order to yield better performances or different properties—iron into steel, timber into paper or plywood; but now we are in the early days of a new age in which we shall tend to use such cheap, natural materials less and less, because the features of the more expensive man-made materials will be so vastly superior and will be tailored specifically not only for the performance-in-use of the finished article, but more particularly for the performance-in-fabrication.

These materials will tend to be created in order to lend themselves particularly to a mass-production process, the efficiency of which would be very limited if it were to be confined to the properties of natural materials. For example, present-day so-called industrialized systems of construction rely heavily upon concrete and timber. Concrete is heavy, crude and cures slowly in the mould. Timber can hardly be moulded at all (in this context) and its unidirectional strength characteristic dictates its application.

Contrast this with the speed and efficiency of the mass-production of units in thermoplastics materials. A tool which may contain a hundred or more impressions can have a curing time of seconds, and even this may be boosted by the use of several tools so that the injection barrel is in constant use.

Here we have materials well-suited to a mass-production fabrication technique, but they have a restricted range of properties and are incapable of performing certain functions. So other new materials possessing more desirable properties are pressed into use with these fabrication techniques, and we have the extrusion and injection-moulding of the thermosets.

This is still not quite good enough, so the next step is for further new materials to be developed incorporating the desirable moulding performance of the thermoplastics with the performance-in-use of the thermosets.

All this is very crude and not unduly spectacular except to the enthusiast, but it does illustrate the potential for the future—the fact that what we now know as the plastics industry may well become simply the supplier of materials to all the industries of the world, because it will be increasingly capable of producing materials for specific purposes, and these materials will tend to oust those of the past.

This then sets the general background for and development of the plastics industry in the future. Its opportunities in the building industry will surely be more extensive than anywhere else. What other industry relies so heavily on naturally-occurring materials? How has it come about that sticking bits of burned clay together with slop, by hand, is still the cheapest way we have of enclosing space in the second half of the twentieth century? All this excavation and laborious placing of patch upon patch and yet more patches to cover the gaps in the patches beneath, and juxtapositioning of totally dissimilar materials—which if they do not actually destroy each other by electrolytic action, at least move and decay at dissimilar rates and therefore leak and look leprous. What an impact we could make on this situation!

I have very strong feelings on this subject. Running a practice which is half designing components for production by the plastics industry and half general building work from the muck-and-rubble of modernizing substandard houses upwards is a schizophrenic pastime which I can recommend to anyone who thinks there is anything at all reasonable in the way in which we operate our building industry nowadays.

It is good to be a little detached though, and necessary to be more than a little ignorant, as expertise can be an emasculating commodity. Barnes Wallis says something like this when he claims that the last organization capable of judging the potential of an idea is the panel of experts, who tend to be so blinded by the mass of problems which technically could arise during development that they lose sight of the grand objective. This is how such a panel came to tell Harry Whittle that his jet engine would not work, way back in the thirties.

I have come to believe that a certain level of ignorance is an essential ingredient of innovation and technical advance; armed with this ignorance the innovator can keep a clear view of his goal and can solve the technical problems one by one as they arise, rather than be defeated or deflected by them at the outset.

What better illustration of this exists than the present world-wide state of the building industry? A massive demand which we try to meet with what are virtually stone-age materials and techniques. And yet on the other hand an accelerating technology of mass-production. If only we could adopt this objective—to harness technology to the production of buildings in the speediest and most effective way possible, and to use the opportunities created by this revolution to question and re-assess not only the built environment, but also our whole way of life.

bibliography

CALVERT, T. 'Plastics—from the beginning', *Plastics and Rubber Weekly,* 13.11.70
COUSENS, E. G. and YARSLEY, V. E. *Plastics in the Modern World,* Harmondsworth 1968
DIETZ, A. G. H. *Plastics for Architects and Builders,* Cambridge, Mass. 1969
 Modern Plastics Encyclopedia, New York 1970
 'Building with Plastics', *Shell Plastics,* London
 'Plastics Materials Guide', *Plastics,* London 1969
EMMERICH, D. G. *Géométrie Constructive,* Paris 1970
HENDRY, A. W. *Photo-elastic analysis,* Oxford 1966
KAUFMAN, M. *Giant Molecules,* London 1968
 'The First Century of Plastics', *Plastics Institute,* London
 'Landmarks of the Plastics Industry', *Imperial Chemical Industries,* London
MCHALE, J. R. *Buckminster Fuller,* Englewood Cliffs, N.J. 1962
FREI OTTO (ed.) *Tension Structures* (2 Vols.), New York–Washington 1970
PHILLIPS, L. N. 'Carbon-fibre-reinforced plastics', *Transactions and Journal of the Plastics Institute,* VIII, London 1967
POWELL, D. 'Plastics' *Specification,* 1, London 1969 and 1971
REBONE, P. and MITCHELL, R. G. B. *Plastics in the Building Industry,* London 1968
 Plastics Today, 38, London 1970
 Fibreglass Reinforced Plastics, Fibreglass Ltd, St. Helens
ROLAND, C. *Frei Otto—Spannweiten,* Frankfurt-am-Main 1965

list of illustrations

1 A chronology of plastics, with one hundred dates. M. Kaufman, *The first century of Plastics*. Plastics Institute.
2 Common plastics materials. A. G. H. Dietz, *Plastics for architects and builders*. M.I.T. Press, Cambridge, Mass 1969.
3 Molecular structure diagrams.
4 The main properties of plastics. David Powell, 'Plastics', *Specification*, 1. The Architectural Press. 1971.
5 Typical properties of cellular plastics used in building. Shell Chemicals, *Building with plastics*. May 1966.
6 Properties of reinforced plastics materials. David Powell, 'Plastics', *Specification*, 1. The Architectural Press. 1969.
7 Extrusion of thermoplastics.
8 Injection moulding in thermoplastics.
9 Vacuum forming.
10 Filament winding.
11 Sandwich injection moulding. *Plastics Today* no. 38. I.C.I. Plastics Division, England.
12 Properties of typical g.r.p. laminates. *Fibreglass Reinforced Plastics* section 3. Fibreglass Ltd.
13 Carbon fibre reinforced plastics: specific strength and stiffness of various aircraft materials. L. N. Phillips, 'Carbon-fibre-reinforced plastics', *Transactions and Journal of the Plastics Institute*, VIII, 1967.
14–16 The first all-plastics house. Ionel Schein with R. A. Coulon and Yves Magnant.
17 Motel cabin. Ionel Schein, with R. A. Coulon and Yves Magnant.
18 Mobile library exhibition units. Ionel Schein, with R. A. Coulon and Yves Magnant.
19 Vacuum-formed acrylic window. Ionel Schein, with R. A. Coulon and Yves Magnant.
20, 21 House of the Future. Alison and Peter Smithson. Photos *Daily Mail*.

22–24 Monsanto House of the Future. Hamilton and Goody.
25 Component housing system, Cesare Pea. Photo Publifoto.
26, 27 Vaults. Roberto Menghi.
28 Plastics house. Rudolf Doernach.
29–31 Relay Room system for British Railways. Arthur Quarmby with David Appleby.
32–34 Relay Room at Thameshaven Junction, Essex. Fabricated and assembled by Mickleover of London Ltd.
35 Electricity substation. Mickleover of London Ltd.
36 Telephone exchange for Bakelite Limited. Costain Ltd., with Mickleover of London Ltd.
37 Biological Research Laboratory, Signey Island. Mickleover of London Ltd.
38 Vehicle washing bay for Schweppes. Mickleover of London Ltd.
39 Pneumatic patent drawing. F. W. Lanchester.
40 Porpoise suit patent drawings. O. W. Neumark.
41 Para-foil, with O. W. Neumark.
42 Mobile, articulated caterpillar structure. O. W. Neumark.
43 G.r.p. stores building. Scott Bader Services Ltd.
44 Scalloped dome. William R. Orr.
45, 46 Dubai Airport. Page and Broughton, with Costain Civil Engineering and Mickleover of London Ltd.
47, 48 Sulphur plant, Rome. Renzo Piano.
49, 50 Motorway service area bridge. Mickleover of London Ltd.
51 Swimming pool enclosure. Scott Bader Services Ltd.
52 Motorway vault. Arthur Quarmby.
53 Swiss National Exhibition, Lausanne. Florian Vischer.
54, 55 Covered market at Lezoux. Yves Chaperot. Photos Document Neuf, Pierre Beaune, Brussels.
56 Factory roof. Renzo Piano.
57 Stadium at Laval. Saint-Arroman and du Château, with Yves Chaperot.
58–60 Factory at Forth Worth. William R. Orr. Structural Plastics Inc.
61 Experimental roof model, Renzo Piano.
62 Factory roof, Genoa. Renzo Piano.
63, 64 Italian Pavilion, Osaka. Renzo Piano.
65, 66 Derby Castle Solarium. Gillinson, Barnett and Partners, with J. Phillips Lomas and Partners.
67, 68 Heating plant domes. Stéphane du Château. Document Neuf, Brussels.
69 U.S. Pavilion, Expo '67. Buckminster Fuller.
70 Bloedel Conservatory, Vancouver. Lenning Chemicals Ltd.
71 Gloop house project. Rudolf Doernach.
72 Emergency housing in Peru. Bayer Chemicals.
73 Spiral generated dome. Dow Chemicals.
74 Plydom housing. Herbert Yates, with the International Structures Corporation.
75, 76 Hexagonal dome, Arthur Quarmby; folded and unfolded.

77 Unfolded square-based dome, Arthur Quarmby.
78 Octagonal-based dome. Arthur Quarmby with students of Bradford Regional College of Art.
79–91 Folding structures, models and details, basic range. Arthur Quarmby.
92–94 Details of folding structures, second range: Arthur Quarmby.
95 Suspension hangar for NATO. O. W. Neumark.
96 Service station at Lancaster for Shell-Mex and B.P. Arthur Quarmby.
97 'Trisail' structure. Irving Air Chute Co. of Great Britain Ltd.
98, 99 Kuwait stadium model. Otto, Tange and Kamiya.
100 West German pavilion, Montreal. Frei Otto.
101 Swiss National Exhibition, Lausanne. Frei Otto.
102 Retractable awning. Frei Otto.
103 Folding umbrellas over open-air concert hall. Frei Otto.
104–106 Shell roofs by John Zerning.
107 Spray technique. Dr Richard Baringer and students of Illinois Institute of Technology.
108–110 Spray technique and models. John Zerning.
111 Scene from 'The Touchables' by 20th-Century Fox. Photo *Daily Mirror*.
112 'The Touchables' dome. Arthur Quarmby. Photo 20th-Century Fox.
113–15 Project for the French Pavilion, Expo '70. Le Couteur and Sloan.
116 Inflated church, Montigny-les-Cormeilles. Hans-Walter Müller. Document Neuf, Brussels. Photo 'M'.
117 Wembley stadium enclosure project. Arthur Quarmby for Polyplan Ltd.
118 U.S. 'Atoms for Peace' exhibition inflatable. Victor Lundy with Birdair Structures Inc.
119–21 Boston Arts Center Theatre. Koch and Ross, with Weidhinger and Birdair Structures Inc.
122 Landscape enclosure project. Frei Otto.
123 Stadium roof project. Birdair Structures Inc.
124 Large span enclosure patent drawings. O. W. Neumark.
125 Tube structure. O. W. Neumark for the Frankenstein Group Ltd.
126 Clamshell articulated shelter. O. W. Neumark for the Frankenstein Group Ltd.
127 High pressure rib radome erecting device. O. W. Neumark for the Frankenstein Group Ltd.
128 Inflated tube radome. Birdair Structures Inc.
129–31 Fuji Pavilion, Expo '70. Yutaka Murata.
132 Panel inflated structure. M. L. Aviation Ltd.
133 U.S. Atomic Energy mobile exhibition. Joseph Eldredge and Birdair Structures Inc.
134 Taipo River 'Fabridam', Hong Kong.
135 Compression tube structure. Aubert, Jungmann and Stinco of the Beaux-Arts School, Paris under D. G. Emmerich.
136–38 General purpose enclosure. J. Aubert, Beaux-Arts School, Paris, under D. G. Emmerich.

139 Gas-lifted roof project, Wembley Stadium. Arthur Quarmby.
140 Inflated tube apartment block project. Pohl and Smith.
141, 142 Pavilion housing project. Arthur Quarmby.
143, 144 'Corn-on-the-Cob' suspended apartments project. Arthur Quarmby.
145 Variable housing system. Pascal and Claude Hausermann.
146 Industrialized housing system. Pascal and Claude Hausermann.
147 'Hotel Mobile' project. Gernot Nalbach.
148, 149 Variable housing system. Pascal and Claude Hausermann.
150 'Rondo' housing project by Casoni and Casoni.
151, 152 'Futuro' house. Matti Suuronen.
153 Prototype housing unit, Chanéac.
154, 155 'Aixilia' floating town. Chanéac.
156 Stacking shell unit. Chanéac.
157, 158 'Cascaron Argentino'. Jean Manéval.
159 Component housing project for Isago. N. Kurokawa.
160, 161 Ski lodge unit. Komatsu Plastic Industry, Japan.
162–64 Spheroid housing project. Guy de Moreau. Photo Luc Iweins.
165–67 'Maison 12E'. Atelier 4. Photos Documents Neuf, Brussels.
168, 169 Spatial housing project. Wolfgang Doring.
170 Industrialized urban habitat. Domenig and Huth.
171 Transportable units. Angela Hareiter.
172, 173 'La bulle six coques' Elevation and plan. Jean Manéval.
174, 175 Terminal 3 building, London (Heathrow) airport. Pascall and Watson. Photo Colin Westwood.
176 'La bulle six coques'. Jean Manéval.
177 Cladding units. E. H. C. Inskip with Polyplan Ltd. Photo Scott Bader.
178, 179 Façade panels. João Honorio. Document Neuf, Brussels. Photo J. R. Nonato.
180 New faculty building, Lyon-Bron. M. Detland with Prouvé-Petroff.
181, 182 SFI cladding panels, Department of Architecture, Greater London Council.
183–85 'Maisons par éléments' Andreas Christen.
186 Shell Service station. Compagnie de l'Esthétique Industrielle, Paris.
187 B.P. service station. Arthur Quarmby with Polyplan Ltd. Photo Freddie Squires Ltd.
188 Minimum service station. Arthur Quarmby.
189 'Kunststoffhaus fg 2000' Wolfgang Feierbach.
190 Bus shelter project. Students of the Hochschule für Gestaltung, Ulm.
191 Revolving bathroom. R. Bucher.
192, 193 Packaged bathroom. Arthur Quarmby.
194 Bathing cabin. Mario Scheichenbauer.
195 Bathroom unit. H. G. Müller Kunststoffwer.
196, 197 'Bloc sanitaire monobloc'. Mario Scheichenbauer. Photo Cera
198 Unita bathroom block. Alberto Rosselli. Photo Publifoto.
199 Bathroom tower. Farrell/Grimshaw Partnership.

200, 201 Soft bath. Arthur Quarmby.
202 'Les Jours Mailleurs' house. Jean Prouvé.
203 Decorative panel. Photo Greaves.
204–206 Sculpture by William Mitchell. Photos Hans Snoek (204) and Crispin Eurich.
207 'Ensculptic III' spray polyurethane house. W. E. Wedin.
208 Sculptured wall at Viry-Chatillon. P. Kowalski.
209 'Sprayform' house project. John M. Johansen.
210 Pneumatic pouffe. Arthur Quarmby.
211 Plaster model of housing component. Chanéac. Document Neuf, Brussels.
212–14 House and Garden project, Arthur Quarmby.
215–17 'Yellow Heart'. Haus-Rücker-Co, Vienna.
218, 219 Furniture carpet. Gernot Nalbach.
220 Utopian pneumatic town. Gernot Nalbach.
221 Roman leather airbed. Photo Graphische Sammlung Mathys, Basle.
222 Flyhead. Haus-Rücker-Co.
223 Mind-Expander chair for two. Haus-Rücker-Co.
224 Balloon-for-Two. Haus-Rücker-Co.
225, 226 Living pod. David Greene.
227, 228 Dyodon habitable pneumatic. J. P. Jungmann, Beaux-Arts School, Paris, under D. G. Emmerich.
229 Biotecture 70.6. Rudolf Doernach.
230 Wrapped coast. Christo. Photo Shunk-Kender.
231 Cloud. Eventstructure Research Group. Amsterdam.
232 'Projekt Canaris'. Herbert Distel. Photo Scott Bader.
233, 234 Dome over Manhattan project. R. Buckminster Fuller.
235, 236 Arctic City project. Otto, Bubner, Arup, Tange and Urtec.
237 Interplanetary city project, Frei Otto.
238 Suspension roof, Expo '64. Frei Otto.
239 Cartoon 'System Building'. Alberto Longoni.
240, 241 Hunstanton Leisure Centre project. Gillinson, Barnett and Partners.
242 Biotecture. Rudolf Doernach.
243 Hydropolis 1. Rudolf Doernach.
244 Biotecture house. Rudolf Doernach.
245 Hydroponic Biotecture. Rudolf Doernach.
246 Summerland. Kinji Fukuda and Minoru Murakawi. Photo Y. Futagawa.
247, 248 Cushicle. Michael Webb.
249, 250 'A home is not a house' project. Reyner Banham.
251 Asteromo. Paolo Soleri.
252 Novanoah A. Paolo Soleri.
253 Drive-in housing. Michael Webb.
254 Novanoah B. Paolo Soleri.
255, 256 Floating house. Masayuki Kurokawa.
257, 258 New town for the Seine valley. Miasto Group.

259 'Instant City'. Archigram Group.
260 'Control-and-choice living'. Archigram Group.
261 'Walking City'. Archigram Group.
262 'Plug-in City'. Archigram Group.
263 'New town—vertical'. Aldo Rossi and Donatella Mazzoleni. Document Neuf, Brussels.
264 Plastics floating city. William Katavolos.

name index

Amsterdam, 'Cloud', 159; fig. 231
Anmac Ltd, Nottingham, 65; fig. 51
Aquarius, New York, 152
Arctic regions, 161, 164
Arcueil, 49
Archigram Group, 176, 177; figs. 259–62
Ardrey, Robert, 164
Arup, Ove, figs. 235–6
'Asteromo', fig. 251
'Atelier 4', figs. 165–7
Aubert, J., figs. 135–6
M.L. Aviation Co., fig. 132

Baekeland, Leo, 13, 14, 17
'Balloon for Two', fig. 224
Banham, Reyner, 131, 132, 188; figs. 249, 250
Baringer, Richard, 69, 107
Batelle Institute, 28
Battersea College of Technology, 65
Bayer, 16
Bayer Chemicals, fig. 72
Beaux-Arts School, Paris, figs. 135–8, 227–8
Bedford store, fig. 177
Bezou, figs. 257–8
'Biotecture', 170; figs. 229, 242, 244

Bird, Walter, 60
Birdair Structures, figs. 118–21, 123, 128, 133
Bloedel Conservatory, Vancouver, fig. 70
Bobrowski, Jan, 183
Boston Arts Center Theatre, figs. 119–21
Boyle, Robert, 11
Bradford College of Art, parabolic dome, 98–9; figs. 77–8
British Railways, Relay Room, 52, 134; figs. 29–34
Bubner, figs. 235–6
Bucher, R., fig. 191
Building Plastics Research Corporation of Glasgow, 45

Caisse des Dépôts, Arcueil, 49
'Canaris', 159; fig. 232
Cardington, R.A.F. research establishment, 107
'Cascaron Argentino', figs. 157–8
Casoni and Casoni, fig. 150
Chalmers, William, 14
Chambéry, fig. 153
Chanéac, 148, 177; figs. 153–6, 211
Chaperot, Yves, 69; figs. 54–5
Charbonnages de France, 46
Christen, Andreas, 138; figs. 183–5

Christo, fig. 230
'City by the Sea', 45
CLASP, 185
'Cloud', 159; fig. 231
Compagnie de l'Esthétique Industrielle, fig. 186
'Control-and-choice living', fig. 260
Cook, figs. 259–60
'Corn on the Cob', figs. 143–4
Costain Civil Engineering, figs. 45–6
Coulon, R. A., 46–7; figs. 14–16, 18, 19
Crompton, figs. 259–60
Cross, 13
Crystal Palace, London, 183
'Cushicle', 158; figs. 247–8

Dartforth, James, 134
Derby Castle Solarium, 169; figs. 65–6
Detland, M., fig. 180
Distel, 159; fig. 232
Doernach, Rudolf, 52, 170; figs, 28, 71, 229, 242–5
Domenig and Huth, fig. 170
Doring, Wolfgang, 152; figs. 168–9
Dow Chemicals, fig. 73
'Dropolis', 170
Dubai Airport, figs. 45–6
Du Château, Stéphane, 73; figs. 67–8
'Dyodon', figs. 227–8

Einhorn, 13
Einstein Tower, Potsdam, 44
Emmerich, David Georges, figs. 135–8, 227–8
'Ensculptic III', fig. 207
'Enviro Machine', 152
Eventstructure Research Group, 159; fig. 231
Expo '67, Montreal, U.S. pavilion, 73; fig. 69
Expo '70, Tokyo,
French pavilion, figs. 113–15

Fuji pavilion, figs. 129–31

Farrell/Grimshaw Partnership, p. 138; fig. 199
Fasani, Antoine, 46
Feierbach, Wolfgang, fig. 189
'Flyhead', fig. 222
Fort Worth, Texas, figs. 44, 58–60
Frankenstein & Sons Ltd, Manchester, 62; figs. 126–7
Fresnes, 146
Fukuda, Kinji, fig. 246
Fuller, R. Buckminster, 73, 141, 161; figs. 69, 233–4
'Futuro' house, figs. 151–2

Genier, 146
Genoa, factory, 76; fig. 62
Gillinson, Barnett & Partners, 73; figs. 65–6, 240–1
Goody, 50; figs. 22–4
Goodyear, Charles, 11
Gray, 13
Great Exhibition, 1862, 11, 12, 13
Greater London Council, Department of Architecture, 134; figs. 181–2
Greene, David, 132; figs. 225–6

Hamilton, 50; figs. 22–4
Hancock, C., 11
Hara, Hiroshi, 176
Hareiter, Angela, fig. 171
Hartley, Herbert, 30
Haus-Rücker-Co., Vienna, 152; figs. 215–17, 222–4
Hausermann, Pascal and Claude, 78, 148, 177; figs. 145–6, 148–9
Herron, Ron, figs. 259–62
Holzer, 13
Hong Kong, 'Fabridam', fig. 134
Honorio, João, figs. 178–9
HUD 'Operation Breakthrough', 123
Hunstanton, Leisure Centre project, figs. 240–1
Hyatt, John Wesley, 12, 13, 17

'Hydropolis', 170; fig. 243
'Hydroponic Biotecture', fig. 245

Ideal Home Exhibition, 1956, 49
'Induction House', 176
Inskip, E. H. C., fig. 177
'Instant City', 177; fig. 259
International Structures Corporation, 79; fig. 74
Irving Air Chute Co., fig. 97
Isago, Yokohamo, fig. 159
Isle of Man, Solarium, 169; figs. 65–6

Johannsen, John, 44, 148; fig. 209
John, Hans, 14
Johnson Wax structures, 45
Jungmann, J. P., figs. 135, 227–8

Kamiya, figs. 98–9
Karcewski, figs. 257–8
Katavolos, William, fig. 264
Kennedy, T. Warnett, 45
Komatsu Plastics Industry, figs. 160–1
Kowalski, P., 146; fig. 208
Kurokawa, Musayuki, figs. 255–6
Kurokawa, N., fig. 159
Kuwait stadium model, figs. 98–9

Lancaster, service station, fig. 96
Lanchester, F. W., 60; fig. 39
Larkin Building, 45
Lausanne, Swiss National Exhibition, 89; figs. 53, 101
Le Couteur, figs. 113–15
Leeds School of Architecture, onion dome, 99
Lefevre, figs. 257–8
Lezoux, covered market, figs. 54–5
'Living pod', 132; figs. 225–6
Lomas, see Phillips
London (Heathrow) figs. 174–5
Longoni, Alberto, fig. 239
Lundy, Victor, fig. 118
Lyon-Bron, faculty building, fig. 180

McNicholas, J. B., 92
Magnant, Yves, 46–7; figs. 14–19
'Maison 12E', figs. 165–7
Maisons par Eléments, 138
Makowski, Z. S., 65, 69
Manéval, Jean, 148; figs. 157–8, 172–3
Manhattan Island, Fuller dome, 161; figs. 233–4
'Maritime Society', 170
Mazzoleni, Donatella, fig. 263
Mendelsohn, Eric, 44
Menghi, Roberto, 52; figs. 25–7
'Mesa city', 177
Miasto group, 177; figs. 257–8
Mickleover of London, figs. 31–8, 45–6, 49–50
Milan Triennale, xIth, 52; figs. 25–7
Military Engineering and Experimental Establishment, Christchurch, 107
Millard House, 45
'Mind-Expander', fig. 223
Minke, Gernot, 89
Mitchell, William, 146; figs. 204–6
Moeller Sanitar unit, 138, 141; fig. 195
'Monsanto House of the Future', 50–2, 116; figs. 22–4
Montreal, Expo '67, U.S. pavilion, 73; fig. 69
Moreau, Guy de, figs. 162–4
Müller, Hans-Walter, fig. 116
H. G. Müller Kunststoffwer, fig. 195
Murakawi, Minoru, fig. 246
Murata, Yutaka, figs. 129–31

Neumark, Otto Walter, 61–2; figs. 40–2, 95, 124–6
'New town-vertical', fig. 263
Nalbach, Gernot, 152; figs. 147, 218–20
Norwich, Connecticut, Lutheran Church project, 148
'Novanoah A', fig. 252

'Novanoah B', fig. 254
Novo Iraja, fig. 178–9

Orr, William R., 69; figs. 44, 58–60
Osaka, Expo '70, Italian pavilion; figs. 63–4
Otto, Frei, 89, 106; figs. 98–9, 100–3, 112, 235–8

Page and Broughton, figs. 45–6
Panton, Werner, 158
Paris Exhibition, 1956, 45; figs. 14–16
Parkes, Alexander, 11–12, 13, 17
Pasadena, Millard House, 45
Pascal, 148; figs. 145–6, 148–9
Pascall and Watson, figs. 174–5
Pea, Cesare, 52, 134; figs. 25–7
Phillips, J., Lomas and Partners, figs. 65–6
Piano, Renzo, 65, 76; figs. 47–8, 56, 61–4
Plover Cove Water Scheme, fig. 134
'Plug-in City', fig. 262
Plydom housing, fig. 74
Pneumatic Tent Company, 61
Pohl and Smith, fig. 140
Portmeirion, 144
Potsdam, Einstein Tower, 44
'Projekt Canaris', 159; fig. 232
Prouvé, Jean, fig. 202
Prouvé-Petroff, fig. 180

Quarmby, Arthur, 78; figs. 29–34, 52, 75–94, 96, 111–12, 117, 139, 141–4, 187–8, 192–3, 200–1, 210

Relay Room System, 52, 134; figs. 30–8
R.F.D. Company, Godalming, 61
Rio de Janeiro, Honorio façade panels, figs. 178–9
'Rondo' housing project, fig. 150
Rosselli, Alberto, fig. 198
Rossi, Aldo, fig. 263
Royal Air Force Research Establishment, Cardington, 107

Scheichenbauer, Mario, figs. 196–7
Schein, Ionel, 45, 46–7, 115, 134, 143; figs. 14–16, 18, 19
SCOLA, 185
Scott Bader Services Ltd, 51; figs. 43, 51
Siegfried Line, 76
Signey Island, Biological Research Laboratory, fig. 37
Skeist, Irving, 60
Sloan, figs. 113–15
Smithson, Alison and Peter, 49, 77; figs. 20–1
Soleri, Paolo, 177; figs. 251–2, 254
'Sprayform', fig. 209
Stinco, fig. 135
Summerland, Tokyo, 169; fig. 246
Suuronen, Matti, figs. 151–2
Swiss National Exhibition, Lausanne, 89; figs. 53, 101

Taipo River 'Fabridam', fig. 134
Tange, Kenzo, figs. 98–9, 235–6
Thameshaven Junction, Essex, 52, 134; figs. 31–4
Thompson, D'Arcy Wentworth, 106
Tokyo, Summerland, 169; fig. 246
'The Touchables' dome, 99–100; figs. 111–12
Turner, Kenneth, 69

Ulm, Hochschule für Gestaltung, 134; fig. 190
U.S. Atomic Energy mobile exhibition, figs. 118, 133
Urtec, figs. 235–6

Vancouver, Bloedel Conservatory, fig. 70
Viry-Chatillon, sculptured wall, fig. 208
Vischer, Florian, fig. 53

'Walking City', fig. 261
Webb, Michael, 158; figs. 247–8
Wedin, W. E., fig. 207

Wembley Stadium enclosure
    project, 107, 114; figs. 117, 139
West, John, Design group, 65
Weston, Conn., spray concrete
    house, 148
Woods Hole, Mass., figs. 119–21
Wright, Frank Lloyd, 44–5

Yates, Herbert, fig. 74
'Yellow Heart', figs. 215–17

Zagreb, U.S. pavilion, 148
Zandfoss, figs. 257–8
Zerning, John, 65; figs. 104–6

subject index

A.b.s., *see* acrylonitrile butadiene styrene
acetal copolymer, 21
acrylic, 19, 21; *see* polymethylmethacrylate
acrylonitrile butadiene styrene (a.b.s.), 22
architectural profession, future of, 188–90

Bakelite, 13, 14
bathroom units, 138–43
building industry, future of, 185–8

Calendering process, 36
carbon fibre reinforcement, 43
casting, rotational, 36
Cellophane, 38
Celluloid, 12–13, 21
cellulose acetate, 21
cellulose nitrate, 11–12
chemistry of plastics, 18–20
cladding panels, 134
cocoon-spray techniques, 65, 69, 98
component construction, 115–43

Decorative applications, 143–58
dough moulding compound, 38

Environmental design, 189

epoxide (epoxy) resin, 25–6
extrusion, of thermo plastics, 31–2; fig. 7
of thermosets, 32

Fibreglass, *see* glass reinforced polyester
filament winding, 38–9; fig. 10
foams, 27–8
folding structures, 79–89
Formica, 22, 25
functioning cores for housing, 138–43

Glass reinforced polyester (g.r.p. or Fibreglass), 22, 26
glazing materials, 14
g.r.p., *see* glass reinforced polyester
guncotton, *see* cellulose nitrate

High density polyethylene, 20
high molecular weight polyethylene, 20
high pressure pneumatics, 107–14
high-stress membranes, 89, 92, 98
holiday resorts, 107, 164, 169
housing, component construction, 115–43

Indulex panels, 134

injection moulding, in
    thermoplastics, 33–4; fig. 8
    in thermosets, 34–5
insulation, 27

Laminated boards, 79, 89
lamination, low pressure, 36–8
low pressure pneumatics, 98–107

Manufacturing processes, 31–43
'Matra 2' cladding, fig. 180
melamine formaldehyde
    (melamine), 13, 14, 24–5, 35
membranes, high stress, 89, 92, 98
monomer, 18
moulding, blow moulding, 20, 32
    filament winding, 38–9
    injection, 33–5; fig. 8
    low pressure lamination, 36–8
    rotational casting, 36
    vacuum forming, 35–6; fig. 9

Nylon, *see* polyamide

On-site enclosures, 77–8

Panel construction, 134–8
Parkesine, 11–12
p.f., *see* phenolformaldehyde
phenolformaldehyde (phenolic or
    p.f.), 22–4, 27, 35, 45
phenolic, *see* phenolformaldehyde
plastics industry, future of, 190–1
pneumatic structures, 60–2
    high pressure structures,
        107–14
    low pressure structures,
        98–107
polyamide (nylon), 21, 27
polycarbonate, 13–14, 22
polyester laminates, glass
    reinforced, 36–8
polyester resins, 13, 26
polyethylene (polythene), 16, 20
    high density, 20
    high molecular weight, 20
    low density, 20

polyethylene terephthalate, 22
polyimide, 22
polyisobutylene, 76
polymer, 18
polymethylmethacrylate (acrylic),
    14, 21
polyolefins, 20
polypropylene, 16, 20
polystyrene, description, 21
    foam, 27
    invention of, 15–16
polytetrafluorethylene (p.t.f.e.), 22
polyurethane, 16
    foam, 27
    rigid foam, 30
polyvinyl acetate (p.v.a.), 21
polyvinyl chloride (p.v.c.), 13, 16,
    20–1, 27, 28
    spray, 98
polyvinyl fluoride (p.v.f.), 22
pre-impregnated glass mat
    ('pre-preg'), 38
production methods, 31–43
p.t.f.e., *see* polytetrafluorethylene
p.v.a., *see* polyvinyl acetate
p.v.c., *see* polyvinyl chloride
p.v.f., *see* polyvinyl fluoride

Radiation cross linking, 26
rotational casting, 36
rubber, 11
    synthetic, 16

Sandwich panels, 38–9
sculptural applications of plastics,
    143–58
shell assemblies, frames with shell
    infill, 73–6
    pure shells, 63–9
    trussed, 69–73
silicone plastics, 26
simulation of traditional materials,
    143–4
spatial enclosures, 63–143
styrene, 13, 15
sunlight, artificial, 107, 169–70
suspension structures, 89–98

Tape, cloth, fig. 107
    plastic, 79
tensile structures, 89–98
thermoplastics, 19–22
    disposal, 28
    extrusion, 31–2
    injection moulding, 33–4
    photosensitive, 28
    reinforced, 26–7
thermosetting plastics, 20, 22–6
    disposal, 28
    extrusion, 32
    injection moulding, 34–5
    reinforced, 27
trussed shell assemblies, 69–73

Ureaformaldehyde (urea), 13, 14, 24, 35, 45

Vacuum forming, 35–6; fig. 9
vinyl chloride, 13
vulcanization, 11

Warerite, 22, 25
waste, plastic, 28–30, 170
weathering, 76–7
windows, power operated, 126